911
is
Disconnected

So This is Rock and Roll

Adam Bomb

NEW HAVEN PUBLISHING LTD

Second Edition
Published 2018
NEW HAVEN PUBLISHING LTD
www.newhavenpublishingltd.com
newhavenpublishing@gmail.com

Cover design © Pete Cunliffe
Second edition editing by Taylor T. Carlson

newhaven
publishing

For Claire….
The greatest writer I've ever known

Claire O'Connor with Jimmy Page in Chinatown, NYC 1986

Content

Introduction	5
Altneuland	7
An Unexpected Souvenir	12
Inflammable Angel	18
School Daze	27
Smoke on the Water	39
So This is Rock and Roll	43
Junior High Rock Stars	57
Eddie Van Halen	71
CaliFFornia World Music Festival	84
The Senior Keg	93
The Battle of the Bands	100
Backstage Kiss	105
Barracuda	111
Crashing Rush	117
The Day Night Came Early	120
Homegrown Rockfest	131
Technical Knockout	138
Honolulu Danger City	149
The End Zone	161
MetalFest II	174
The Last Party	178
911 is Disconnected	183
No Quarter	189
Shape of the World	200
End of the Line	213
The City That Never Sleeps	223
Super Rock '84	238
The Beverly Sunset	248
1985	255
Just Check Out These Names	269
High or Low	278
Acknowledgements	286
Discography	288

Introduction

It's 2017, and I find myself in Las Vegas, a widower, supporting my 16-year-old daughter, Blaise. We moved here from New York City with my 23-year-old girlfriend from Amsterdam, Anne-fleur. We met while I was on tour, and had been living together in secret as a couple in Holland since 2014. Blaise was starting to get in trouble at school in New York City. My whole life was being investigated by social services. It all stemmed from the death of her mother.

After 24 years of marriage, I lost my wife Claire to lung cancer. She died in my arms on July 28, 2011. Ever since that day, my roller coaster life has been one catastrophic event after another.

The same year, my father died and my stepmother sent me his ashes in a cardboard box by UPS. The following year, my eldest daughter, Darian hired a lawyer whose strategy was to put a restraining order against me in attempt to cut me out of my wife's life insurance policy. It had already gone into court proceeding because of forged signatures. I was sued for $500,000 by a court appointed guardian for my 90-year-old aunt. I got married to a girl named Geroge on July 4, 2014, and got divorced less than a year later. I went through 20 different band lineups. I decided to quit touring to get my daughter through school, so Blaise, Anne-fleur, and we tried to start a new life in a new city, Las Vegas.

After months of chasing guitar auditions around Sin City like a cabaret showgirl, I landed a job as a guitar tech for an impersonator show band. The producers of the show don't know anything about me. They thought I worked at a music store chain, so they hired me.

In the land of make believe, where everyone pretends to be rock stars, I could pretend to be a roadie. I saw a fake Steven Tyler sitting in the audience watching a mock Axl Rose perform, and a phony Billy Idol wandering around while a guy dressed as Paul Stanley was chatting up an imitation Joan Jett. As a faux Elton John was playing *Funeral for a Friend*, I wandered back to my tech room, through the casino kitchen, past the showgirls and bikini-clad cocktail waitresses, and I glanced at a text that read: "Sorry, we have to let you go..."

I started to wonder how I ended up here. Was everything I had done in my life for real, or was it all just a crazy dream?

Altneuland

On the eighth day of my life, my father threw a party. It was August 22, 1963. On this hot day, there were about 50 people drinking in the sunshine by the pool in formal attire. In attendance was every employee of Brenner Brothers Bakery, a business that was started by my father, Joe Brenner, in the early 1950s. Everyone was there to witness the bris of Adam Daniel Brenner. Everybody got drunk, and ended up in the pool with their clothes on. The bakers talked about that party for the next decade.

I was named for my Grandfather Abraham Brenner, and my Uncle David, who was killed in World War II. We lived in a middle-class suburb of Seattle called Seward Park, in a big two-story house with a swing set in the front yard and a huge pool in the back. My dad's business, Brenner Brothers Bakery, was the most popular kosher bakery in Seattle. It all started with my great grandfather Chaim.

Chaim Brenner was born in 1860, in Mielec, Austria-Hungary, a small village 80 km south of Krakow on the Vistual River. When he was 17, he fell in love with a beautiful girl, Rahel Machenias. They met on the Corso, a Main Street hotspot where Jews in Mielic could pick up girls in the late 1870s. He pulled Rahel in the Stranzica, a beautiful garden surrounding the local firehouse, and she got pregnant. To avoid scandal, they married, and had another seven children in eight years. Chaim joined a gang of reckless youths who started a theater ensemble called Trupe Mielic. Jewish kids from across Europe were starting theater troupes. It was the dawn of a dramatic new art form called Yiddish Theater; a combination of satirical Yiddish humor, original music and the popular Yiddish cover songs of the day with instrumentation, singing, dancing, and a message. A typical troupe could be quite large, with sometimes over 30 people in an entourage. Theater posters would often show 14 performers or more on a handbill, and surround them with colorful Hebrew lettering.

Like all 21-year-old males, Chaim had to serve in the Austro-Hungarian Army for three years, but the troupe carried on, and Yiddish theater broke big all across Eastern Europe. The theater troupe interpreted the writings of Solomon Rabinovich, who went under the stage name Sholem Aleichem. The troupe had developed a stage act taken from the Jewish stories and political propaganda of the 1880s. Trupe Mielic had a hit in 1893 with *Tevye the Dairyman*, a play which ultimately became known as *Fiddler on the Roof*. They traveled all over the Galician province by train, doing the circuit, performing all over the region. The theater troupe became so popular that Mielec became a town of distinction.

On March 13, 1881, Tsar Alexander II was assassinated by revolutionaries before he could enact a parliament. The Russian press blamed 'The Jews' for his death. Pogroms, or gang riots, were staged all over the Russian provinces, in an attempt to wipe out Jewish life in revenge attacks perpetrated by business competitors and railroad workers. By the year's end, 40 Jewish deaths were recorded, 17 of which occurred during the 225 incidents of rape that were reported. Alexander III blamed it on 'The Jews' and made 'May Laws' forbidding Jews to buy or own property.

In Warsaw, Christmas Day 1881, a false alarm of fire started a stampede in Holy Cross Church. Two kids ran inside and screamed, *"fire,"* used as a ploy to cause panic so they could pickpocket the fleeing crowd, but it went horribly wrong. 29 people were crushed to death. A mob gathered at the scene, and two Jewish kids who were never inside the church were accused by the real culprits. The mob started to riot, attacking and destroying the Jewish businesses on the street next to Holy Cross. Gangs all across Warsaw carried on their pogrom, and attacked Jewish shops and homes for three days. The Russian army arrested 2,600 people. Only two were killed, but it devastated a thousand families. Many left for America - the myth of hope to escape the persecution.

In 1894, the new Russian Tsar, Nikolai Alexandrovich Romanov, who was known as Nicholas II or 'Nicholas the Bloody,' inherited power. He went to England to become godfather to the future king of England, King Edward VIII. Nikolai admired the mobs, and he believed anti-Semitism was a useful tool to unite his regime.

Like all Jewish men, Chaim Brenner wanted revolution, and for Jews to have equal rights. Yiddish theater and writings became the most powerful tool of communication, in the hope of reaching others. Yiddish Theater performances were considered threats to the social order. Religious teachers in the yeshiva would inspire discussion for a young Yosef Brenner from Ukraine, who grew up with the pogroms.

Local boys would cut off a finger to avoid being drafted, which often meant being ordered to destroy Jewish homes and businesses. The Mielec factories made guns, bombs, and ammunition. Mielic was a strategic point of land, desirable to Russia, Poland, and Germany. Signs were everywhere the world was heading closer to war.

The threat of pogroms made Chaim and Rahel want a better life for their three youngest sons; Abraham, Harry, and Israel. In the sub-zero winter of 1899, Chaim got sick, and his dying wish was for the boys to leave Mielec and start a new life in the Altneuland, the land of hope, America. Chaim Brenner died on December 31, 1899.

Chaim and Rahel's seventh son, Abraham, or Abe as he was called, born on January 1884. He worked at a local bakery in Mielic with his brothers. His father told him, "No matter how much the world changes, baking bread will never go out of style. People always have to eat."

Yosef Brenner

A cousin from the Ukraine, Yosef Brenner, was a writer. He published an article that made him famous, *Pat Lachem - A Loaf of Bread,* in 1900. Yosef was drafted into the Russian Army. He escaped to London during the Russo-Japanese War with the help of The Bund, a group of revolutionaries from Vilnius who founded the Vilna Troupe and performed in Warsaw. Yosef emigrated to Palestine where he became a leading figure in Yiddish writing and mixed dialects. He was killed during the Jaffa riots in May 1921. The Brenner Prize, one of Israel's top literature awards, is named after him.

Abe, Harry, and Israel, who they called Izzy, went to a Yiddish theater performance in 1903. There Izzy ran into a man who worked with his father. He gave them all jobs on the crew, and they traveled with the troupe as far as Hamburg, Germany. The three brothers boarded the German ship Graf Waldersee, and they sailed to America.

Israel, Harry, and Abraham Brenner were all processed at Ellis Island on Sept 10, 1903.

Abe, Harry and Izzy arrived in New York City. They took a train to Virginia to stay with their uncle, Max Brenner, who immigrated in 1881. Izzy stayed in Maryland, while Abe and Harry ventured down to Silver Springs, near Baltimore. Harry got a bad case of the yetzer ra, Yiddish for 'evil impulse.' He got extremely attracted to a really pretty girl, but in those days, there was no sex without a wedding ring. She was the youngest of three sisters, and the only good-looking girl in the family.

In those days, the Orthodox Jewish tradition was that the older sister would have to be married first. After Harry proposed, the bride's family tried to cover it up within the community to avoid a scandal. It was a religious ceremony, and Harry did the badeken (veiling). They gave him wine as he danced and he marched down to the chuppa (wedding canopy). All the guests were clapping their hands and stomping their feet to the festive music as the band played on. His beautiful wife-to-be, waiting at the chuppa, had the prettiest face he'd ever seen.

Harry slowly covered his blushing bride's face with a heavy veil. And in the 3,500 year old Orthodox tradition, she danced in circles, spinning around Harry in the chuppa seven times. The crowd cheered her with every spin. On the final spin, she put her hand on her face, overcome with dizziness. She fell into the crowd, knocking over the guests closest to the chuppa. They all went down like bowling pins. Everyone still standing pushed Harry out of the way, and swarmed around her. After the chaos, the covered bride returned to the chuppa. The rabbi recited the ceremony. Harry Brenner smashed the glass, closed his eyes, and took off the veil to kiss his new wife. When he opened his eyes, he was shocked to see that he'd just married the older sister.

After a while, Abe wanted to date the younger sister. Harry still wasn't over it. There was a fist-fight, and Abe got his ass kicked. Abe went to the train station and said, "Get me as far away from here as fucking possible." Seattle, Washington was the last stop on a three-day train journey, and he took the 2,750-mile ride alone. Abe's first residence was a boarding house run by a single lady with three daughters. When Abe came looking for a room to rent in 1905, there was a little girl bouncing a ball in the yard. Her name was Bessie Rosenthal. She was 11 years old.

On February 4, 1912, after she turned 18, Abe Brenner married Bessie Rosenthal. They proceeded to have seven children. Barney, Itsey, Sammy, Charlie, Yetta, David, and my father Joey, who was born on May 8, 1925.

Abe started a business, A. Brenner Bakery, on 12th and Jackson in downtown Seattle. It became successful, and it soon moved to a better location at 18th and Yesler Way. Abe added a delicatessen to the bakery, which was a pioneering idea for the Seattle area in the twenties. After that, the business boomed and became a Seattle institution.

Bessie Brenner, Charlie, Yetta, Joey, David

Abe Brenner's Bakery truck 1912

An Unexpected Souvenir

My dad's first job was cracking eggs for his Uncle Harry, who traveled from Baltimore to Seattle to attend Abe's wedding. He reconciled with his estranged brother, and he came to work after Abe became successful. Abe Brenner was a dapper dresser who always wore a suit. He was a drinker and he liked the plum brandy slivovitz. He loved to gamble, but he usually lost. He lived next door to a card room, and he went there every day for years.

My dad's earliest memories of his big brothers were watching his mother removing lice from his brother Barney's head, and Itsey always complaining about working. Joe Brenner recalled, "We all slept in one big room. Itsey hated to get up at four in the morning to go to work the bakery, so he'd go over and fart in our father's face while he was sleeping."

When Joe Brenner was 14, his mother died from cancer. She suffered in horrible pain for the last six months of her life. Abe remarried one year later to Ruth Lutkoff, who worked at a neighborhood butcher's shop. They had a son, Mark. None of the older Brenner kids fully accepted Ruth but Joey, who wanted his father to be happy.

David Brenner was the best-looking of all the brothers, and the star of the family. He was a football hero at Garfield High School in the days before players wore helmets. All the girls went crazy for him. Although Barney and Sammy were always making jokes and were very funny, the other Brenner brothers were raised to be cold. Everything was done out of obligation. They worked long hours for very little money. Abe would usually take back what he paid Joey, and he'd gamble it away. While the Brenner family flourished in America, their European friends and relatives were much less fortunate.

On September 13, 1939, the eve of Jewish New Year, the Germans targeted Mielec as a strategic base, five days after Germany invaded Poland. The Nazis rode in on motorcycles, terrorizing Jews at prayer, and burned a slaughterhouse and the synagogue in the town center. 40 Jews were killed as they took refuge inside. Those who tried to escape the fire by jumping out a window were shot. Mielec was the first to go since it was home to the PZL or State Aviation Works. The Nazis used it to build planes to attack French and British soldiers.

Mielec became a ghetto. On March 9, 1942, all the Brenner family still left behind, as well as every other innocent Jew from town, (around 2,800 people), were herded up and shipped off to death camps. Adolf Brenner, a grandson of the brother of my great-grandfather, was on Schindler's list, and records show he lived in the Mielec area. He lived to see the end of the war.

To this very day, there are no Jews in Mielec. It was the first town in Poland to be judefree. There's no trace of Jews from the past, no signs of Jewish life, and no Brenner history left behind to touch. Only a gate with a Star of David in an empty field where the synagogue used to be, with a plaque that reads, 'There are no bodies, no graves here because the Nazis destroyed them all.'

Joey Brenner wanted to fight in the war as soon as he graduated from Garfield High School in the class of '42. Charlie was drafted, and fought on D-Day in Normandy. Sammy and David enlisted voluntarily. David was stationed in London, and he spent three months working on airplanes with the ground crew. He went to bars in Soho at night, and he hooked up with British girls who liked American soldiers.

David got promoted to be a 'belly gunner.' He trained to shoot a machine gun from a ball turret in a B-17. On his first mission, a run over France on May 14, 1944, his plane took Nazi fire somewhere over the French coast. David got hit with shrapnel, and he started to bleed from his chest. The bleeding was so severe that by the time they got back to London, David Brenner was dead.

David Brenner was buried twice: Once in England, then, after the war, the US Government exhumed his body, and flew him back to Seattle. As a child, I used to play with a large American flag that had been draped on his coffin at his second funeral. That was the only memento left behind of my dad's favorite brother.

Joe Brenner joined the Navy in 1943, and he was stationed in Corpus Christi, Texas. He had a perky girlfriend he called Grapefruit. After they dated a few times, she asked him to loan her $20. He gave it to her and he never saw Grapefruit again. Years later, my father gave me some great advice, "If you ever want to get someone out of your life forever, just loan them $20."

After the war, Joe Brenner went back to Seattle to work for his father. He liked running the bakery, where he mixed the dough, greased the pans, and made sure the bread was displayed perfectly in the storefront, as the scent of cakes and cookies filled the store. If an employee didn't do something right, Joe just did it himself. He took great pride in his work. Baking was in his blood.

Joe Brenner (center) in the bakery

My grandfather showed my dad how to operate the business so he could eventually take it over. All the older brothers were off getting married and doing other things. Only my Aunt Yetta worked at the bakery, and, just like my dad, she worked there most of her life.

Abe spent less time working and more time gambling. His compulsive nature led him to lose the bakery one night in a heated card game. But he won it back the following night. Abe eventually got sick, and he died of clogged heart on August 27, 1952. There was a meeting at a lawyer's house with all the brothers and his widow Ruth to discuss his will.

Abe Brenner leaving a card game

Joe Brenner said in his last interview in 2011, "It was left in such a way that my dad wanted me to run the bakery and help out his wife Ruth. Then the bakery would have been solely mine. Otherwise the bakery would go to Ruth and be put up for auction. I felt so guilty that I got it all and my brothers got nothing. They worked just as hard as I did when they worked there. So I said, 'screw it,' and told the lawyer to put it up for auction. The old bakery was worth $28,000, which was about the same amount it took to start up a new bakery. So we split it up, and I got a bank loan to start up a new business. We opened a place on Yesler Way. It was a success right from the bang."

Ruth tried to run the bakery herself, as Abe Brenner Bakery, but it went out of business after Itsey, Charlie and Joe Brenner opened Brenner Brothers Bakery in the winter of 1952. It took off like gangbusters.

My dad's best friend, who was always hanging around the bakery in the 50s, was Alin Wigodsky. They called him Wiggle. My dad said, "We used to laugh and joke around as kids. Alin got carried away with a woman from Spokane, Roberta Warshaw. He married her, and had three kids. I went with them on a train back to Spokane. Out of the blue she tells Wiggle that she wanted a divorce. I tried to talk her out of it but she went through with it. Then she set her sights on me. She had her wilds out for me and next thing you knew I did what I shouldn't have and what I didn't want to do, and married her."

Roberta Warshaw was born on April 19, 1929. She was the daughter of Harriet and Samuel Warshaw from Spokane.

Joe and Bobbie's wedding, 1960

On November 10, 1960, my parents had a wedding at Temple De Hirsch, but the rabbi forgot to come. There were around 20 guests, and my dad always donated big money to the temple. My father had just enough time to have second thoughts, but he stayed and married her. The rabbi had fallen asleep from too much wine, but he finally picked up the phone and rushed to the synagogue to perform the marriage.

In November 1962, my father took his new wife, Roberta Brenner, who everyone called Bobbie, to Honolulu for a vacation. He was now a father with a built-in family of three kids; Janice, Cathy, and David. My dad supported them and loved them as if they were his own. He bought a house in Seward Park, a suburb of Seattle, at 6400 57th Ave South, and they all took the last name Brenner. There were never any plans to have another child, nor did Bobbie think she could have more kids. But, when they returned from Hawaii, Bobbie was pregnant. My father told me, "You were an unexpected souvenir."

Happy Family 1964 - David, Janice, Baby Adam, & Thumper

Inflammable Angel

I was born on August 14, 1963, at the Swedish Hospital in Seattle. My father said it was the happiest day of his life. Everybody at the bakery was thrilled for Joe Brenner. He was the overall boss, and his two partners, Itsey and Charlie, were in charge of the baking and deliveries. They had over 30 employees at that time. Everybody loved my dad. He was full of humor and not a mean boss like his brother Itsey. Joe's big sister Yetta, worked the retail part of the bakery and

Yetta

always dressed up in full makeup like a 1930s movie star. Sammy was offered a partnership in the business, but he backed out at the last minute and moved to Oakland to start his own bakery. The business on Yesler Way grew so much, they relocated to a bigger space in the Seattle area of Cherry Street and Empire Way.

My sister Janice took care of me when I was very small, and my parents hired a nanny to look after me. As soon as I learned how to walk, my parents made we wear a corrective shoe brace to stop me from running into things. I was an accident-prone baby, constantly knocking over vases and bookcases. My mother said I was an inflammable angel because I left a trail of destruction wherever they took me.

My dad spent most of his time working while my mother threw lavish parties in the living room. They went on vacation, and brought me back a ukulele. They went to Spain, and brought me back a plaque with the head of a bull that killed a matador. They put it on a shelf in my room. I tried to climb on a dresser to play with it but the dresser collapsed, and the shelf toppled over on me. I was trapped for 20 minutes before my brother came down and lifted it off of me.

I was raised by a black woman named Eva. She'd push my stroller down to Lake Washington to pick blackberries from the sticker bushes. She lived in the projects, was dirt poor, and worked 14 hours a day. I loved Eva; I always felt safe with her, and she could cook the best fried chicken in the world.

My sisters were both in their teens, and they shared a bedroom with white canopy beds. Cathy, who we called Thumper, had a stereo. I would sneak into her room and look at her records. I tried to put one on, but it made a big scratching noise. I got scared, and ran out of her room.

In 1967, there was a race riot in Seattle, and the bakery got vandalized. There was also a bad fire. My sister Janice was working there, and a robber with a gun shot a bullet that ricocheted and hit her in the leg.

My father decided to gamble on building a new bakery in a safer location. He picked an undeveloped area east of Seattle, in the suburb town of Bellevue, Washington. Bellevue was located just across a new floating bridge that ran through Mercer Island over Lake Washington. They built the new bakery at 12000 Bel Red Road on the corner of NE 8th Street.

I was closest with my sister Thumper. She had really long black hair. Her best friend was the girl next door, Jeri Lee Cunningham. Jeri Lee would come over and play our piano. She would also lie out topless by our swimming pool and drink Tab. In the summer she went on a mountain climbing trip, fell off a cliff, and died. She was our next-door neighbors' only child. Jeri Lee was 16 years old when she died. Her parents, Leo and Vernette Cunnigham, were never the same after that. I could understand their heartache even at that age. I cried for Jerri Lee and I never forgot her. She was the first girl I ever saw topless.

When Eva left for the day, Thumper would take care of me. She sat me in front of the TV, and spend her summers getting a tan, and her winters watching soap operas. There was always some relative over at our house raiding the booze from a wooden cabinet that opened into a bar in the living room.

Adam and Jeri Lee Cunningham

My dad bought my mother a Lincoln Continental. On the very first day she had it, my mother, Janice, and Sammy's son Daryl, ran a stoplight, and crashed into another car. The brand new Continental was completely totaled. My mom was in the hospital for two weeks in a full-body cast. When she got out of the hospital, my mom got a new Continental, while my dad drove an old green station wagon with plastic wood panel siding.

My dad would take me to the movies once in a while, usually old films at Venetian Theater. He tried to share with me things he liked as little boy, like The Marx Brothers. He took me down to an older section of town called Pioneer Square. He showed me there was a secret entrance to Underground Seattle behind the kitchen of the restaurant Brasserie Pittsbourgh. They served my dad's bread there. We went through a vault in the back of the café and crawled down a ladder into the old city Seattle was built on top of. It was dark and musty, like a crypt full of relics.

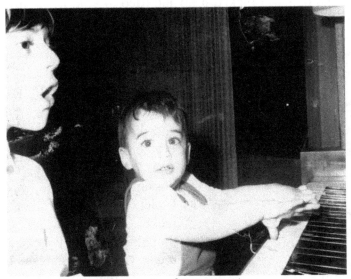

Thumper teaching me to sing

I felt a connection to things from the early 1900s, like old candy brands and old silver coins. I loved Farrell's Ice Cream Parlor, with its 1920s décor, player piano, and aisles of candy. Every time we went, I said it was my birthday, and they'd sing at our table while beating a big bass drum.

I wanted to be a cowboy, a fireman, or an astronaut. My dad took me to see *Sylvester the Mummy* at the Ye Olde Curiosity Shop on the Waterfront. He took me to visit his friend, Ivar Haglund, an old sailor man who reminded me of the cartoon *Popeye*. Ivar owned a fish restaurant. He patted me on the head and told me, "Keep Clam."

My father took me shopping in the stores underneath Pike Place Market. Seattle was full of history from old life. You could see it everywhere downtown, but we lived in the suburbs. I dreamed someday I'd get to see the whole world.

When I was five years old, my brother David and I shared a room. He had a classical nylon string guitar, was a big fan of The Beatles, and could play the intro to the song *Day Tripper*. When he was at school, I opened the guitar case and hit the strings. I watched them vibrate and hit them again. They made strange waves. The more I hit the strings, the stranger they looked. I did it very fast, and it made a huge racket. I picked it up and tried to hold it like my brother did, but it was too big, and it crashed on the floor with a big sound like the cartoon, *El Kabong.*

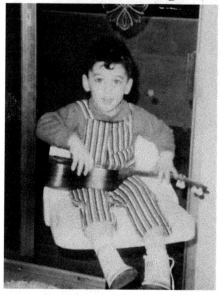

There was a little crack in the bottom of the guitar. I was scared because I thought I'd broken it. Carefully, I put it back in the case, and placed it back underneath my brother's bed. That was the first time I ever played a guitar, and possibly the first time I broke one. I picked up my brother's tennis racket and played air guitar. I thought it would be harder to break, but I still managed to bust a string on that too.

A 19-year-old kid on our block, Steve Perringer, told me about a rock band called The Who, and this thing called FM radio. I was only seven. These groups sounded too wild for a little kid to understand. Like most kids I loved The Jackson 5, but everything else sounded too grown up to care about. All I knew about rock bands was by watching The Monkees on TV. They ran around on beaches playing leapfrog, jumping up and down, and wearing funny costumes. At the end, they'd act serious, and sing a song.

My brother David went to see to The Monkees in concert, and he brought me home a concert program. David Lee Brenner was a popular kid, and I thought he'd grow up to be famous.

The centerpiece of our living room was a round white marble coffee table. I hit my head against it, and I had to go to the hospital to get stitches on the corner of my left eye. It happened again, two weeks later, on my right eye

Then, around Halloween, I wanted my father to take me to a haunted house. He said he'd take me if I got him a glass of ice water. I went to the kitchen to fill up a glass, and my head barely reached over the counter. My mother walked by and slapped me on the back of the head, and I hit the bridge of my nose on the edge of the counter. I had to get more stitches, and I never got to go to the haunted house. My mother told my father she didn't hit me, and I must have cut my nose by myself.

When I was eight, I had my first girlfriend. Her name was Vicky Calvo, and everyone called her Chummers. Our parents would set us up for play dates. We used to go to her room and play with her dolls. One time, she lifted up her skirt to show me what was between her legs. Then I showed her what was between mine. After that got boring, we went back to playing with her dolls.

Chummers and I went trick-or-treating together, and I got a whole pillowcase full of candy. Somebody put a needle in one of the candy bars, but we saw it and threw it away. There were always news stories about some sicko poisoning candy.

Chummers always came over to my house to play records on the big stereo in the living room. We would dance to routines we made up to the songs, *Spinning Wheel* by Blood, Sweat, and Tears, *Up, Up, and Away* by the 5th Dimension, and Herb Alpert and The Tijuana Brass.

We rode our bikes to an abandoned school on our block that had acres of property. Once there we threw rocks at the windows, and Chummers always said we'd get married someday. We were best friends, but she moved away, and I never saw her again.

My brother went to Garfield High School, the same school my father had attended. I heard chatter about a famous guitar player who went there, called Jimi Hendrix. My dad told me he went to school with Jimi's dad. Jimi played a big concert at the local baseball stadium down on Rainer Avenue called Sick's Stadium. It was the home of the baseball team, the Seattle Pilots. I remember seeing Jimi Hendrix concert posters all over town on the telephone poles. Not long after, I heard he'd died of a drug overdose.

My mother was always partying while my dad spent his days and sometimes his nights working at the bakery. I thought it was normal for parents to ignore their kids. Eva, my nanny, did everything, and there were also three other teenagers to cook and clean for. I thought it was a happy home until my parents starting arguing.

I idolized my dad, with his shiny black shoes and the big fat wallet he kept in his back pocket. He greased his hair with Brylcreem, and he had all of his belts hanging on a piece of furniture in his bedroom. I was always threatened with getting spanked with 'the belt' to keep me in line, but he never hit me once. My dad wouldn't talk to me about grown up things. When I asked him, "What does it mean when my thing gets hard and big?" His answer was, "It means you have to go to the bathroom." I had to figure that out on my own.

He took me to Pike Place Market, and all the merchants knew him. Many places sold Brenner's bread. We were walking on First Avenue once, and he took me to a place that had pinball machines. A guy that looked like a bum on the street stopped him. I asked, "Hey Pops, who was that guy?" He answered, "That was Wiggles, Alin Wigodsky. He's David, Janice, and Thumper's real father." I never knew my siblings were adopted, and I was stunned at the revelation. It felt like everything everyone ever told me was a lie. At last, I understood why we weren't a close family.

My dad took vacations without my mother, and he'd take me with him. He once took me to Las Vegas, where he stuck me in the arcade all day with a pocketful of quarters. I got hooked on pinball, with all the flashing lights. My dad wasn't a heavy gambler like his father, but he'd take me to the race track in Seattle. It was called Longacres, and he'd ask me to pick horses for him. The first time I tried it, I picked two horses, and he bet the exacta. He won $70 on a $2 ticket.

My dad would always make the worst jokes and laugh with the bakers. They all loved him. My Aunt Yetta was a socialite. She looked like a movie star, but she always lived alone. Auntie Yetta was always surrounded by her six brothers growing up, so she always said she was happy to be living by herself. But when she took me downtown to the department stores like the Bon Marche or Frederick & Nelson, she would always introduce me as her son.

I had two friends who lived across the street. Brandt Luke, a Chinese boy who was two years older, and Steven Vincent, a black kid my age who moved to the neighborhood. Brandt's mother could not speak English, and they were very traditional. Brandt would give us Chinese candy, which was not really candy, but dried ginger, or something called sour balls, that you could buy at the Chinese shop called Uwajimaya. The only things we talked about were sports or girls, and what we thought boys were supposed to do with them.

Steven Vincent's father would always talk neighborhood gossip and joke around with my father. Sports were the big thing, and every father wanted their son to be a baseball, football or basketball star. I was too small to be a sports star, but I was real good at making noise. My dad bought me a toy drum set to stop me from setting up pots and pans and banging on them with wooden spoons. I also used to set up the empty pickle drums at the bakery and go to town.

My brother David and his friends would make model rockets and shoot them off in the street. Some of them were quite expensive, and I loved to watch my big brother put them together. He collected Hot Wheels cars, and made models with glue and paint. I had a big chemistry set, and I used to make plastic creatures called Creepy Crawlers with an electric toy called a Thingmaker. It used a liquid called Plastigoop which you poured into molds and baked it until it hardened. If you left it in too long, it could catch fire. I almost burned the house down more than a few times before they took it away.

I loved to stay up late and watch scary movies on TV. I was terrified of monsters. My big brother would always laugh at me for being scared. He'd calm me down by pretending we were astronauts taking off for the moon. He talked me to sleep every night.

My brother David liked a group called The Doors, and he learned how to play *Light My Fire* on the guitar. The older kid from our block, Steve Perringer, took him to see the Rolling Stones with Brian Jones at the Seattle Center Coliseum.

The Rolling Stones had a song on KJR called (*I Can't Get No*) *Satisfaction*. I wondered why this group was singing a song that was a slogan for a Winston Cigarettes TV commercial. 'Winston taste good like a cigarette should. Get satisfaction.' The song was always played constantly. I've never read the connection before, but I always assumed the song was Mick Jagger's answer to that Winston commercial. I didn't know you could take some advertised slogan and use it for yourself. I wouldn't find that out until much later.

Things like watching the president get shot or a man walking on the Moon on TV seemed normal. But cursing or doing anything indecent was considered shocking. It was a great time to be a kid.

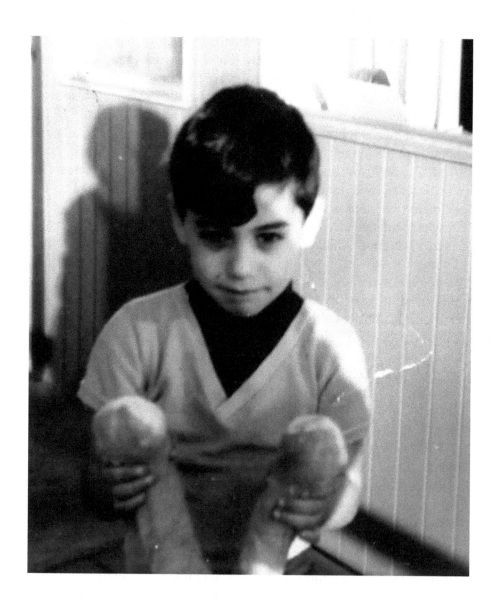

School Daze

I went to a private school called Seattle Hebrew Academy. We were not an extremely religious family like the Sephardic Jews who were decked out in scarves and hats, but the Brenners were a respected pillar of the Jewish community. My father would only take me to the synagogue on holidays. We never celebrated Christmas, but my Auntie Yetta would take me to get my photo with Santa every year

and spoil me with gifts. I was the little boy she never had. She always said I'd grow up to be a lady killer. My Auntie Yetta made me feel like the Moon followed me wherever I went.

My parents made me take piano lessons but I couldn't read sheet music. The teacher was a snobby fat lady who impressed my parents by playing something she called *Honky Tonk*. She taught me how to play *Chopsticks* and a few chords on piano, mainly the C chord. I wanted to play *Honky Tonk*, which was like the ragtime music I heard in a movie called *The Sting* that my father took me to see, but I could barely play *Chopsticks*.

At an early age, the religious people were more like figures of authority. My father had an obligation to appease them, just as he would the Bakers Union or the Health Department. It took strict guidelines to be certified kosher, and it was expensive. I preferred what my dad called crap, which was candy, grocery store cookies, or fast-food hamburger places like Dag's or Herfy's. The bakery had a full kosher restaurant and delicatessen. It was the only one of its kind in Seattle, just like the big Jewish delicatessens in New York and Chicago. But I only really liked crap or Eva's fried chicken.

In kindergarten, we had a teacher named Mrs. Rakavinsky. We called her Mrs. Rotten Whiskey. The principal, Rabbi Katz, was a mean Sephardic, and if you got called into his office, he would open up his desk drawer and show you 'The Paddle.' The paddle was a

27

short wooden bat with three holes cut into it at the top and what looked like Hebrew graffiti in marker pen on the side.

I had to take the bus to school in first grade, and I hated it. The only part I liked was recess. I brought my Monkees concert program or my mother's books for show and tell. I got in trouble for bringing in a book called *The Joy of Sex*, and another time for bringing in a book called *Black Like Me*.

I fell off a stool in class once, and I broke two fingers on my

right hand. I was in a cast so I had to write with my left hand, like my Dad. But, I was right-handed. At recess, the kids signed my cast, and we traded baseball cards. If you had one of a famous guy like Willie Mays, all the kids would be impressed. A kid showed me a card with the picture of a singer on it. He said it was Elvis Presley. I wasn't really that interested in singers or collecting cards; I had a chemistry set and was obsessed with Saturday morning cartoons.

The next year, in second grade, my father came to school, and he brought brownies for all the kids. It was really embarrassing to have my father come to school. Other kids' fathers came and talked about their normal non-Jewish jobs. Learning Hebrew was impractical. I never took to learning anything more than the first six letters of the alphabet. The biggest subject they pushed in school was obedience. They instilled a fear into every kid from day one.

I was in love with a girl at school named Abby Stern. So were my two best friends, Jerry Calvo and Paul Griff. She was really cute, and she had a birthmark on her hand. I tried getting her attention by writing 'FUCK' on the bathroom wall, but it backfired. A kid named Danny Stein immediately ran out of the bathroom crying and told the Rabbi what I had done.

The Fuck on the Wall Gang - bottom row far left to right: Abby Stern, Me, Jerry Calvo
Top row far right to left: Rabbi Katz, two girls, Danny Stein, Paul Griff

The Rabbi thought my two friends were involved as well, but they weren't. Rabbi Katz had us all write out the alphabet so he could compare the writing. I was so scared I pissed my pants, but I thought I could get away with it if I wrote the alphabet with my left hand. I didn't. Whenever someone got a swat you could hear the screams in every classroom. That was the first time I got my ass beaten trying to impress a girl.

I hated going to Seattle Hebrew Academy. It was in a bad neighborhood which was all black and becoming dangerous. They cancelled recess because there were shootings all around the area. I saw a poster of a record called *Superfly* in a store across the street from school. It had a picture of a dead guy with white stuff on his eyes. I was told it was cocaine.

In fourth grade, my parents put me in Graham Hill Elementary. It was a big change. You had to do the Pledge of Allegiance every morning. Most of the kids in my class were black. It was even harder to fit in with them than with the Jewish kids I had been going to school with. I got into fights, and I always got my ass beat. The black kids eventually warmed to me when they saw my nanny Eva, who they thought was my black grandma. I finally made a few friends after I said I liked Michael Jackson and the Jackson 5.

We usually played kickball at recess. It was a game where they rolled a basketball-sized rubber ball, and you kicked it and ran the bases like baseball. To get you out, they would throw the ball and hit you with it. I got slammed in the face when it was my turn. Another game the kids played was called Boodie. For this game you had to take a basketball shot, and if you made it, the next guy had to make the same shot. If he missed, he had to turn around, and you could hit him in the ass with the basketball as hard as you could throw it. I used to get creamed.

That same year, a policeman came to Graham Hill and showed the kids what drugs were. They brought in a display of pot, hash, pills, and cocaine. I looked at everything very carefully. The display made me curious. It looked dangerous, and it was kind of attractive to me. The cops told the kids, "If you ever try this stuff, you will go jail for the rest of your life..... if it doesn't kill you first."

All the kids, myself included, said, "I'll never use drugs when I grow up." The only thing grade school really taught me was how to watch the clock and get my ass kicked.

I wasn't very good at sports, but I joined the Oh Boy Oberto little league baseball team and played football in the 89ers league for eight and nine-year-old kids. If I went to a friend's house from school, they were always really poor. My dad was considered rich because Brenner Bakery was quite famous. There was a lot of segregation between black, Asian, Christian, and Jewish families in the early 70s. It was hard to make friends and keep them.

One day, my brother David went with my sister to Herfy's, and they were supposed to bring me home a hamburger. By the time they got home, my brother had eaten everything. I cried to my mother, and there was some sort of argument. The next thing I knew, an ambulance came, and some guys in white coats entered the house and took my big brother away. I didn't understand why they took him. It was just a hamburger or so I thought. I never saw him go crazy. I didn't even know if my mother loved him, but I did. I cried myself to sleep, and my brother wasn't there anymore to stop me from being scared.

My big brother David was a normal kid, but the psychiatrists thought otherwise. The doctors convinced my parents to consent to an experimental treatment for behavior problems called electro-shock therapy. Nobody in the family ever talked about my big brother's problems to me when they took him away. When we went to visit him, he was like a zombie. He never recovered, and he became a paranoid schizophrenic. They moved him into a halfway house. My mother just gave up on him.

My parents always had parties upstairs, like everything was fine. The day after one wild party, my parents had a horrible argument during dinner. Apparently, my mother was having an affair with a man named Dick Eacho. He had a wife, Rosalee, and four kids who were all teenagers. They were always coming over to our house.

My parents and sisters sat around the dinner table, and everybody screamed at each other. I just stared at the felt wallpaper and cried. A few days later, my Dad pulled up in our driveway in a lime green Porsche 914. He showed me his new Pulsar gold digital watch, gave me a hug, and told me he was moving away. I watched him drive away in his new Porsche, and I continued trying to dig a hole to China in our driveway with a nail.

I wanted to run away, to be anywhere other than where I was, and I never wanted to come home. I only got as far as a tree, five houses up the road. I was only eight, but I wanted to stay under that tree until I was 18.

My mother was never around after my father left, and I turned into a little troublemaker. My Dad picked me up sometimes to take me for the weekends. He moved to a singles-only residence in Bellevue called Sixty-01.

When I went to the bakery I drove my Uncle Itsey crazy. He was a short, fat, red-faced motherfucker. I went up to him and yelled, *"trick or treat,"* kicked him in the shins and ran away. I just hated Itsey from day one. He was the textbook definition of an old fat bastard.

My dad liked to take me on deliveries with him. I was always a handful who couldn't sit still. On one delivery of a wedding cake, I was bouncing around the truck screaming, and he yelled at me, "Sit down and shut up." I said, "okay", and I sat down on the wheel well but something didn't feel right. It felt squishy. Then I realized I had accidently sat down on the wedding cake. I said, "Umm Pops, I think I did something really bad. I'm sorry. You can spank me."

He laughed it off, but he wasn't thrilled. He called a bakery in Seattle that helped him do the repair, and he made the delivery on time. He used to brag that I sat on some couple's wedding cake.

I went to Lenny Wilkens basketball camp in the summer of '72. I was only nine and the minimum age was 11, but they accepted me anyway. My dad let me go for two weeks instead of one. I wasn't very good at basketball, but I loved it when my dad took me to the Coliseum to see the Harlem Globetrotters or the Seattle Supersonics.

Lenny Wilkens was a basketball superstar. I spent the night at his house during break between camp sessions. Lenny drove me to the bakery on the way to his house, but he didn't tell me we were going there. I was embarrassed, and I wanted to stay in the car. He went in, attracted a crowd, and my dad came out in the parking lot to get me.

Lenny took me home to stay overnight with his family. He drove me to camp the next day in his Mercedes. He had a million-dollar house with huge windows, in a forest. I played with his kids, and his wife cooked dinner. I wasn't too good at competing against the bigger kids, but I got an award on Trophy Day. On the final day of camp, I got a certificate that said, 'Smallest Camper - Biggest Voice.'

I loved to look at Thumper's Elton John record *Goodbye Yellow Brick Road.* The guys in the band looked like royalty. My sister's favorite song was *Stairway to Heaven* by Led Zeppelin. I thought it was a true song and it made me sad, but I really loved to hear that guitar sing at the end of the song. Even then, Led Zeppelin was like a magnet that attracted me.

Thumper once asked me, "If you were going to be a rock star, what would you be?" I told her, "I'll be a singer like Elton John." But even then I knew, to be a rock star you had to have talent, and I couldn't sing. I heard my voice played back on a cassette recorder, and I was horrified. Nobody in our family was musically inclined. Besides, all those cool rock stars were from England, which as far as I was concerned, was a different planet.

When I turned 10, my parents decided to sell the house in Seward Park, and my mother wanted to move away from Seattle. My oldest sister Janice had moved out and married a bakery truck driver named Stu Cordoba. David was living in a treatment center, and Thumper was about to move out on her own and get married to a guy named David Zauhar. My nanny Eva stopped working for us. Our family was broken.

Janice's Wedding

After a string of unsuccessful buyers, a man from South America was interested in the house. His name was Mr. Allen. He was in his late forties, wore gold jewelry, and had greasy black hair. He told my parents stories about life in his country, and he showed them and me a stack of Polaroid pictures of people that had been killed or tortured. He was a loud flashy man and he scared me.

On his second visit to our house, I was sitting in the living room, lighting a match and blowing it out. He came up to me, and said, "Don't play with matches." I replied in a snotty tone, "Gladly," and got up to walk away. That set him off, so he started to chase me. I ran down the stairs, and I tried to hide in the bathroom. He forced open the door, and proceeded to beat the shit out me.

I screamed for help as the big man from South America started hitting and kicking me. I cowered on the floor and thought he was going to kill me. He grabbed and twisted my hand and said, "If you were my kid I would break your fingers." When I told my mother what had happened, she just laughed it off. They continued to deal with Mr. Allen, and he bought our house.

I was having problems dealing with the divorce, and they figured counseling was the answer. I didn't want to see a psychiatrist, but I learned that if you told them what they wanted to hear, you could get out of there sooner. My dad thought it was a waste of time and money, but I think that was an easier solution for them than trying to explain things to me themselves. I swore that I would never get married after living with what my parents put me through. I didn't want to understand it.

My mother ended up marrying Dick Eacho, the man she was having an affair with. They decided to move to Mercer Island, a small town between Bellevue and Seattle. She tried to convince me that my father was a bad person. She told me, "Your father's going to bring Mr. Allen over here to beat you." She had me so scared he was going to do something bad to me I hid in a treehouse with some older boys from the neighborhood.

My mother talked so bad about my father I didn't know what to believe. I was too young to know she was extorting him, threatening that she'd never let him see me again unless he gave her more money.

The treehouse boys, Joel and Bill Skok, made short films to the music of The Beatles. The first music video I ever saw was their student films. They made clips to *A Day in the Life* and *The Fool on the Hill*. I'd never heard these songs before, and the films had lots of effects where their faces would change color. They filmed Joel sitting on a mound of dirt that was down the road. The camera followed him around the forest and going up the treehouse. They had a screening in their basement. I was blown away.

School in Mercer Island was an easier place to make friends if you were from a white middle-class family. I was best friends with a kid named Tad Salvator. I told his mother I was Catholic so I could go to church with them. I stood in line, and I got the Holy Communion. His mother called my mom and said, "I didn't know you were Catholic." When my mother told her we were Jewish, she wouldn't let Tad be

35

friends with me anymore. I was let down. I bought him a $13 toy airplane for Christmas and his mother returned it.

I had a crush on a Jewish girl, Maryanne Stusser, a skinny blonde with blue eyes and a crooked nose. I won a contest to take a small plane ride with our science teacher by guessing how many jelly beans were in a jar. Maryanne won second place, and she got to come too. The science teacher was a hippie. He had a Cessna Skyhawk airplane that could sit three people. He asked us, "Would you like to do a stall?" He pulled the throttle back to its lowest setting, and we started to fall to the ground. Maryanne grabbed my hand. Then he kicked on the engine and took the plane back up. I figured if I was I going to die, at least I'd be holding Maryanne Stusser's hand.

It wasn't always fun at school. I had words with a kid in class who got insulted when I said he was stupid. He got up from his desk and slapped me. The teacher broke it up but after class, I followed him outside and tapped him on the shoulder. When he turned around I punched him hard, right in the face. The teachers got there quickly after I hit him, and they broke it up before he could hit me back. That kid was a lot bigger than me. We both got detention.

I didn't have many friends, so I started some hobbies. First collecting stamps, then collecting coins. I spent hours at this shop called Pennies & Postage where I used to look at the coin books, steal some of the coins, and give the books back. Then I'd sell the coins back to them the next day, and buy more coins. Once they got wind of what I was doing, I stopped hanging out there and collecting stuff. There wasn't much else to do in Mercer Island.

My father took me to visit Eva in the projects, and a few months later, he took me to Eva's funeral. That was the first time I saw a dead person. She only made $50 or $80 a week taking care of me, cleaning and cooking for my entire family. Eva May Bryant was 80 years old when she died.

Divorce was common in the 70s, compared to the decades before. I didn't understand why my family fell apart, and everybody took sides. My dad was taking care of my brother, who was working at the bakery, even though David wasn't his biological child. They lived together for a while until David had more episodes. He complained Uncle Itsey was out to get him, and had become increasingly paranoid, putting newspapers all over his bedroom walls and windows. David went back to the halfway house, and he's lived in a facility ever since.

My dad took me out of school frequently to go on vacations. We went to Ocean Shores on the Washington coast. I liked the sea, but it wasn't my calling. We also drove down to Los Angeles. Somewhere in California, he fell asleep at the wheel, and spun off the road. I was in the back of his new Chevrolet hatchback sleeping, and I woke up to the car spinning. We hit a guard rail. I wasn't hurt and neither was he, but the car was wrecked.

When we got to Hollywood, it seemed dirty. It had a certain air about it that was very different from Seattle. We stayed at the Saharan Motor Hotel on Sunset Boulevard. There were burlesque clubs, strip bars, and music venues all along the Sunset Strip in 1974. I was only 11 years old. My dad took me to Knott's Berry Farm and Disneyland. While waiting in line, a woman came up to me. She asked if she could look at my eyes. I said okay, and she just stared at me. I loved going to Disneyland. It was my favorite place, even though it was full of strange women.

We went to Honolulu, and my dad hit on an Asian lady named Grace, who worked in a jewelry shop. He asked her, "What do you recommend for a pretty lady?" She showed him a pink coral necklace. He bought it, and she wrapped it up and gave it to him. He put it in her hands and said, "Would you like to go out sometime?"

My dad went to Waikiki often, to see Grace. He always stayed in the same hotel, The Waikikian. It was just like the TV show *Hawaii Five-0*. I loved my dad, but my mother got custody of me in the divorce. After our Hawaiian holidays, I usually went right back to Mercer Island to live with Mom and Dick.

Dick Eacho always had these get-rich-quick schemes. He designed a disposable barbeque called The BBQ. It consisted of a foil pan, briquettes, and a metal grill wrapped in a plastic bag. It was stapled together with a tag that required a hole punched into it, to attach it to a display rack. To save time, I used a hammer on the puncher so I could do 10 tags at a time instead of one. I broke his custom $20 hole-punch tool. and he kicked the shit out of me when he found out.

The BBQ never took off. He got it in a few local grocery stores. Then we saw in another grocery store, some big company had made the same thing. He only got it in a few local grocery stores. Later, we saw in another grocery store, some big company had made the same thing. Dick was a bad drinker and a horrible stepfather. I hated him, and wanted to live with my dad.

Smoke on the Water

For the summer, I went to live with my father in Bellevue, and after my twelfth birthday, I went back to live with Mom and Dick. They moved to a small town called Friday Harbor, on San Juan Island. It was a two-hour drive and a two-hour ferry ride from Seattle. The town was so remote that the nearest neighbor lived a mile away.

There was an older girl that I crushed on, named Lynn Buck. Lynn would catch baby rabbits for fun. One day I took one home. The poor thing choked itself to death trying to get out of a cardboard box.

I got interested in motocross from our neighbor, Slick. He rode a Kawasaki 125, and went to motocross races. I got an XR75 motorbike which I used to ride around on a track we made on Lynn Buck's farm. I crashed a few times, and gave up riding motor bikes.

Friday Harbor was a fishing village, so I started to hang out with the kids at the docks, and they got me to smoke cigarettes. While I was smoking, the older kids would burn holes in the back of my blue down jacket. I was starting to be pegged as a troublemaker.

When my Mom and Dick went away, Slick, our closest neighbor, stayed over. He was 16. I invited one of the girls from my grade to come over. Her name was Pam, and she was the baby of three sisters. One day, we poured a little bit of every bottle that was in the wet bar into a glass. That's what I thought a mixed drink was.

We both got way too drunk, and Pam and I decided to have sex. We did it, but I didn't know what I was doing, and neither did she. We just stuck ourselves together for a few minutes, but nothing really happened.

We also got extremely sick. When my Mom returned the next day, there was vomit all over the house. At school I was quizzed by Pam's older sister who asked me, "What did you do to my sister?" and I said, "Nothing." She said, "Pam said you fucked her." All of a sudden, the older school girls started to talk to me.

Dick and my mother thought I was getting out of control, so they sent me back to live with my father. My dad got an apartment in Bellevue, at a complex called Heatherstone. I got enrolled into Highland Junior High School. It was easier to make friends there.

I used to go to the bakery after school. The employees took to me pretty well. At the bakery, I was the only one who could get one over on my Uncle Itsey, who was meaner than ever. I drove him crazy. He'd complain to my dad, and my dad would tell him to leave me alone. Out of all the machines, the bread slicers were the ones I liked the best. Sometimes my dad would ask the drivers to take me with them when they did their deliveries.

One of the drivers I did a delivery with was a tall white guy with a Jewfro named Dave Pierce. He was 24, and I thought he was cool. My dad asked him to take me with him on a trip downtown. While we were driving, he pulled out a brass pipe and asked me, "Have you ever smoked marijuana?" I shook my head "no," and he lit it up and passed me the pipe. I took a few puffs, and he told me to hold it in. By the time we got back to the bakery, I had to go in my dad's office, shut off the light, and lie down on the couch. I was spinning and seeing colors. It was frightening, but I liked it.

I used to wait on customers at the bakery, but all I really wanted to do was go down the street to this pinball arcade. I would take money from the register to go play pinball, but I got caught, so my dad wouldn't let me wait on customers anymore.

One day after school, I saw a guitar case in the office. It belonged to Dave Pierce. Dave came into the office, and opened the case. He told me the guitar was called an L6-S. It looked like a guitar that I saw on Led Zeppelin posters. He started to play it, and it blew my mind. He told me, "Check it out; I just got it." He let me hold it. My dad was filling out the orders at his desk, and it was a quiet afternoon. He showed me how to play *Smoke on the Water* on one string. When I played it, I felt a shock, and my eyes grew wide. Pierce said, "You know what, I got an old guitar that I don't use anymore. It's just a Japanese copy of a Les Paul, but you can have it. I'll bring it by tomorrow." I didn't know what a Les Paul was, but it sounded pretty cool.

The next day, he brought in a black guitar with gold pickups. I took it home, and took it apart with a screwdriver. A few days later, I brought it back to him in a bag. It was in pieces.

Thumper took me to see the movie *Tommy* by The Who, because Elton John was in it. I'd never seen anything of The Who before that.

Seeing that movie as a child was really intense. I liked Elton John's songs, but I was really taken aback by the lead singer in the band, Roger Daltrey, and the rest of the stars.

With all the Hawaiian vacations, Disney cartoons, TV, and the occasional R-rated movie, I was really confused about what real life was supposed to be like. It made me want to grow up even faster than I already was.

I was making friends in my new school, Highland Junior High. One kid, Dave Olsen, met me in the woods next to the school on the night of a school dance. He had a joint, and we smoked it. We were running through the football field, and everything seemed like it was in slow motion. After we smoked that joint, it was like I was dreaming, but I was awake.

There was another kid in my class, Chris DeGarmo, who used to smoke with us. Chris was a skinny kid with a shag haircut and a pointy nose. Rock bands ruled the world, and it was all that anybody at school talked about. Dave, Chris, and I all had a dream to start a band. Dave wanted be the singer, and he drew pictures of what he thought we should look like. We smoked pot in the woods during lunch, and I was really starting to be happy in this new school.

Unfortunately, my dad had to send me back to Friday Harbor to live with Mom and Dick because my mother wanted to use me for child support to pay for the house they were living in.

I was starting to feel like a Duncan yo-yo, being dragged up and down the state. After a while, I got used to the traveling, I even started to like it. People were always happy to see me when I returned from a trip, but I never got used to living with Dick. I usually cried myself to sleep at night and swore, "When I get older, I'm never going to get married. Never ever."

It was a new school year on Friday Harbor, and a new girl came to the island. Her name was Holly Bacon, and she was the hottest girl in our grade. She was a 12-year-old blonde bombshell. She had boobs, and she hung out with the smokers. We were set up together, but all we did was a bit of kissing and groping. She was the first girl to stick her tongue in my mouth. I was too afraid to do anything else. Eventually, the older boys snatched her up, and she started to go out with them.

My neighbor Slick took me to the motocross track to watch him race, and we rode around the farms. Bands didn't play in Friday Harbor, so none of the kids were interested in music. It was sports, motorcycles, or marijuana.

Slick had an electric guitar in his room. It was some cheap Japanese guitar, and he said I could have it. I took it home, and I took that guitar apart too. I couldn't play, so I guess I thought taking them apart was the next best thing.

By this time, I had become a seasoned pot smoker. One day, I was walking back from school, and obviously high. Dick saw me, and stopped his car. He saw that I was really stoned, took me home, and beat me up. It was a huge crisis that a seventh grader was smoking pot, and the solution was to have me enrolled into a strict boarding school in Vancouver BC.

Dick drove me to Canada, and I had to present myself to the Headmaster to be accepted to this establishment of higher learning. We entered his office, and I sat down on the couch facing him, but I just looked down. He was wearing some sort of uniform.

He asked me, "So Adam, why do you want to go to this school?" I stretched out my legs and put my feet on the coffee table in front us, looked him dead in the eyes, and said, "I don't want to go to your fucking school." The Headmaster calmly got up and told Dick that I could not be accepted, and asked us to leave.

Dick and my Mother were fed up. I was dragged out by my ears, and taken back to Friday Harbor. It was a very silent, miserable ride home. A few weeks later, I went back to live with my father, and I never looked back.

So This is Rock and Roll

It was the summer of '76. I was back with Dad, and free from the abuse of Dick Eacho. The bakery was always busy, so I'd go down the road to the pinball arcade. When I ran out of quarters playing pinball, I went next door to a music shop called Bandstand East.

I wanted a guitar. A salesman introduced himself as Charlie Kester. He showed me a Fender Mustang; a good starter electric guitar. They plugged it into a Fender Champ amplifier. My dad didn't want to buy it; he thought an electric guitar would be another hobby like collecting stamps that I'd lose interest in, but I really wanted a good electric guitar, so I went to my aunt.

A few days later, I went back there, and I met another salesman named Mike Lull. He had long hair, was young and cool, and he also repaired guitars. As an early birthday present, my Aunt Yetta bought me the Fender Mustang, the Champ Amplifier, and a red wah-wah pedal to go with it.

I went back home, and sat down. Once I was in my room, I plugged it in and started making noise with the wah-wah pedal. I tried to pick the strings and play some notes, working on it for eight hours a day for weeks, just making noise with that guitar plugged into the wah-wah pedal.

I couldn't figure out how to play anything but *Smoke on the Water* on one string. After a while, my fingers hurt so bad I wanted to cry. It was frustrating. I couldn't make music, but I felt like I had something brewing inside of me that was dying to get out. I really wanted to figure out how to play it. When I set it down, I'd stare at the guitar like it was looking back at me. I was taunted.

I was just about to turn 13, and my father was taking me to Israel with Thumper so I could have my bar mitzvah at the Wailing Wall. I couldn't read Hebrew, and I didn't want a bar mitzvah. But I studied how to say my recital phonetically to make my dad happy.

I didn't like to spend my time at the bakery, but my father taught me the trade anyway. I learned to fold cheese buns. I scooped bagels out of the pot they boiled them in first to proof them before baking. I saw how they mixed the dough, and painted egg on the bread or pastries to make them shine. I got burned a few times taking things

43

out of the oven. It was expected that I would work in the bakery like everyone else in the family, but I saw how hard my father worked, and I wanted a different life than he had.

Before the trip, I loaned my Fender Mustang guitar to Chris DeGarmo. We had sleepovers and talked about the girls at school, rock bands, and which one of us was further up the puberty chain. We went to see our first concert, Yes and Gentle Giant, at Seattle Coliseum on July 23, 1976. We smoked pot in a downtown park before the show, and we went on the Wild Mouse and Flight to Mars rides at Seattle Center. We were best friends. Yes was supposed to be the most amazing concert ever, and they even have a three-headed-dragon. We had really bad seats, and by the time Yes played, the music bored me, and I fell asleep.

On August 14, 1976, my 13th birthday, I had my bar mitzvah ceremony at the Jerusalem Wall. I wasn't religious, but I figured if I was going to talk with God, that was my moment. I prayed to make my dreams in life come true. I wrote a few wishes on paper, stuck it in a crack, and kissed the wall.

Now, in my father's eyes, I was a man. In my eyes, it was a great big world, and I wanted to see it all.

We went to all of the holy tourist spots, and I rode on a camel. In a pizza shop, I saw a poster advertising a Ted Nugent concert in Tel Aviv. I went to an Arab market, and I saw little kids walking around with machine guns. We also went to London, and my sister took me to Carnaby Street. Once there, we bought the ugliest pair of platform shoes ever made. The plane stopped in New York, and we went outside long enough to feel the muggy air of the city in the summer of '76, while Son of Sam started his year-long reign of terror.

When I returned to Bellevue, I called Chris DeGarmo to get my guitar back. He told me, "Listen to this," and over the phone, he played the guitar intro to *Over the Hills and Far Away* by Led Zeppelin. I didn't believe he could do it. I thought he was playing the record.

When he returned the Fender Mustang, he showed me that he had really learned how to play it. He said, "I figured it out by listening to the record over and over." I was amazed.

Just before school started up again, I went with Chris DeGarmo and his brother Mark to the Seattle Kingdome to see Aerosmith. The opening acts were Jeff Beck, Derringer, and Starz. We made our way up to the front of the crowd. The mass of people swayed back and forth as the band hit the stage, and Chris and I got split from each other.

Derringer's guitar player, Danny Johnson, did a guitar trick, and put both hands on the guitar neck. The bass player was Kenny Aaronson, someone I would get to play with later in life. The drummer was Vinny Appice who later played with Dio and Black Sabbath. At the time, Rick Derringer's band and career were on fire.

Jeff Beck was incredible. There was no singer; he sang with his guitar. *Freeway Jam* and *Scatterbrain* were a little heavy for my inexperienced ears, but I got it. His music was extremely emotional. I had never heard a guitar cry like that before. At the end of his show, he played *Train Kept a Rollin'* which was one of Aerosmith's big songs on the radio.

The crowd swayed, and I got pushed into girls. I grabbed a girl's chest to retain my balance. You could grope the girl in front of you while trying to push your way forward. It was a sea of crazy people.

Aerosmith were fantastic, but not as exciting to me as the bands who played before them. Joe Perry moved his arm like a locomotive during *Train Kept a Rollin',* and he used a talk box in the song *Sweet Emotion.* I stayed up front the whole time. After the show was over, I looked at all the amplifiers, lights, and sound gear, as the roadies were tearing down the stage. I couldn't find Chris or his brother, and I didn't know how I was going to get back home. I wandered out of the Kingdome, and just followed the crowd.

I was stranded in Seattle, but I didn't care. I was on a new high inspired by this rock and roll, and those super cool guys on stage with the long hair. There were thousands of people in the streets coming from the show, and the whole world seemed happy. People were screaming, singing, and cheering. I'd never been alone in downtown Seattle by myself, and I didn't even have any money. I just followed everyone else and got on a bus without paying to get myself back to Bellevue.

All of a sudden, everything seemed possible. I just had to figure out this guitar thing. After that show, I decided to get serious about learning how to play guitar. I asked one of the bread slicers at the bakery, Lee Moore, if he could help me. Lee said, "I know this guy, Chris Jacobson, he can play like Jimmy Page of Led Zeppelin, even the double lead on *Black Dog.*" I never heard of a double lead before. Chris Jacobson was in his late 20s. He had really bushy long hair and looked like a rock star. He came over to the bakery for lunch. We sat in the restaurant, and he started playing stuff on my guitar. He knew how to play everything. Chris was known as one of the best guitar players in Seattle. but he never stayed with any band for very long. He was in a band called Marilyn, and joined another band called Krakatoa, quit after a few months, and joined Jax. He took me to his house in Seattle, and showed me his Goldtop Les Paul. There was just a couch and a stereo. Beer cans and records littered the floor. One record I saw was by a band called AC/DC. Chris said to me, "Hey, would you like to go see a really good band next week at the Paramount? They're called Rush."

I went to the Seattle Paramount on Oct 28, 1976. I had never heard of Rush before. The opening act was a guitar player named Tommy Bolin. He was bluesy; I didn't think much of it. But then Rush came on. It was like a tidal wave of magic swept over me. A feeling I never felt before that transported me into a new dimension. They opened with a song called *Bastille Day*. The opening guitar riff was the most badass thing I'd ever heard. I hadn't imagined a guitar could sound so powerful, so emotional. It spoke to me. It was overwhelming. I had never experienced anything that made such a direct impact straight into me.

Their song lyrics had no mystical message that was over my head like Yes, nor were songs about girls like Aerosmith and Rick Derringer. This message was just pure rock and roll. The singer was so confident, and the way he played bass in time with the guitar player was masterful. Everything sounded so tough, so big and dynamic, and at times so beautiful that it made me cry. They did this thing called *2112,* and Geddy Lee sang, "Listen to my music and see what it can do."

The music went from really quiet to really loud, and from slow to really fast. It was like a roller coaster. At the end of the song, a voice came out and said, "We have assumed control" over and over. At that moment, something changed in me forever.

I was floored. I never imagined that anything, not just a band, but anything on Earth, could be so powerful. The guitar player was the most attractive person I had ever seen on a stage. He covered his face with his long blond hair while playing a Gibson ES 335. They had giant Marshall amps stacked on top of each other, and a chrome drum set with two bass drums. I stood on my seat when Chris would stand up, and when Chris applauded, I did too. He loved the drum solo. When they announced the song *Working Man,* I screamed and applauded like I knew it. When the house lights came on, I felt like I had found God. I was baptized by Rush. From that day on, I was instantly and completely addicted to rock and roll.

After the show, we waited by the backstage door, and watched the band go into a waiting black limousine. When the band came out, I tried to give the guitar player, Alex Lifeson, a guitar pick, but he just right walked past me with this girl on his arm. She was all dressed up like a movie star. Chris said, "That's Gail. She's a notorious groupie." I'd never seen a groupie before.

The next time I went to Chris Jacobson's house, he had the Tommy Bolin album on the floor. Tommy Bolin died of a drug overdose six weeks after that show.

I had destroyed my Fender Mustang. I got frustrated and threw it against the wall. The only thing I could play was *Smoke on the Water.* I hated the way it looked with its tiny pickups. It was a toy compared to the guitars in the music stores.

Chris Jacobson gave me a Japanese Les Paul copy as a gift. He took me to Guitar Center to look at the instruments. They had amps that were stacked as high as the ceiling. There was a Gibson Doubleneck hanging on the wall, like Jimmy Page from Led Zeppelin used. The guitar shops during the 70s were my temples. I had my eye on a guitar that was shaped like a V. I just needed $500 to buy it.

I thought up the brilliant idea to collect pot seeds and add them to some commercial weed. I would divide it up into plastic bags which I cut in half and sealed with a lighter in a phone book. I sold them for 50 cents. I sold a few bags to some older kids and they wanted to know what the catch was. When I said, "There are a lot of seeds," they said, "Good, we'll grow them."

A lot of kids sold parsley as weed, but I thought mixing it with seeds was a better idea. One morning before school, I sold one to Billy Biggs, a short kid with a Jewfro. Later that day, I got called into the vice principal's office. There was a man there with a large birthmark on his face and I saw Billy Biggs crying.

The vice principal said, "His morning teacher caught him showing this bag of marijuana to the person sitting next to him, and Billy said you sold it to him." I freaked out, denied it, and I was arrested. I was taken out of school in handcuffs. My dad was livid.

A few weeks later I went to court, and I still denied it. I was shaking my head while Billy Biggs was giving his testimony. My dad hired a lawyer. He told me, "Don't shake your head. The judge will know you're guilty. Just be still." I got sentenced to 30 hours of community service, which consisted of picking up litter off the streets in Bellevue. That was the end of my drug-dealing career.

There were some really beautiful girls at Highland Junior High. One was Jil Rivet; she was absolutely stunning. I went over to her house and tried to impress her with a Buzz Bomb, this firework I got at an Indian reservation. She wasn't impressed.

All the pretty girls only went out with high school kids, so I let guitars take over my interest. I hung around after school with my best friend, Chris DeGarmo. We went to music stores, talked about records, played video games and pinball, and tried to say impressive things to each other about guitars.

School dances were fun, and they usually had live bands. One band was called Shifter. They had a blond guitarist and bass player who were twins. Their brother was a bass player who wore white fur boots in a band called Rail & Company, the biggest local band in Bellevue.

Rail & Company had two guitar players. Andy Baldwin, who played a Gibson SG, and Rick Knotts, who played a Gibson Flying V. DeGarmo and I went to see them, and we watched the show from the front row. Rick Knotts could play every solo note for note. His sound was perfect. They both had Marshall 50-watt amps, and their guitars sounded just like the songs on the radio. They were managed by a small local company called Unicam. The man in charge was Craig Cooke, a guy with a permed mullet and big glasses. He booked all the bands that played at Lake Hills Roller Rink.

Shifter played covers. I studied the guitarist's hands as he played *Rock and Roll Band* by Boston, and *Last Child* by Aerosmith. Nobody danced at these school dances when the bands played. We were middle-class white kids so nobody could dance very good, but my friends and I loved to watch these rock bands play. It was an immediate form of communication.

The disco dances without bands were all about trying to hook up with a girl. Some kids would dance, but the stoners didn't. I just stood around like a wallflower. At one of the disco dances, I asked a really pretty girl, Lisa Soloman, to dance. She was a cheerleader. By blind luck, it turned out to be the slow song, *Love Hurts*. She put her arms around me, and put her face right against mine. I fell in love in six seconds. After the song was over she kissed me on the cheek and walked away. We never spoke when we saw each other at school, but I never forgot that dance.

At another dance, Jeff Rivers, one of our stoner school friends, had an older brother, Corey Rivers, who played guitar and was the singer in a rock band. He looked like *The Greatest American Hero* in the daytime, but on stage he became dark. He wore a black cape, played lead guitar, and sang Black Sabbath. It freaked us out. I never knew someone could change so much when they played on stage with a band.

I started hanging around a music store called Bandwagon after school. I usually stayed there until it closed, when my father or my aunt would pick me up and take me home. I looked at the guitars and the watched the people trying them out. I always walked around holding my black Les Paul copy that Chris Jacobson gave me.

There was a Gibson book on the counter with a picture of Keith Richards wearing no shoes and playing a black Les Paul. All the rock stars in that book played the same guitars you could buy in the store. I could stare at guitars for hours. I still couldn't play, but I saw a guy pick up a Les Paul and bend a string back and forth.

The store manager Joe Griggs and the guitarist for a band called Rite of Spring would plug in the amps and play loud guitar for me. He played the riff to *Rock Bottom* by a group called UFO. My dad let me bring them free food from the bakery, so they didn't mind me hanging out there all day long.

A guy came up to me and said, "Hey kid, you're always around here wearing that fucking guitar and you don't ever play anything. Why don't you learn a couple of chords?" He showed me a D chord, and I practiced bending the middle string back and forth. From there, I started to understand the fretboard and the strings like it was a new language.

I took home a Mel Bay guitar chord book and after a few weeks, I started to know more than Chris DeGarmo. I got good enough that I convinced my dad to buy me a Gibson Flying V, one that I'd been staring at for months in the shop window.

Rick Knotts offered guitar lessons at Bandwagon. It cost $5 per 30-minute lesson. Chris and I took some lessons together, and my dad paid for it. Rick answered all of our questions. He showed us how to play chords, and taught us scales. The blues scale was very important. 99% of rock and roll guitar solos were based upon it.

The goal was to learn the solos to *Train Kept a Rollin'*, *Stairway to Heaven*, *Freebird* and the solo to Led Zeppelin's *Heartbreaker*, which had a strange guitar trick done at the top of the neck. We started with the chords and scales, but DeGarmo knew all the right things to ask. He knew these guitar terms like barre chords, pull-offs, and hammer-ons. Rick showed us picking techniques, and how to get different harmonics out of one note like ZZ Top, by holding the pick very close to the string. We stopped taking lessons when we were good enough to understand the guitar on our own.

Rick Knotts taught us how to learn on our own, because once you knew the basics, it was about record copying. Instead of showing us how to play a song, he wanted us to be able to learn how to play things on our own. I wanted to learn exactly how guitarists like Alex Lifeson of Rush played guitar.

Rick Knotts had tricks like slowing down the record speed to 18 RPM so you could hear really fast guitar licks being played back slow, an octave lower. Once he taught me the basics, I was off to the races. Every new song I learned was like a prize. I was completely in love with playing the guitar.

In school, we would do nothing but talk about guitars and bands. There was a new band called KISS who wore clown makeup. They had a double live album that was really popular. DeGarmo said he liked the guitars and I was curious. There were a lot of people saying, "KISS sucks." I wanted to form my own opinion.

After school we'd go at a pinball arcade called Foosball, next to a tavern called The Mustard Seed. Just down from there, in a parking lot, was a record store in a portable trailer. I went in, took a look around, grabbed the KISS *Alive!* record from the rack, stuck it under my jacket, and walked right out the door.

I thought the guitar playing on KISS *Alive!* was not as cool as Led Zeppelin or Rush, but there was something more that I liked. The feeling of rock n roll they had from everything they sang about. I liked the lead singer and the way the lead guitar player made his notes sing.

When the Led Zeppelin movie, *The Song Remains the Same,* came out, it played in a midnight movie theater in Crossroads. It was the most exciting thing that ever came to town. I went with Chris DeGarmo. We were too young to see Led Zeppelin when they played concerts in Seattle, but the movie had a huge impact on me.

Looking at Jimmy Page on the big screen playing guitar was unlike anything I had ever seen before. I had no idea how he was doing what he did. Led Zeppelin had this huge mystique with kids and there were all these crazy rumors about them. Jimmy Page seemed to be not of this Earth. When I saw the bassist John Paul Jones with his wife telling stories to his daughters, and he said, "Ahh, the tour dates.... This is tomorrow," I knew he was a normal guy. I dreamed about meeting them someday.

I knew I could play single notes really well and I could make them sing like the guitarists I heard on the radio. The term for it was vibrato, and it was a lot harder for DeGarmo to make those single notes sing and sound in key. Eventually, I started to get really good. I could play all the solos I heard on the radio.

Rail & Company sold their 50-watt Marshall amps to Bandstand East to upgrade to 100-watt amps. I got my dad to buy me one, and got my aunt to buy me the other one. At the time, they were only a couple of hundred bucks each. I still use those amps to this very day.

I spent a lot of time at Bandstand East, since it was so close to the bakery. I was occasionally working at the bakery, but I couldn't get along with Itsey, and I hated working. The only thing I wanted to do was hang out at the guitar shop.

I started to become friends with the guitar repair man, Mike Lull. I brought him lunch from the bakery. Mike invited into the back of the store where he worked on guitars, and he smoked pot with me. He taught me about building and setting up guitars, dipping pickups in paraffin wax, and how to use a strobetuner. He told me, "You need to get PAF pickups for the V, It's a vintage Gibson pickup from the late 50s, with a sticker on the back that said 'Patent Applied For.' I'm going to find you a couple but they're kinda pricey, around $250." I got two of them and started to hang out at Bandstand East every chance I got.

Rush was still my favorite band at the time. I could play every guitar riff on *2112* and most of the other songs from the double live album. Chris Jacobson came around and taught me some chords I couldn't figure out.

Chris Jacobson's new band, Jax, were doing a show at the Seattle Paramount, opening for the Ramones. Chris took me to the show, and I sat in the third row to watch him. He was super cool. He played *Walk This Way* by Aerosmith, and other cover songs with his Goldtop Les Paul through a Marshall stack. After he played, I sat there and waited to see the Ramones. I'd seen the movie *Rock and Roll High School* and they reminded me of the 60s bands my brother David liked.

Next to me was a young couple who looked like students from the early 60s - a girl in a nice dress with bobby sox and saddle shoes, and a college guy wearing a buttoned-up white shirt with Buddy Holly glasses. When the Ramones went on, it was like a 747 jet had just taken off inside the room. It was 100 times louder than anything I ever heard in my life. It was so loud that it was scary.

From the very first 1-2-3-4, the guy next to me with the glasses started to go into spastic convulsions. I thought he was having an epileptic fit. He was throwing his arms in the air, jumping sideways violently, and bumping into me and everyone else around him. It was his way of reacting to the music. His girlfriend kept apologizing because I thought he was having an epileptic fit. He did it to every song.

Chris Jacobson and his Goldtop Les Paul Deluxe

Chris Jacobson came and got me after the show. I asked him, "Why can't the guitar player play any solos?" Chris told me, "I saw Johnny Ramone warming up on the side of the stage before he went on and he was playing leads. They just don't have any leads in their songs." I still have never heard a group play louder than the Ramones at the Seattle Paramount.

Chris DeGarmo and I had a friend named Rick Balch. His dad was a Chevrolet dealer named Dick Balch, who was famous for smashing new cars with a sledgehammer in TV commercials. Rick lived with his mother. His parents were divorced, and we never saw his father.

His mother let us smoke pot in their basement. We blasted the stereo, and cleaned the seeds from the weed off of a Ted Nugent album. We bonged out for months, and listened to all the big rock of the 70s. Chris and I would pass my guitar back and forth.

Rick Balch didn't play anything. He was a goofy guy with freckles and wire frame glasses. He was a year or two older than Chris and I, and he could do whatever he wanted at home. He constantly yelled at his mother, telling her to fuck off. She always just left us alone.

I got caught smoking pot one too many times by my dad, and it was becoming a problem. He wanted to send me back with my mother, but I talked him out of it. There was nothing to do but hang out at the pinball places or go to Rick Balch's house with Chris DeGarmo and smoke his bong. I convinced my dad to let me stay over at Rick Balch's house for a few weeks, and it was okay with Rick's mother.

Balch was a control freak and a bully. He grabbed my V guitar from out of my hands, and pretended he wanted to learn how to play it. When I asked for it back, he threw the guitar across the room and nearly broke it.

Balch had a fancy sports car from his dad's car lot. Sometimes he was really cool and funny, other times he was mean and vicious. He would talk shit about me behind my back to Chris DeGarmo, and do the same to him. We were a group of friends and we took a lot of shit from Rick Balch, but he always had really good pot.

Led Zeppelin were coming to Seattle that summer to play at the Kingdome. Rick, Chris and I waited in line all day and got 100 level general admission tickets. Because I was staying with Rick, he wanted to hold the tickets for safekeeping. A few days passed, and Rick said to me, "I checked on the tickets, and it's the strangest thing. Mine is there, but yours isn't." I asked him, "What happened?" He was telling it to me like he thought I believed him.

I begged him, "C'mon, don't do this to me," but he just insisted that it wasn't there. It was no use. I started complaining, and then Rick Balch proceeded to hit me in the face. I got a bloody nose and a cut lip. I fell down to the ground, and he started kicking me. He threw me out of his house and said, "Fuck off you little piece of shit. I'm keeping your guitar."

His mother came out, and asked what happened. I was a bloody mess, crying in her front yard. I asked her to please get me my guitar back, so she went back inside. Rick came out and threw the guitar case on the grass and said, "You just had to tell my mother, didn't you? I was going to give your ticket back but not now. Go away, you little fucking baby."

I walked back home to my dad's apartment, and I never did get my ticket back. That was the last time Led Zeppelin played in Seattle.

I listened to a show called *The Next Best Thing* on the radio. They played the songs Led Zeppelin recorded in the order they performed them in Seattle. I stopped hanging around Rick Balch and Chris DeGarmo after that.

I didn't have a crystal ball, but 24 years later, I played lead guitar on Led Zeppelin bassist John Paul Jones' solo album, *The Thunderthief.* We performed together live on multiple occasions, and I became a close personal friend to him and his family. But on July 17, 1977, I was home alone practicing my guitar, trying not to feel sorry for myself, dreaming about meeting Led Zeppelin.

After that, I blocked Rick Balch out of my life forever. I never knew anything about his life, but his death was in The Seattle Times, reported by John de Leon of The Associated Press in 2013.

"EVERETT — No charges will be filed against an Everett woman who at one time was suspected of suffocating her boyfriend with her chest.

Snohomish County Deputy Prosecutor Travis Johnson told The Herald there was insufficient evidence from police and medical examiner reports to go forward with a manslaughter charge.

The medical examiner concluded that 51-year-old Richard Balch, of Auburn, died Jan. 12 of alcohol poisoning. He also had heart and liver disease. A struggle may have contributed to his death but was not the cause.

Police noted the size difference between Rick Balch and his killer Donna Lange, she was 5-feet, 6-inches and 192 lbs, he was 5-feet, 7-inches and 175 lbs. Deputies, called to the Airport Inn trailer park at 12:45 AM for a disturbance report, found medics performing CPR on Lange's 51-year-old alleged boyfriend, who was later pronounced dead at Swedish Hospital.

Witnesses said several people were drinking and smoking marijuana at the mobile home when Balch and the 50-year-old woman argued over an ex-girlfriend. Witnesses later found her on top of Balch in back of the trailer. She was intoxicated and said she didn't remember."

Apparently, Rick Balch's demise was something the authorities thought best to leave unsolved.

Junior High Rock Stars

Sometime in 1978, I was sitting on a small amp at Bandstand East, playing my Gibson V through a Marshall. I saw two guys get out of a car from the storefront window. As they walked in, I was playing the riff to *Finding My Way* by Rush. Sometimes people would just watch me play and say nothing, but these guys came right up to me. A kid with long blond hair about my age said, "Hi. I'm Gary Thompson. I play drums. Do you want get together and play sometime?"

We exchanged numbers, and got together to jam in Gary's parents' basement. Gary was 15, and one school grade above me. He was almost old enough to drive a car.

Gary Thompson had a chrome Ludwig drum kit just like Neil Peart of Rush. We were into the same type of music. He read magazines like *Circus, Hit Parader,* and *Creem*, and knew a lot about rock bands.

Adjacent to the rehearsal area was his bedroom where he had a Pioneer stereo system and albums by Rick Derringer, Rush, Pat Travers, Angel City, UFO, Queen, Scorpions, Peter Frampton, Led Zeppelin, Ted Nugent, and Aerosmith. We put together a list of songs, and went about learning them.

Within a few weeks, we got a local kid from Gary's school, Scott Earl, to come over and play bass. Scott had curly brown hair, rosy red cheeks, and a black Fender Mustang bass. He was just learning how to play. Bass was easier than guitar; you only had to play one string. We didn't have a singer, but we figured we'd find one. We got some songs together, and that was the start of our first band.

We wanted a one-word name with four letters like KISS or Rush so we called the band Rage.

Rage rehearsed in Gary's basement for months. I started to get to know Gary's friend, Mike McCrea, who lived with his grandparents on a mink farm in Woodinville. McCrea was a 16-year-old stoner with long hair. He had a Cherry Sunburst Gibson Les Paul that he couldn't play. He just wanted to be the guy behind the scenes. McCrea told me, "You need a singer like Steven Tyler from Aerosmith because most of his lyrics have double meanings. He writes songs about drugs and anxiety."

We listened to *Rip It Out* on the Ace Frehley solo album, and McCrea pointed out, "Most rock lyrics like Ace or KISS are all just simple, stupid poems. Like nursery rhymes, but about fucking chicks, or heartbreak. That's the formula. That's how you write songs."

I looked at all the Aerosmith, Ted Nugent, and Scorpions records, and the name that was on all of them was Leber-Krebs. It was a management company out of New York. We would read every detail on the back of the albums like we were looking for clues. McCrea told me. "Jack Douglas, the record producer in the credits, is the greatest record producer in the world. You've got to work with him someday."

We wanted a singer who could sing the high notes like Rush and Led Zeppelin. Nobody in our schools could carry a tune. Getting a real front man was going to be the hardest thing. We thought a star lead singer like Steven Tyler in Aerosmith was the key to making it.

Some of the kids at school were musicians. One drummer, Mark Welling, was talented enough that everyone said he'd make it big. Other kids like Chris DeGarmo and I played guitars at school, but this was ninth grade so nobody took themselves too seriously.

I was getting a good reputation as the best guitar player in school, and a kid in my class named Michael Wilton asked me for guitar lessons. He came over to my dad's apartment, and paid me $12 to teach him some scales. I didn't like teaching; it was too much like work. I wrote him out the scales on paper, and spent the money on weed.

I was pretty particular about what bands I was into, and only liked guitar hero bands like Rush and Led Zeppelin. Not surprisingly, I didn't want to be in a two-guitar band. KISS and Aerosmith I liked despite dual guitarists, but I idolized Alex Lifeson and Jimmy Page. They played all of the guitars on their albums. I thought if a band had a second guitar player, it just meant the lead guitarist wasn't good enough to do it by themselves.

I told my father, "When I grow up, I'm gonna be a guitar hero."

My dad took me on another trip to Hawaii. This time, he brought along a new girlfriend, Mary Kolle. He met her at a swingin' 70s singles party at Sixty-01, an adults-only condominium complex for singles and divorcees. Mary was around 40, and worked as a teller at Peoples Bank.

I spent most of my time in Hawaii trying to buy weed, which was kind of dangerous for a 14-year-old kid on the streets of Honolulu. The only way to score was to ask the local kids.

I followed three kids into a parking garage and they showed me a bag of Hawaiian buds that looked beautiful. When I gave the guy a $20 bill, the other guy snatched the bag out of my hand and ran. Eventually, I met a Hawaiian hippie, who just gave me some pot. When I asked him to sell me some on another day, he took my $20 and never returned.

Hawaii was full of Asian culture. I bought a blue silk kimono with a dragon on it. I thought it looked like an outfit Jimmy Page would wear, but it was really just an Oriental bathrobe. I had it wrapped in a brown paper bag, and taped it shut. I wanted my dad's girlfriend Mary to carry it on the plane, but she refused to take it through security because she thought it was marijuana.

When I got back from Hawaii, Gary set it up a gig for the band to play in the basement. We invited about 40 people. We used Gary's bedroom as a dressing room, and as we walked out, everybody cheered like a concert audience. We did every cover song we could play, opening with *Tie Your Mother Down* by Queen. From there, we played *A Passage To Bangkok* by Rush, *Train Kept a Rollin'* by Aerosmith, and *The Ocean* by Led Zeppelin. Our set also included Aerosmith's *Seasons of Wither*, on which we used a dry ice fog machine we'd built. Truly, we'd transformed the basement into a concert hall We played instrumental versions of songs by Scorpions, Judas Priest, Angel, Pat Travers, and other groups that nobody in our school had heard of before. That was going to be our thing. We were going to expose this music to kids our age by playing it live.

We had just one original song called *Out of Faze*. It was just a Rush type riff, a bridge, and a guitar lead. We were just teenage kids trying to play loud rock and roll, having to figure it out on our own as we went along. We were cute, but far from cool. My Gibson Flying V was bigger than I was. We didn't even have a singer. I was a little kid, but I had big dreams.

Rage Against Junior High – Scott Earl, Gary Thompson, and Adam Brenner

Playing guitar was taking up most of my time. If I wasn't rehearsing with Gary and Scott, I was at a music shop or sitting at home teaching myself Rush songs from a cheap cassette deck. I didn't pay much attention to school or girls. I was into guitar bands, and if some group's music was so simple that anyone could play it, it didn't interest me. The only other thing that mattered besides rock and roll was learning how to drive a car.

I started getting into guitar effects, and I bought a tape echo unit from Chris Jacobson called an Echoplex. When I moved the lever, it made all of these crazy sounds like a train wreck or a UFO landing. Rush and Led Zeppelin used the same one onstage. There were guitar players who used flangers and phase shifters on songs we learned, so I had to get one of those too.

The MXR flanger was small, and it cost around $300. I tried one out at Bandstand East, and after a few hours, I put the thing in my pocket and walked home. I got a call from Charlie at the music store asking me to bring it back, but I never did. Charlie Kester started a band with Mike Lull called Charlie & The Tunas. He also started a speaker cabinet company called The Energy Group. Then Charlie became the manager of Rail & Company. He fired singer Chris Kincaid, and had bassist Terry Young take over as lead vocalist Then he put them in three-piece business suits, and made them cut their hair. They all took vocal lessons from Maestro David Kyle, a 60-year-old flamboyant gay man who worked as voice coach and lived in Alki Beach. Rail & Company went into a recording studio and cut the Harry Nilsson song *One,* popularized by Three Dog Night. They started to play bigger places, and they even became an opening act at the Coliseum.

I stopped hanging out at Bandstand East and started going to Mike Lull's new shop called Guitar Works. It was just a repair shop for guitars and amps. I went there every chance I could. I loved to set up my V on the workbench, and clean the frets with steel wool and change the strings. I'd bring him huge bags of food from the bakery, and he'd always get me really stoned. He always had much better pot than I could get at school. Sometimes he let me buy some of it. We went in on 1/4 pound of weed soaked in hash oil with Roger Fisher of Heart.

One time we tried cocaine. I only did a little bit, but it had a strong effect. Mike Lull was a good friend and a great teacher. Drugs were just a normal part of the music world. I was privileged that these older musicians let me be a part of that.

The amp repair guy at Guitar Works, Andrew Cannon, put in a master volume knob on both my Marshall heads. He built a pedal board for my wah-wah pedal and my flangers. I bought an ADA Flanger from Bandstand East so they didn't say anything about the MXR. Charlie Kester never brought it up.

Guitar Works did a lot of work for Roger Fisher, the lead guitarist in Heart. Roger would come in once in a while. He really acted like he was a big rock star, so Mike always had to ask me to leave when Roger arrived. He'd run in the back to avoid being seen, and make some pot deal, or check out a new guitar he wanted to buy.

We never found a singer. Scott Earl moved to California, and that was the end of my first band. We tried out a kid from school called

Eddie Jackson on bass, and played *Bad Motor Scooter* by Montrose. I made the guitar sound like a motorcycle by using a metal slide. It didn't last more than a few days with Eddie. Gary and I put a message in the want ads for a bass player, and it was answered by an older guy named Randy Nelson. He was 28, and he could play bass better than the kids our age. He had a red Fender bass and an Ampeg SVT amp. He didn't mind playing with younger guys, and we were better than most players his age. Randy Nelson joined our band, and we started rehearsing four times a week.

Around the same time, I learned to how to drive a car. Chris Jacobson gave me a cassette tape of this group called Van Halen. I put the tape in, and cranked up the car stereo. I didn't know what to expect. When I heard *Eruption*, I flipped out. The guitar sound was everything I ever imagined a guitar could sound like. The guitarist shredded like nobody on Earth, and the band had such a fun sound. I had no idea how he made the guitar sound like that. I could play the chords from simple groups and sound just like AC/DC, Ted Nugent, KISS, or Rush, but I couldn't begin to figure out what this guy Edward Van Halen did on guitar.

Van Halen were playing a show opening for Black Sabbath at the Seattle Center Arena. Chris Jacobson took me to the show. We went to the front row, and I stood right in front of Eddie's amps. He had a white guitar with black stripes and Marshall speaker cabinets with car headlights on them. He could stretch his fingers further apart then anyone I'd ever seen before.

He could pick one note so fast that his right hand looked like a hummingbird wing. He constantly smiled and posed with his guitar.

My face melted. I was hooked on him. Edward Van Halen was by far the coolest guitar player on Earth.

When Black Sabbath went on, Chris Jacobson pointed out that Edward Van Halen was just a few feet away behind a curtain that bordered the backstage. I got his attention. He gave me a guitar pick, and somebody gave me the round cardboard insert from a *Led Zeppelin III album*. Edward autographed it for me, 'To Adam, Make Your Mama Scream For Me.'

I didn't watch any of Black Sabbath; I just stared at Edward Van Halen through the curtain like he was The Wizard of Oz. He was the most beautiful and charismatic person I ever saw. He looked nothing like the blurry photo of him on Van Halen's first album. He was just an older kid, no more than 22. He had bad skin and long black hair. He'd occasionally look over and smile at me. He was chatting with people and I watched through the curtain for 30 minutes.

I found the hero of my life. That's what I wanted to be. I wanted to be him.

Chris Jacobson was really impressed with the way Eddie Van Halen played with his right hand on the guitar neck. Chris said, "Edward Van Halen can do a whole guitar solo with both hands on the neck. Nobody has ever done that before." For me it was if I had just seen Superman, God, and the Pope. It seemed impossible, but I wanted to learn how to play guitar just like him.

I loved Rush, but Van Halen seemed more in touch with fun. The band made their California lifestyle seem so attractive. Eddie Van Halen radiated rock and roll. My search for the ultimate guitar hero was over. I tried to figure out how to make my guitar sound like Eddie Van Halen.

I met Greg Stock, a guy with a great sounding 100-watt Marshall. He had a handball court on his property. I went over after school and practiced guitar solos with his amp on 10, and it sounded huge with natural echo. I was starting to get noticed by older guitar players.

There was a record store near Crossroads called Easy Street. They sold bongs, and there was one bong called an Aqualung that was three feet long with tubes sticking out of it like a Crazy Straw. It cost $20. I bought it, and my dad came home and caught me and three friends smoking out of this bong. At first, he didn't know what it was. When he found out, his girlfriend Mary wanted to call the police.

My dad didn't call the cops, but he threw out the bong. He took the weed that was in an ashtray, and just set it down gently in the dumpster. He didn't even spill the bong water. After they left, we took the bong out of the dumpster and carried on. I gave the bong to a kid named Alan McDonald, as my dad would just have thrown it away again. It was way too big to hide.

Playing music with guys in older grades had benefits. You could go to older kids parties, but you were still just a little shit if you were younger than the high school kids. Eventually, between Gary and myself, our clique had a circle of friends that covered three schools, and everybody was into hard rock music.

Our bass player Randy found a singer. His name was Jake, a 38-year-old construction worker. Jake came down to the basement, and we were really excited to finally have a singer. It took a lot of coaxing by Randy to get him to come down. He looked like Eddie Money. Everything sounded right when Jake sang into a microphone. Gary booked us at our first gig at Redmond High School. We called the band Spectrum. Some girls made up posters with markers that hung in the hallways at school. It was our first real gig, and I could hardly wait.

One of Gary's friends, John Boghosian, helped do our sound. John was a preppy guy with short hair, and his dad coached for the Oakland Raiders. John's dad, Sam Boghosian, was friendly with my father. Sam came to our house and flashed his Super Bowl ring like he was the Pope. John was studying to become a sound engineer, and helped us set up the PA in Gary's basement. Gary's parents had just bought him a $500 mixing desk, and we started experimenting with recording the rehearsals.

After the band did the soundcheck, John introduced me to Brenda Lane. She was a grade below me but I didn't care. I went wild when I saw her for the first time. She was like sunshine, sugar and spice and everything rock and roll was supposed to be about. I was never like that before, but I wanted to be. I immediately grabbed her, and we ran away holding hands, laughing and running down the empty school hallway.

I dragged her into a locker room. She had this really great giggle. We started kissing, and I felt her up. She made out with me even though she had a boyfriend. Playing rock and roll just made me feel adventurous. Brenda Lane and I became friends, and we dated a few times, but she was never my girlfriend. We were a forever couple. I'll always love Brenda Lane. She was my first groupie.

After disappearing with Brenda. I had to go and play. Right before I went on, I changed into a pair of white boots. The stage floor was slippery. I fell face-first the moment I walked onstage, and broke the headstock on my Flying V. It was hanging on by a screw and the guitar strings.

I quickly got up, and changed guitars. We were smart enough to bring Mike McCrea's Les Paul as a spare. It was an embarrassing entrance, but because it happened so fast, nobody really saw it. There was no delay; just a quick guitar change. I got away without being humiliated, but I did break my V.

We did *Hot Legs* by Rod Stewart, *Kings and Queens* by Aerosmith, and whatever else Jake sang. Every song he sang, he sang great. A friend from my junior high school, James Tolin, came to the show along with 10 other kids from Highland Junior High. Redmond High School wouldn't let students from other schools into their dances. They all watched the show from the lunchroom window.

Scaring the teachers at Redmond High

Older people could get in, and a couple of girls in their twenties came, invited by Randy Nelson. Their names were Debbie Ward and Susie Wimberly, and Jake introduced me to them. Susie was a hairdresser and she teased my hair backstage before the gig.

After that show, Gary and I got an impressive reputation as a couple of young kids who could play rock and roll like the big boys. I noticed that girls were starting to pay attention to me after that, and all the other kids wanted us to play at schools.

I got rubber soles attached to the white boots so I wouldn't slip again. Mike at Guitar Works fixed my V back with wood glue and a clamp. He said, "That happens a lot with Gibson guitars, and it's no problem to fix them. You'll have it back in a couple of days." That was the first of a hundred broken guitar necks.

For our second gig, we changed the band name to Anthem, after the song by Rush. Jake did a few more shows with us at schools and then he stopped coming to rehearsals. No one could get him on the phone. When Randy finally did, I picked up the phone and started yelling, "Jake, you gotta come to rehearsal right fucking now. This is bullshit. Unacceptable! Get here now or fuck off."

I had zero diplomacy skills. He hung up on me, and I never heard from Jake again. He went back to doing construction work. We had to find a new singer.

My dad bought a condo right near a drive-in movie theater on the border of Kirkland and Bellevue. I had to change schools, and was enrolled into Kirkland Junior High. Once there, did a report on Led Zeppelin and got an A.

I had a crush on a girl who sat next to me in math class. Her name was Donna Donaldson. She was pretty and had developed early. She was a really bossy bitch outside of class, but in class she would flirt with me constantly. She'd lean over into me and rub her breast against my arm, then ask me for math help. Donna always asked me about math problems I had no idea how to solve. I got hypnotized when I looked down at her cleavage, and I felt her breath on my cheek. I had to be careful when I got up from my desk.

She occasionally got dropped off after lunch by high school guys. She was always glassy-eyed and looked like she'd just been fucked when she got out of someone's car. High school guys had all the fun.

I brought my Gibson V into school with my Marshall, and tried to fit into music class. The music teacher, Jack Kunz, hated me. He boasted about himself. He printed sheet music of compositions he wrote. Kunz knew I was a stoner, and tried to discipline me. I set up my guitar and my Marshall amp in the school music room. It was so loud they could hear it all across the school.

I didn't last very long in the school band. I failed because I refused to learn to read music. Kunz said, "You'll never amount to anything." I told him, "Fuck off. You're a plastic musician." I had no fear in telling off my teachers.

I made new friends in Kirkland. My new best friend was David Morris, a toothy short kid with long hair. We met by the school bus stop while I was sneaking a toke off a joint.

Soon I was the terror of the school. I was always getting into trouble with the principal, Mr. Carson. I saw him peeking through cracks in the bathroom stall, trying to catch me smoking weed with David Morris. We used to pass a little pipe underneath the stalls. Mr. Carson saw us smoking, and David tried to hand the pipe back to me along with some hash that was in a little film canister. Mr. Carson tried to pry it out of my hand, and I broke free and threw the pipe across the hallway. They never found it, but he called David's parents. They didn't care. They just laughed and hung up on him. They smoked pot and so did their whole family. Mr. Carson couldn't get my father on the phone. He was too ignorant to just call the bakery. My dad ignored all the hoopla about marijuana. It was everywhere.

One day at school, I bought an M-80 firecracker from a guy in our class named Roger Harrington. I stuck it in the vending machine after school, and lit the fuse. David Morris kept a lookout. There was a massive bang. The buttons flew off of the machine. Some of the candy fell down to the bottom, but there was no major damage.

The next day, my dad took me to Hawaii. I was out of school for two weeks before I had to answer for it. When I returned from the vacation, I got called into the office. I only got told not to do it again. David Morris took the rap. He got suspended for three days, and had to go up in front of the Kirkland School Board to get reinstated. His punishment - he had to write a 500-word essay on the errors of his ways.

I spent a lot of time at David Morris' house. His parents took us on a week-long camping trip. We lasted one day, and came home. There was always somebody smoking pot at David's house. He had an older sister, Karen, and a big brother, Chipper. They had lots of friends who were all potheads. David's mother Carol and his stepfather Chuck were very liberal. They didn't care who smoked or got drunk or took drugs in their house. It was in a nice area surrounded by neighbors with nicer houses whose yards were more kept up. Everyone would go in David's yard, and pick magic mushrooms with blue rings around the stem. When they found enough of them, they boiled them in a pot on the stove, and made mushroom tea. David and I were like the babies in the house, so the older kids usually wouldn't give us anything harder than bong hits. When the big kids got high and weren't paying attention, we drank some of their tea.

I collected marijuana. You could say I was a pot fan. I had a cigar box at home full of little baggies that contained all kinds of different exotic grass. I had a jar full of roach weed from all the joints I smoked. I made a joint smoker with a little foil tube, and put weed in it to make it resonated and stronger. In ninth grade, I was smoking pot every day. I got stoned before, during, and after school.

We watched a lot of TV. I liked *Saturday Night Live,* and David's big brother Chipper would make us listen to Cheech & Chong or *Let's Get Small* by Steve Martin. He'd sing along to *That Smell* by Lynyrd Skynyrd while he was cleaning his room. They had big parties at the house, and crammed 60 people into their basement. On New Year's Eve, we got to kiss all the girls at midnight. Some older girl got pissed off and told Chipper, "Adam's been going around trying to kiss all the girls twice."

Morris Gategnio and his little brother Eddie were always hanging around at David's house. Morris was a guitarist. He was obsessed with Pink Floyd and the band Journey. He turned me on to Neal Schon who was a blazing lead guitar player, but Journey wasn't a pop band yet; they were progressive with a lot of keyboards. I wasn't really into keyboard bands.

David and Chipper Morris, Me in a Heart shirt, Morris and Eddie Gategnio

Pink Floyd's *The Wall* had just come out, and they sat around the kitchen table smoking pot, discussing the meaning of it all. Morris said, "Pink Floyd has a real airplane that crashes into the stage during the concert." I wanted to see their movie, *The Wall.*

I was never a big Pink Floyd fan. That was a group for guys who took LSD. I heard them constantly on the radio, but something struck me when I saw the movie of *The Wall.* Part of me thought that what I was seeing on the screen could be my future and I really loved the guitar solos.

David Morris couldn't play guitar. I tried to teach him how to play a chord or two by pressing his fingers until it hurt, very hard on the neck. He couldn't get it. He could only associate playing music with pain. I taught him how to tune my guitars with a strobe tuner and he became my roadie instead.

Before school, David and I worked at the bakery together for two hours. One of the truck drivers would drive us to school. Whatever money we got was spent on weed, records, and concerts. If my dad drove us to school, David and I would sit in the back of the car and sneak hits off a joint. My father said he had no sense of smell, so he didn't even notice. He became more tolerant. If we got caught from then on, he would just shake his head and say, "What do you wanna smoke that shit for?"

Once I got my dad to take a puff by telling him, "It's not that bad, everybody does it," but he wasn't at all interested. My dad smoked Camel non-filters for 35 years, and had just quit around that time. He never got really shitfaced drunk around me. Once in while he'd have a beer, and he was always funny. He was just my dad, Joe Brenner, and everybody loved him. We were a family. As long as his girlfriends didn't get in the way.

Mary Kolle called the police after she caught me with pot when my father wasn't home. The cops came to the apartment, and they took me down to the Bellevue Police Station. They put me in a holding pen for 20 minutes. My dad came to get me. I wasn't charged with anything. My dad was pissed at her for calling the cops. He broke up with Mary not long after that. I hated jail, even for 20 minutes. I was only 15 years old, but I swore to myself I'd never do anything stupid enough to put me back there - like get caught.

Eddie Van Halen

In the summer of 1978-79, I was in tenth grade at Lake Washington High. I had three interests – Playing guitar, smoking pot, and girls. The older high school girls wouldn't look at me, but girls were easier to talk to when I was playing guitar at shows. I decided to concentrate on the band with Gary so we could play more gigs.

On our hunt for lead singers, we put out an ad, and it got answered by a guy from Tacoma. His name was Jeff Tate. He had a brown Jewfro and pockmarks on his face. He was in his early 20s, which was still really old compared to Gary and me. The idea of two old guys and two kids seemed to sit okay with us. We couldn't really find anyone our age who was at our level.

At the audition Jeff came into Gary's basement and said, "I'm really impressed by the gear and lights you have set up. You've really created a mood in here." Jeff was kind of a hippie. He drove an old garbage-filled brown VW van, and he had a high singing voice. He was not into heavy metal at all. Most of the groups we wanted to cover, he had never heard of before. He was into Yes and Genesis, while we were into heavy metal.

We ran through a couple of songs that we had him learn for the audition. *Long Live Rock and Roll* by Rainbow, *Loving You Sunday Morning* by Scorpions, and *Victim of Changes* by Judas Priest. It wasn't very magical, but it was good enough. In the basement everything sounded really loud, and very tinny. We were desperate for a singer who could cover these groups, and Jeff fit the bill.

We offered Tate the gig, and went about rehearsing. He was not a trained singer, and had not really done anything in music before that. He could scream really high, and his voice was very shrill. He didn't have much control over his voice, but at moments, he'd spit something out that sounded like it could be on the radio. Tate wore jeans and his girlfriend's blouse. Randy wore a Japanese jacket or a kimono like the *Solid Gold* disco groups of the 70s. Gary and I tried to dress like Van Halen. We didn't have much of an image, but we all wanted to rock.

Gary and I thought Jeff was gay at first. He had a hairy chest. and liked to show it. He was very effeminate. He told Mike McCrea and me that he wanted a more mystical name, and said, "I want to change my name to Jeff Waterfall." We gagged and choked, trying hard to not fall down laughing. The nickname stuck, but only as an inside joke for me and my friends. He decided to call himself Jeffery Djarmony instead, but everyone just knew him as Tate, or in our case, Waterfall.

Jeff was more comfortable singing Queen and Scorpions than Judas Priest or Rush. He was not the instant superstar singer we were hoping for. We were impatient high school kids, and we were very demanding. Every little detail was a big deal to us. If you did something stupid, you got picked on mercilessly. The older guys had thicker skins, but Gary and I took everything way too seriously.

We only had ourselves and our friends at this point for guidance. We thought we knew everything since we studied these bands day and night. When I played guitar and Gary played drums, we sounded just like our idols. We worked really hard on practicing like a band, and we started to get good at it. To help Jeff out, my dad gave him and his girlfriend Sandy jobs at the bakery. They both lived together in Tacoma. Jeff was a bread slicer, and my dad had him do truck deliveries as well.

Since Van Halen had a Fender-shaped guitar with one pickup and a tremolo bar to make all of those dive bomb noises, I had to get one too. I had Mike Lull put together a Boogie Body Strat with a Charvel guitar neck. We installed a spring tremolo bar, and I got a vintage PAF pickup. It was around $300 for the guitar, 300 for the pickup that I bought from Mike's business partner, Ron Van Ryn.

I was going to a lot of concerts. It was my obsession. I saw Michael Schenker with UFO who were opening for Blue Oyster Cult at The Hec Edmundson Pavilion. I watched Judas Priest, Pat Travers, and Frank Marino & Mahogany Rush play at the Seattle Paramount. I saw bigger concerts in the Coliseum like UFO, opening for Rush on September 17, 1977. I saw AC/DC with Bon Scott opening for Ted Nugent on August 30, 1978. I also went to see Pat Travers open for Rush on November 7, 1978. Queen played on December 12, 1978. I saw Freddie Mercury sing *Bohemian Rhapsody* on the piano, when he had long hair. It was an amazing time to see rock shows.

We'd always get to concerts early in the day, and wait around in line or by the backstage. Hanging out all day for concerts was a ritual. We watched the roadies, tried to meet the bands, and get guitar picks. I usually went with Mike McCrea. He got Michael Schenker's pick at the Blue Oyster Cult show. It was just a brown Herco pick, like Chris Jacobson used. I kept it.

Susie Wimberly and Debbie Ward, the two girls we met through Randy and Jake, said they could help me meet Edward Van Halen. Debbie was a secretary for John Bauer Concert Company, a big Seattle concert promoter who had an office near the bakery in Bellevue.

Susie and Debbie were both really pretty. Debbie whispered to me, "You know, Susie had a romp with David Lee Roth." Susie giggled and said, "Ooh la la," then she whispered in my other ear, "Debbie fucked Eddie Van Halen." I didn't care who they slept with; I just wanted to meet Edward. Mike McCrea had a huge crush on Debbie Ward. I thought Debbie was hot, but I wanted these girls to help me, so I didn't try to hit on them. Susie and Debbie were my rock and roll big sisters.

Debbie had inside information on the next Van Halen tour. We got their hotel and flight details, as well as the fake names they used to check into hotels. She was the one who made their reservations for John Bauer. Eddie's hotel name was Justin Time, Alex was Justin Kase, Michael Anthony was Biff Malibu, and David Lee Roth's hotel alias was Hugh Jazz.

The first show was in Tacoma, just an hour south of Seattle at the University of Puget Sound. It was Van Halen's first headline tour, and their second album had just come out. Debbie gave us all the details, and Mike McCrea and I booked a room in Van Halen's hotel, the Rodeway Inn. It was April 3, 1979.

The concert was incredible. We were in the front row and there was no pushing, I took photos on McCrea's shoulders with a 35mm camera. Eddie wore yellow pants and a black vest. Michael Anthony did a bass solo, bathed in blue light with clouds of dry ice. The whole band played drums in the middle of *Feel Your Love Tonight*. During the quiet part of *Ain't Talkin' 'bout Love,* David Lee Roth shouted, "I been to the edge.... Tacoma! Who likes to get high around here?"

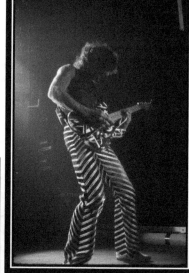

Van Halen – Tacoma - April 3, 1979

Edward started off his guitar solo doing *Spanish Fly*. He did a lot of scales starting slow, and going faster up neck. He picked and held his highest note a thousand times per second. He ran across the stage and smashed into his amp stacks, and made the guitar moan like a sick elephant. Then he blasted into *Dead or Alive*. I was a little surprised that he didn't play *Eruption*.

We got to the hotel about 30 minutes after the show. the Rodeway Inn was just a cheap two-floor motel in Tacoma, near the concert. As we were going to our room on the first floor, there were about five roadies throwing pizza at each other. All of a sudden, we spotted Michael Anthony and I ran up to him with my Gibson Flying V guitar in my hand and asked him, "Would you put your teeth marks in my guitar?" He said, "Sure kid," and we went into his doorway and he bit the headstock. That was Mike McCrea's idea, to get rock stars to put their teeth marks in the wood on my guitar's headstock.

Van Halen bassist Michael Anthony with my Gibson Flying V while the roadies fought in the background

I asked Michael Anthony, "Do you think you can get Eddie to sign it?" He said, "Why don't you ask him yourself?" Pizza was flying up and down the hallway. The walls were splattered with pizza sauce. Drunk roadies were screaming, laughing, and spraying beer at each other. Michael Anthony dodged a flying pizza slice, banged on the door of Room 138, and said, "Hey, Ed. Sign this kid's guitar."

Edward Van Halen cracked open his door and glanced at me. I ran right up to him. He sort of retreated back behind the door and peeked out and I said, "Eddie, would you please sign my guitar?"

He opened up his door all the way and said, "Sure, c'mon in." Pizza was still being thrown. Someone chucked a slice, and it just missed us and hit the wall next to the door of Eddie's room. McCrea came in right behind me and we walked in and looked around. Edward Van Halen had a metal suitcase. There were girls' panties that had 'Edward' written on them, laid out on the floor. There were a few clothes around the room, but he was just in there by himself watching TV. He was wearing a white V-neck t shirt, blue jeans, and the coolest shoes I ever saw.

McCrea sat on one of the beds, and I handed my V to Edward. I asked him to take a pen and just scratch his name into the back of it. I also asked him to put his teeth marks in the headstock. He laughed, and bit the top of my guitar. He grabbed a hotel pen, and scratched his name on the back. It was permanent.

When he handed the guitar back, I asked him, "Is this right?" and I started playing *I'm the One*. Eddie grabbed the guitar from me, and started showing me the rhythm of *I'm the One*, how he was keeping the rhythm with the open A string while muting it the whole time, even when he was doing the crazy riff. He explained how important it is to keep the rhythm going constantly on one string while you hit the others.

We sat down on the beds across from each other, and I kept asking how to play things right. Even though the second album had just been released a week earlier, I knew how to play parts of almost every song on it. "How do you play *Dance the Night Away*?" I asked. He started doing the tapping middle bit. He was just hitting the strings with his right hand 12 frets above where his left hand was.

I said, "Is this how you play *Light Up the Sky*?" and I took the guitar back, and played the intro and the first riff. He looked at me and said, "Yeah," then he took the guitar back and showed me how to play the bridge, and the quiet part before the guitar solo.

He played the intro to *Women in Love* on my guitar; my eyes were just a few inches from his fingers. It was beautiful and perfect. He could make every note stand out. When he played *Jamie's Cryin'*, he made my V sing, just like he sounded on the first Van Halen album. He said, "It doesn't matter which guitar I play. It's all in the fingers. I sound like me on any guitar."

We didn't need amps; my V was very loud acoustically. Every note and harmonic rang clear as a bell. When he played the quiet intro on *Bottoms Up!* it sounded just like it did on the record. Eddie made me feel like I was just hanging out with my big brother, playing a guitar in a hotel room while my buddy watched.

Eddie was smoking cigarettes, and played whatever I asked him to. He was only 24; the Warner Brother's press kit shaved off a year. He had some bad zits, and long messy black hair. He looked like he had just got out of bed. McCrea told me, "It's rock and roll to look like you just got out of bed, 24 hours a day." Edward's eyes sparkled, and he had the nicest smile you could ever see on a rock star. He had a small envelope of cocaine. He opened it up, took his Van Halen guitar pick to scoop up a hit, and snorted it. He said, "I'd offer you some but I only have a little bit." I told him, "That's okay; I'm really just a pot head." He said, "I got a roach but I need it to get to sleep later," and he showed me half a small joint in a matchbook. I'd seen cocaine at Guitar Works and some parties, but it didn't interest me at the time. I was as high on electric guitar as anyone could ever get. I was in love and in awe of Eddie's playing. Everything about him was so cool.

After trading off back and forth with my guitar for about 30 minutes, he opened up his metal suitcase, and he pulled out a guitar body and a guitar neck. He took a screwdriver, and put this Danelectro guitar that he carried with him together in front of us. Then he pulled out a set of Dean Markley strings, and strung it up. After that, we started tuning up together, just sitting on the beds facing each other.

Mike McCrea and I looked at each other and freaked out every time Eddie looked the other way.

We started playing Van Halen songs together. I played *I'm the One,* and then he stopped and I played the little solo bit. Eddie shook his head in approval. He looked at a McCrea and said, "Wow, this kid really rocks."

I had impressed Eddie Van Halen. I'd worked really hard, trying to learn all of his songs and leads, but watching him do it up close explained it all. We'd played practically every guitar riff on both of his albums. Most of the chords in his songs were just two or three strings, like when he showed me how he played *Runnin' with the Devil.* And a lot of his leads were just based around simple arpeggio chord progressions. When I watched him play the lead to *Somebody Get Me a Doctor,* my eyes got wide.

He showed me how he warmed up for shows. He played a major scale starting on the low E on the third fret, then when he got to the high E string on the fifth fret, he moved it up half a step and did the scale backwards. Then he moved up another fret, and repeated the scale, going a little faster each time, until he went all the way up and down the guitar neck.

I wanted to know how to properly play the song *On Fire.* I was shocked to learn that the harmonic bit was on the sixth fret. He played the chord riff before the solo, and it just sounded totally badass. The solo was like his warm-up scale, and when I saw him do it, I got it right away. He played all of these fast harmonics on the three high strings, just by moving the ring finger of his left hand up and down the guitar neck, and he explained it. "There are open harmonics all over the neck, not just on the fifth, seventh, and twelfth frets. They're everywhere; you just have to find them."

I asked how he did the crazy harmonic hand slide in *Somebody Get Me a Doctor.* He took the edge of his pick, and slid it up the G string while he did pull-offs on the second and fifth frets. He did the same trick in the solo for *You're No Good.* Eddie could spread his fingers apart farther than anyone I'd ever seen before. He didn't have to adjust the position of the guitar. He played the seven-fret spread guitar solo in *Ice Cream Man* like it was nothing. Eddie showed me his superfast hummingbird picking technique, but that was a talent only he was born with. It was almost like a nervous tick that he had complete control over how fast he could flutter a pick against a string. He could probably hit one note 20 times per second. He liked simple licks instead of just playing as fast he could all of the time. He understood rock and roll guitar better than anyone. He said, "It's not about how fast you can play or how many notes you can put in a solo. It's about feeling. Guys who play a million notes in one solo are just fucking clowns. They sound like they're jerking off."

He showed me how he did tap-on harmonics with his right hand, and all of the two-handed guitar tricks that was making him famous. He put his right thumb on the left side of the neck, and his ring and pinky fingers on the right side. He slammed his right hand index finger on the B string- tenth fret and pulled the string to let the left hand note ring. His left pinky finger was on the B string-fifth fret and his left index finger was on the second fret. He pulled off and hammered on a note with his left hand, and hammered back with his right hand like a sixth finger. He kept repeating it faster and faster. I was hypnotized.

Eddie liked to do pick slides on the high strings while doing pull-offs. He told me, "Just break the rules, there are no rules." He showed me how he played the beginning of *Atomic Punk*. Eddie used the edge of the palm of his right hand, which was all calloused, and scraped it hard across the strings like a wood saw. He showed us riffs that were not on albums yet, all the while taking little bumps of cocaine with his guitar pick. He lit up a cigarette, put the filter behind the strings of his Danelectro headstock, and let it burn. Then he played me a riff he said was called *Hang 'em High*.

His hands were beautiful. The shapes his fingers made as he touched the neck almost looked like shadow puppets. He showed me, in detail, how he did *Spanish Fly* and *Eruption*. He was really a patient teacher, and between McCrea and myself, we had enough questions to keep him from even thinking about being bored. I understood everything that he showed me and he knew I got it, even if I couldn't quite perfectly imitate everything he did just yet. He was actually interested in teaching me things. He probably knew it was the most important guitar lesson of my life. My whole universe was in that hotel room. Guitar was his whole life too; you could really tell that. We had all the time in the world. Edward was just about to become the most famous guitarist in history, but in April 1979, he was just a 24-year-old kid from California that was elated to be on his first headline world tour with his big brother on the drums. His dreams were coming true.

We asked what groups he liked. He preferred to talk about the groups he didn't. "I like Clapton and Allan Holdsworth, but I don't play like them. I don't really like Hendrix; he's too flash. I used to like Ritchie Blackmore until I saw him with John Bonham. It was a couple years ago at the Rainbow in Hollywood. I went up to him to say hello and he looked at me like, 'Who the fuck are you?' He told me to fuck off. I hate that motherfucker."

Edward made fun of Foghat, Bad Company, Montrose, and KISS. He called them clowns. He liked Randy Hansen, a Jimi Hendrix impersonator from Seattle. He told us, "I saw Randy Hansen blow Ritchie Blackmore off the stage."

I asked him, "Where did you get those cool shoes?" He was wearing white leather shoes with no laces. He answered, "I got them on tour in Paris. My favorite thing on Earth is playing live. I'd sell my guitars to go on tour."

I could talk non-stop about the guitar riffs of *Van Halen I & II*. I played him my original riff, *Out of Faze*, and he told McCrea, "I think he's better than that clown from Bad Company."

He talked for a long time about building guitars. He said, "I only learned how to do it by tearing them apart and rebuilding them. I destroyed a few guitars in the process. My main guitar cost only 150 bucks to make. I decorated it with electrical tape and Schwinn bicycle paint. I put some bicycle reflectors on the back, to reflect the stage lights." He loved to talk about his guitar. "It's got a DiMarzio pickup that I rewired with an old PAF. magnet. I had it rerouted so the jack could be rear loaded and I think it just looks cooler without a pickguard. Don't ya think?"

McCrea agreed with everything Eddie said, like he already knew these things.

His guitar, the one he ultimately called *Frankenstein*, became a rock and roll icon. He went on, "I just finished painting it again last week from black to red. All these guys in LA are copying my stripes so I have to keep changing it. I put in two fake pickups to fuck up the guitar companies. They're all coming out with one pickup guitars."

He got a little confiding, "I'm a loner; I don't get along with people. People think I'm unsociable and call me an ego'd-out motherfucker because I don't show my face at parties, but I'm just quiet. I'd rather be alone and just play the guitar. Everything I have to say is in notes anyway."

He showed me how to play the song *Beautiful Girls,* and we played it together. We also played *Ain't Talkin 'bout Love, Feel Your Love Tonight,* and *Little Dreamer,* from Van Halen's first album. Jamming with Ed was better than anything, even sex. When we talked about pickups, I told him that I had a PAF, and he was actually jealous. Edward said he was ripped off by Seymour Duncan. They were selling guitars with his exact same stripe design in Hollywood. Even big guitarists like Tom Scholz of Boston and Rick Derringer were blatantly copping Edward's solo at huge festivals, and it wasn't in tribute. It was something that really got Eddie pissed off.

Before we left, he asked me to do him a favor. He explained that everybody on the Sunset Strip was trying to copy him. He had a serious, sad look in his eyes, like he was afraid he wasn't going to get credit for being the big guitar star that he would eventually become. He said this, "You're gonna go on in life and make music. Everybody in Hollywood is trying to copy me. Whatever you do, just do me a favor and take the music somewhere else, wherever that is. Just don't copy me. Be yourself. Take it somewhere new. Okay? You're gonna be just fine." He looked at McCrea and said, "And you make sure that he does."

He took out a piece of hotel stationary, and wrote down in the corner, *'April 3, 1979, Rodeway Inn, Room 138, ADAM Keep Pickin' your ass off, EDWARD VAN HALEN.'*

I was star-struck, and electrified from that experience. He was the nicest, most humble rock star that I'd ever meet in my life. No matter what he would become, I was his devoted fan forever. He was like the big brother I wished I had. I wanted to be just like him. He said, "I'm gonna go upstairs and find a squeeze." McCrea and I thanked him. I hugged him, and I told him he'll see me again. Then I picked up the V, and we walked out the door.

Back in the hallway, I saw Alex Van Halen and he put his teeth marks in the V, and signed the hotel stationary. Michael Anthony was floating around, and he signed the paper that Eddie signed. Pizza sauce got on it from the hallway wall. The roadies were still running around the hallways screaming.  Someone sprayed a fire extinguisher in one of the rooms.

I was a 15-year-old kid who just saw the mighty Van Halen at the beginning of their first headline world tour, unobstructed from the front row. I had just spent three hours learning guitar tricks, riffs, licks, and lifelong advice that I'd never forget from Edward himself. That was the day I was, without a doubt, the luckiest fucking kid on Earth.

Eddie Van Halen 1979   Photo by Adam Brenner

CaliFFornia World Music Festival

We flew to California with Scott Earl and saw the Van Halen show in San Rafael. We stayed in the same motel, which was just a little place on the side of the road. We stopped by Edward's room in the morning, and the door was open. He was eating room service breakfast of bacon, eggs, and toast. He invited us in, and his road manager Noel Monk came in and said, "You kids leave him alone. Can't he eat his breakfast? Get out." Eddie said, "Nah, it's cool, I invited them in. They can stay."

Noel Monk was a Warner Bros. subordinate. He started out as a sound engineer at Fillmore East, and he ran the boards at Woodstock. His father owned a bookstore in New York called Mad Monk. He tour managed The Sex Pistols across America in 1980, and was with Sid Vicious when he took a knife and sliced 'Gimme a Fix' in his chest, and walked through a plate glass window.

Eddie cared about his fans. He made us feel important, and he always remembered how he felt when Ritchie Blackmore told him to fuck off. We told Eddie we were going to the two-day CaliFFornia World Music Festival. It was the first big outdoor rock concert of my life. Van Halen were playing on the second day with Aerosmith. We took a Greyhound bus to Los Angeles to go the festival. There were supposedly 100,000 people there. We went up in the front to see some of the bands like REO Speedwagon and Toto. It was a hot sunny blue-sky day. Everybody was really mellow, just sitting down in front of the stage between bands, passing joints around. All of a sudden, the people next to me started to get up and back off because a naked black man was running through the crowd, freaking out on acid, and jacking off on the crowd. McCrea, Scott, and I got separated for a while, so I wandered around the festival.

There was an indoor food court with a giant screen that played movies of rock bands. I watched The Kinks' *Celluloid Heroes,* David Bowie's *Ziggy Stardust,* and *Pink Floyd in Pompeii* on the big screen. There was something these English bands did on screen that captivated me far more than the American bands like The Outlaws or Head East who were on the stage. As I watched Ziggy sing *All the*

Young Dudes, I wondered what life had in store for me. Just then, I heard the roar of the crowd from outside in the stadium.

For Cheap Trick, I went up in the front row. They were really exciting, and bright since they played at night. The guitar player was a bit goofy, almost like a clown. The songs were so loud and poppy that they were instantly memorable, and they really rocked. The singer, Robin Zander, wore a white suit, and had the crowd in the palm of his hand from the moment he said, "Hello there ladies and gentlemen." Cheap Trick owned the first night of the festival.

The sea of people swayed. It was tough to get up towards the front, but I was small enough to break through the crowd to the third row. During the song *Dream Police,* the crowd got extremely hyper. Strobe lights were flashing, and the crowd moved in waves. People got pushed around 10 feet left to right and back again. You could almost feel it coming.

The people from behind were pushing towards the front, while others pushed side to side. I lost my balance, and fell to the ground. My heart was pounding in fear of getting crushed. I thought I was going to be trampled to death just as soon as the next wave hit. Just as the crowd made another massive sway, a girl picked me back up. That was enough for me. I backed out of the mob to where it was safe.

I stayed on the side to watch Ted Nugent, but after two songs I went out of the crowd and towards the back of the stadium. Somehow, I found Scott and McCrea again. After the show, everybody left the stadium, and we slept in the park. About 10,000 other people slept in the park with us.

Day two of the *CaliFFornia World Festival* had UFO opening, with their new guitar player, Paul Chapman. We saw them a week later from the front row in the Seattle Paramount, and we all gave him the finger. We were merciless when it came to the guitar parts of Michael Schenker. They were better at the festival than at the Paramount, but without Schenker, it wasn't UFO. The scoreboard lit up the band names as they played, with a backdrop of corporate ads and American flags. Cheech & Chong went on between the bands and told jokes, but they really couldn't get the audience to focus on them. It was way too big for a comedy show. We saw a bit of April Wine's set, and then we went up front for Van Halen. They did the same set as Tacoma, and they looked great in the lights at night. It had a different feeling than their indoor shows. They played like they were out for blood.

After Van Halen's set, McCrea and I met a guy who looked like Punky Meadows of Angel. He said he was the singer in a band called Lips. He got backstage, and saw Steven Tyler yelling at his band. He said Tyler was snorting cocaine out of a big plastic bag. We watched Aerosmith from the back of the stadium. Joey Kramer's cymbals were all lit up and perfectly shined. You could see the glow from far away. I was really tired from our two-day adventure. We left the festival after Aerosmith, slept at the airport, and flew back home from LA.

A few days after the festival, Van Halen played at the Seattle Center Coliseum. Debbie Ward got McCrea and I backstage passes. We got there early in the day. I took photos with my 35mm camera for a photography class I was taking at school. I caught Michael Anthony coming out to a limo, and McCrea photo-bombed the shot. After the show, I took a few pictures backstage, and when I pointed the camera towards David Lee Roth, he put his hand up over his face and turned his head. I took the photo anyway, so I got a few photos of Diamond Dave's hand in his face.

Van Halen's guitar roadie Rudy Leiren and Michael Anthony

We walked around backstage looking at Eddie's guitars and hitting the strings in the dressing room when no one was looking. We were hanging out in the toilets for a few minutes, sneaking a joint and we heard a toilet flush. Eddie walked out of the bathroom stall, looked at us, and smiled. If we were in the way, we tried not to be, but we didn't care. We were backstage.

Mike McCrea, Michael Anthony, and VH guitar tech Rudy Leiren

I was talking to a guy who had brought in a white Fender guitar with a tremolo bar on it for Eddie to see. His name was Floyd Rose. He had just made a locking system for Fender-shaped guitars by routing in a thicker nut. He attached it by drilling two holes in the back of the neck. Little metal plates locked down two strings at a time, and a little screw turned by a hex key locked it down. The bridge of Floyd's guitar had a tremolo bar. He clipped the ball end for each of the six strings and locked them into the bridge with a hex key. When you depressed the bar, you could get the strings to go completely limp and when you released the bar, it snapped back right in tune. It was quite the invention. I knew it was going to be huge. Floyd Rose made his tremolo bar system with a metal press that he had in his basement. He sold them for $300, and he said he had made about four of them already. I told him I wanted one, and took his phone number. It was the missing link for my Boogie Body guitar.

Edward Van Halen coming out of the backstage toilet
Seattle - April 12, 1979

Floyd showed his invention to Edward Van Halen and his roadie Rudy. We knew all the roadies by name. Most of them were nice enough not to throw us out, but we were always considered little kids who were in the way. We also went to the shows in Vancouver BC, Portland, and Spokane. I studied Edward's every move.

Thanks to Debbie Ward, I had Van Halen's flight details. I went to Sea-Tac airport to say goodbye to Eddie. After Spokane, they were flying out to the next gig from Seattle. In those days, you could go through the metal detector and straight to the gate without a plane ticket. When I got there the whole band was sitting down by the gate waiting for their flight to board. David Lee Roth had on dark glasses. He looked hung over and was slumped in his chair.

I was walking over to Eddie. Alex Van Halen saw me walk up and he said, "Hey kid. Come here, I wanna talk to you." I sat down in the empty seat next to him. He started to interrogate me. I was a little shy when I spoke to him, I wasn't expecting to be grilled for information.

ALEX: "How do you get the money to go to all of these shows?"

ADAM: "I get it from my dad. He owns a big bakery in Seattle, you can eat there for free."

ALEX: "Why do like Van Halen so much?"

ADAM: "I love Eddie's guitar. He's the best in the world. I love the songs too."

ALEX: "How do you know where we are all time?"

ADAM: "I know this chick that works for John Bauer Concert Company. I think Ed knows her too. I have a real cool drummer in my band. He plays just like you, and hits his drums super hard. His snare drum is louder than anyone I've ever heard." I wanted to tell him about my band, but he changed the subject.

ALEX: "I extended my drums and put two bass drums together - they sound like cannons. What do think of Black Sabbath?"

ADAM: "I think they suck."

ALEX: "When we played with Black Sabbath in England, I saw the singer, Ozzy Osbourne, take complete command of 200,000 people. It was insane. They've really got something, I've never seen anyone take control of a crowd that big before. You should really look further into them."

ADAM: "I still think they suck."

Alex Van Halen

Alex was really passionate about Black Sabbath. They blew his mind. We talked until they boarded. I said goodbye to Eddie. David Lee Roth lowered his dark glasses and looked at me like, "Oh it's you kid," as he boarded the plane.

More inspired than ever, we went back to rehearsing and adding new songs like *Light Up the Sky* and *Somebody Get Me a Doctor.* Jeff Tate did not have a real David Lee Roth-style voice, but I loved playing Van Halen songs, and Gary and I became like the Van Halen brothers of the Eastside.

We rehearsed every day in the basement for weeks. Occasionally I would play a warm-up riff, and McCrea would go, "What was that?" I was starting to build up ideas for originals. That's what we read Steven Tyler would say when Joe Perry or Jimmy Crespo played a sound check riff. That's how to write originals.

As soon as we had enough songs to do a show, we got ourselves an outdoor gig at Lake Washington High School during the lunch period. All of the stoners and kids watched us as we set up outside and did our thing. I wore a silver vest that looked like inside of a potato chip bag, and we played *Long Live Rock and Roll, We Will Rock You,* and Van Halen songs. We called the band Tyrant, after the Judas Priest song. We were exposing heavy metal to the kids at school, and the radio stations started playing these groups and promoting the concerts.

In school, I developed my Van Halen photos in the darkroom, and turned them in for credit. I also matted and cropped Van Halen's Warner Bros. black-and-white promo shots that were in their press kit, and turned those in. I got a B on it. At lunch we'd hang out at the house of a drug dealer named Marion Moulton. He lived next door to the school. There was always a party there. We had a wailer after the lunchtime concert.

Marion sold cocaine and pot, and he lived with his girlfriend Julie, a blonde girl who looked like a hag with a big skin tag on her chin. I went there with this girl from class, Cory Houston, who had short wavy brown hair, big brown eyes, a turned-up nose, and a face like a blow-up doll. She had an extremely large chest for a 16-year-old girl. Her tits were the size of watermelons. I became friends with her, but I really wanted to fuck her. So did everyone else. Marion was always trying to hit on Cory. She liked drugs, but she really didn't like him. Marion took pictures of the band, and was making a homemade album cover entitled *'TYRANT: Long Live Rock and Roll.'* Meanwhile, Jeff Tate was fucking Marion's girlfriend Julie with the skin tag in the back of his VW van.

One of the seniors, Jeff Obert, saw us play at the lunchtime concert. He was in charge of putting on the biggest party of the year.

The graduating class of Lake Washington High School held a two-day beer bash in the woods. They had one every year during the 70s. He asked me, "Hey Adam, does your band want to play at this year's Senior Keg?"

TYRANT- Lake Washington High School 1979

Jeff Tate (signed Jeffery Djarmony) and Randy Nelson

Gary Thompson and me (Marion Moulton in background)

The Senior Keg

During my high school sophomore year, I couldn't get a girlfriend. I had lots of girls as friends, but I wasn't sure if I was ever really going to get laid. I had this huge scab from a zit on my chin. This older girl, Carrie Jones, a senior, stopped me on the stairs to ask me why I was hiding my face. She laughed at me and said, "What's the matter?" "Wait a minute. You haven't been with a girl, have you?"

She could see right through me. I said, "Is it that obvious? It's just a pimple." She smiled and said, "Nah, you're gorgeous, I can show you the ropes. We'll go out just as soon as I get back from vacation." She got my hopes up, but she never came back home. She went to Hawaii, and she died in a car wreck. I wanted to write a song about her, but I never found the words.

I was spending a lot of time with a preppy girl named René Rossen. She was a senior, and drove a blue Ford Mustang. We talked every day at school, and on the phone for hours. She wasn't a rock chick or a groupie. Not even a stoner. I just thought she was cool. I really wanted to fuck her but she just wanted to be friends. So for most of that school year, René was my best friend.

Eventually, I got a girl that was known as a local slut to come over to my dad's condo. Her name was Robin Hall. We did it in on the floor in the upstairs bathroom. It took an hour, but when it happened and I came inside a girl for the first time, it felt like how most people described using heroin for the first time. I was instantly hooked.

After that, that I started having sex with lots of girls from school, parties, and rock gigs. They just started coming around to my house. Out of nowhere, the doorbell would ring, and some girl from school would ask if I was home. I remember my dad telling me, "Adam there's a girl named Lucinda at the door for you." The next day, a different girl would drop by, "Adam, Allison is here to see you." There was always somebody at the door. Out of nowhere, I was popular.

Girls started to pursue me, but not always the ones I had crushes on. Some of these girls I wasn't attracted to at all. I was shy, but not too shy to say no. Some girls were really dirty. One named Michelle, from my school gave me the clap. I had to tell my dad, and he took me to the doctor. I got tested, which was extremely painful, and got a penicillin shot, which instantly cured it. Ironically, his name was Dr. Cox. Another girl I had sex with gave me crabs. I had to visit Dr. Cox a few times during my high school education.

I loved to watch late night music shows like *Midnight Special, Don Kirshner's Rock Concert,* and *Night Flight.* Sometimes there were full concert specials like *California Jam* with Ted Nugent and Aerosmith. Late at night on channel 11, there was always this commercial for a band called Triumph. They sounded like a poor man's Rush, but in the 60-second TV spot, they had more pyro than any band I had ever seen. They promoted themselves as The Most Explosive Band in the World. I thought that pyro was super cool, and I wanted to use fireworks on stage someday.

Night Flight showed various things from movies to concerts. I watched a concert by a New York guitarist called Johnny Thunders. I couldn't believe how bad it was, and how this Johnny guy who could barely play guitar was singing and playing on TV. I thought in the back of my mind, "If that guy could sing on stage, then I could too." But at that time, I was way too self-conscious to ever think about being a lead singer.

Gary and his friends really razzed me when I tried to sing *Purple Haze* at a rehearsal, so we stuck to what we did best to build up our following. We were the loudest band in town. We were louder on our own than most local PA systems could handle. They never needed to put a microphone on the guitar or the drums when Gary and I played in school gyms or lunchrooms.

I wanted to get René Rossen a present for her birthday, so I looked in the newspaper for puppies. I read an ad, and drove to West Seattle to pick up a puppy for $8. I picked one that had a little black and gold face. He was so tiny that he could fit in the palm of my hand.

I took the dog home, and showed it to my dad who was in bed. He always went to bed early and got up at 5:00 AM to work at the bakery. My dad fell in love with the dog. He held it and said, "Don't give it away. That's my little Oggie Doggie." I liked the dog too. It broke my dad's heart, but I brought it to school the next day and gave it to René.

René was shocked by the gift, and she took it home. The next day, she drove her blue Mustang over to my dad's condo and gave me the dog back saying. "I love that you gave me this cute little dog but I just can't keep it." Then she sat me down on my bed and started kissing me. I asked her, "What are you doing?" and she put her finger to her lips and whispered, "Shhh," then she started to undress. She fucked me. We stopped being best friends after that, but I was really happy to get the dog back.

When my dad got the dog back, he was overjoyed. We named it Oggie. He took the dog everywhere he drove, and it rode sitting on the back of my dad's neck. Oggie slept under the covers, and barked at anyone he didn't like. The dog went to my rehearsals, and we took him to gigs. He loved to howl along when I played guitar in the apartment through an amp. It was just me, my dad, and the dog. We were a family. That was the happiest time in my life that I was with my father.

Thumper got married, and lived in a house on Lake Washington with her husband David Zauhar. My father loved to take me there. I'd ride on the boat, and spend the day at the lake while Thumper baked in the sun, just like she did at the pool in Seattle. David Zauhar was a slick con artist. He convinced my dad to loan him a lot of money up until the time he divorced my sister, right after they had a baby girl they named Davia.

Their neighbor was girl in her twenties with brown eyes. I stared at her nipple peeking out of her bikini top as we went out on their motor boat. She caught me looking, adjusted her top, and smiled. I wished I had a lake house. I loved summer life in Seattle. We watched the hydroplane races, smoked pot, and listened to rock on KZOK or KISW all summer long.

David Zauhar said he had a friend, Darryl Siguenza, from a band called Mojo Hand who was now a drummer in a group from Seattle called TKO. They were blowing up all over the country. I heard their song *Let it Roll* on the radio. David Zauhar took me to their concert at the Seattle Paramount, and we sat in the third row. The singer came out with skin-tight black pants, and he looked like Steven Tyler. You could tell he was a star. The drummer, David Zauhar's friend, was a Filipino guy. They had two guitarists. One of the guitarists looked cool with long hair, and the bass player looked like his twin. They didn't play full-on distorted guitars; they sounded like the guitarists of Heart.

The other TKO guitarist was this really tall guy with a blond Dutch Boy haircut. He was kind of goofy, like the guitar player who wore the baseball cap from Cheap Trick. He acted a bit psychotic, and yelled at the audience. They played their big song on the radio, *Let it Roll*. TKO was just okay, but the singer was very cool. They were a band from Seattle who made it big, that impressed me.

TKO had some affiliation with the group Heart. I was becoming friendly with Heart's guitarist, Roger Fisher, who I met through Mike Lull. I went to Roger's house in Woodinville near where Mike McCrea lived. Roger had a huge house with a private lake surrounded by a forest.

Roger Fisher – Heart, 1978

I met Roger's assistant, Juliana Roberts, and we became friends. She was like a beautiful big sister. Roger's brother, Mike Fisher, was building a 16-track recording studio in a room they were adding to the house. He had a pool table in the dining room that had an overhead stained glass lamp that had Heart's logo on it. Roger photographed me with his new $1,000 Nikon camera. He had a room with 50 guitars hanging on the wall. He'd just bought a new tremolo bar from Floyd Rose, and he showed me all of his special guitars.

I convinced my Aunt Yetta to give me $300 to get a tremolo bar from Floyd Rose. I was the son she never had. Everyone loved my aunt. She was a local star from the bakery. She dressed like a movie star or a hooker everywhere she went. Yetta never smoked or drank in her life. She drove me and my friends around if we ever needed to go somewhere. She would drop everything, and leave work and bring us food at the drop of a hat. She always gushed about me to anyone who would listen, and told me that I was going to be rich one day. She loved me more than my mother who I hardly ever spoke to after I moved in with my dad. My mother and her husband Dick were no longer a part of my life.

Floyd Rose lived in a small old house in West Seattle, and his workshop was in a small basement littered with power tools, where he designed and made this locking tremolo bar out of metal. I tried to convince him to give me a deal by telling him, "I could take it to rock shows and ask the roadies if their boss might be interested in buying one." I can probably get some interest in it. Floyd told me, "I am giving you a deal, they are normally $350.00."

Floyd built a tremolo bar for Edward Van Halen. Eddie's *Shark* Destroyer guitar was right there in Floyd's basement. My Boogie Body guitar was the seventh one made. He routed two holes at the back of the neck, and I wasn't really afraid that he drilled into it even though it was a brand new guitar. I thought it looked like a vampire bite.

Not only was this invention going to revolutionize the electric guitar; it was also an all-access backstage pass to meet every guitarist in the world who came to town. I got the guitar back just in time for the Senior Keg.

The Senior Keg was a really big deal, and took a lot of planning. Jeff Obert and his partner had a lot of meetings with me after school to discuss what we needed to put on an outdoor show in a field. I agreed to get my band to play for free as long as they got a stage, lights, and a decent sound system.

I thought it was incredible that these seniors were talking to me, let alone taking me seriously. Usually, there were social gaps between kids of different grades. Rock and roll broke the barrier.

The site of the party was remote, and there were no lights or power. It was just a big field next to a forest. They built a stage, hired a sound system with lights, and rented a power generator. We loaded up all of our gear into Randy's car and Jeff's VW van. We set up during the day, and played at night. The party was spread out over a few acres. People set up tents, and camped in parked cars.

The band and me were pretty much VIP; we could hang out with anyone we wanted to. There were 500 pot-smoking, beer-drinking, horny teenagers cruising the fields, hooking up and getting stoned. The weather was perfect. Music was blasting out of car stereos, and a truck brought in 10 kegs of beer.

Anticipating the show was exciting. When it got dark and time to play, everyone crammed against the stage to watch us. It was a crystal clear night under a full moon. Bright white lights illuminated the stage. We blasted through all our songs, and drove the crowd into a frenzy. It was different than indoor school shows; it felt like when I saw Van Halen play outside in California. After the show, Randy went back home, and the rest of us stuck around at the party.

Gary and I went looking for Waterfall. We found him about two hours later when we opened the back door of his van. He was in there fucking Cory Houston. It was dark, but the moonlight shone on her massive chest while Jeff pumped on her. It was really impressive, and I was even a bit jealous. At that moment, I thought my singer Jeff Tate was a total rock star.

I wandered through the party going from clique to clique, smoking pot and drinking beer. Everyone walked around with red cups, and it was a bright, starry night. I eventually wound up with a girl I knew, Heidi Kramer. She was a cute, flat-chested blonde who was popular in the stoner crowd. I had a crush on her. We spent the rest of the night together but she told me she didn't want to have sex. She slept with her head on my shoulder as I stared at the stars in the sky.

I found Jeff Tate in the morning. He was kissing Cory goodbye. She was wearing a skimpy white tube top and blue jeans. It really showed off her camel toe. She winked at me when she walked away. Jeff gave me a ride home, and he was happy to kiss and tell, "I had to lick Cory's pussy for two hours before I could get her wet enough to get my dick inside her. She was so tight, it was almost impossible to fuck her. She did have really great tits. That gig was awesome. I can't wait to start working on originals."

That gig was awesome. It was the last great high school party of the 1970s.

We played another outdoor gig at the baseball field in downtown Kirkland for Moss Bay Days. I hit on a little blonde girl named Kelli Knapp. She was a good girl who wore white fuzzy sweaters, but she liked to smoke pot. We made out by the lake, and watched the fireworks. I was so addicted to rock life. I loved sharing moments with girls that I just met. It made the world seem like magic. They stopped having Moss Bay Days a few years later after the police arrested 137 people. The police threatened to sue the city if the festival wasn't toned down, so they stopped it entirely.

The Battle of the Bands

Jeff Tate and me at the BOTB 1979

In the summer of '79, there was a Battle of the Bands contest at Lake Hills every Tuesday. The prizes were studio time, music gear from Bandwagon, and a deal with Unicam. 16 bands from all over the area signed up for it; Amazon, Amethyst, Artist, Easy Street, Jester, Joker, Mildstone, Orpheus, Oz, Rick Shaw and The Orient, Ridge, Smack, Voyager, Wraith, and my band Tyrant.

That first battle was a circus of guys with long hair. Scott Earl's band Orpheus lost in the first round. So did Chris DeGarmo and Michael Wilton's band Joker. Their singer, Paul Passerelli, was a Van Halen fan, and he could imitate David Lee Roth. He was a little on the fat side to be a lead singer, but he had a great sense of humor and was one of our rock and roll buddies.

At the time, I was miles ahead of the other kids my age on the electric guitar. After the first round, there were no other guitar players still standing who could even come close. I thought we had a big chance at winning it. We were the only genuine looking and sounding heavy metal band in the contest. Everyone else in the scene knew it; we were a powerhouse. The bands we were up against played new wave cover songs like The Knack or The Cars. We were hard rock. We had the edge.

We played songs by Judas Priest, UFO, Queen, Rush, Rainbow, and Van Halen. We started with *Light Up the Sky* into *Man on the Silver Mountain*, *Lights Out* by UFO, and *Virgin Killer* by Scorpions. I wore a ripped animal print T-shirt with black leather pants from a downtown bondage shop.

We changed things around every week just to be different. All of our friends came to every show. So did my dad and my aunt who always went in the front row. The judges always scored us 9 or 10 out of 10 in every category. The scoring sheets and comments for Tyrant read like a five-star review. We were unstoppable.

I thought it was going to be our big break. If we won, something big would happen. The battle was always attracting hundreds of people. We watched the other bands, and everybody watched us very carefully. Gary and I were a mean team, and losing was not an option. This thing meant the whole world to us.

We were paired against Snowblind at our first round, and we won. The next battle was Tyrant, Rick Shaw, Wraith, and Oz. Two bands went on to the semi-finals. It was Tyrant against Oz. Tyrant won that battle as well. It was Ridge vs. Tyrant for the final showdown. Ridge was a band with a new wave guitarist, Ted Pilot, and a decent drummer, Ken Mary. They were managed by Craig Cooke, and they had posters hanging with the Unicam logo like Rail & Company. Their big cover song was *My Sharona*. The audience was hardcore, and all of the kids were into hard rock. Both bands did *Rock Bottom* by UFO, and I knew that solo note for note. There was no way we could lose.

The contest made news in The Seattle Times. They printed Tate's name as Jeff Taylor. I got interviewed, and was quoted as saying, "Our goal is to make it big in one year." All of my friends thought it was presumptuous, but I said stuff like that all the time. That's how I learned it didn't matter what you said until it got in the press.

I didn't see why it couldn't be possible. There were all of these young bands coming out of New York, Hollywood, and England. A group called Def Leppard from the UK was said to have an average age of 18, and was opening for Ted Nugent and Scorpions. Gary and I were envious. We wanted to be those young kids on the radio, but Seattle was not New York or Los Angeles where bands got discovered.

Gary Thompson

The final battle was sold out and promoted by the radio station KISW. There were two stages - one on the side, and one in the back of the skating rink. We played on the side stage. Mike Lull from Guitar Works came down to the finals, and acted as my guitar roadie.

Joker, featuring Chris DeGarmo, Mike Wilton, Paul Passerelli, and a bass player named Brett Miller, played on the floor to open the show. Paul wished Tyrant luck at the end of their set.

The band was amped up for the finals. We had an intro tape that Gary made. We kicked it off with a fast guitar version of *We Will Rock You* like Queen did at their live shows. I did a guitar solo, and brought the house down. We blazed through *The Green Manalishi,*

Long Live Rock and Roll, Light Up the Sky, and *Rock Bottom.* We were as good as we ever played in rehearsal. The whole audience was on our side, and we thought the cat was in the bag. We were really proud of that show after we walked offstage. Gary, McCrea and I thought we had really turned Jeff into a rock stud, far from the guy who was into Yes and wanted to call himself Waterfall.

Ridge came on stage with their skinny ties, and did *My Sharona* and their version of *Rock Bottom.* Their guitar player, Ed Sein, couldn't even come close to playing the guitar solo like Michael Schenker. Ken Mary was a good drummer, but the rest of the band fell short. Ted Pilot was an average rhythm guitarist and a third-rate singer. Jeff Tate was not yet the Grammy-nominated singer he would eventually become, but he showed huge potential. I knew I wasn't just some schlock guitar player from a band who was only good enough to play school dances booked by Unicam. I really felt confident that we had won. At the end of Ridge's set Craig Cooke came on stage to say there would be a 20-minute break to count the scores.

Craig Cooke announced the winner. It was a landslide. Ridge won. Pandemonium struck after that. My heart sank. I saw Ridge going back up on the stage all happy. One of the judges came up to me and said, "I don't know what happened, I gave you guys a perfect score, all 10s. This other band didn't even come close. I don't understand."

Our judges sheets showed ones and twos and fours by every judge but one. We didn't know who the judges were. It wasn't really a factor before. It was obvious just how strong a band we were live. Gary was upset. So was I. Our whole world had just crashed and burned.

I couldn't get my head around why we had lost. It didn't really matter that winning gave you nothing. Ridge was managed by Craig Cooke, a guy who supposedly ripped off bands and lied to them about money. He looked like a used car salesman with a Jheri curl perm. I thought it was rigged since Ridge was already a Unicam band. We scored nines and tens on every category in every previous judges sheet since the beginning of the contest. Some of the comments on our final battle judges sheets were brutal. One just said, "You Suck." Some had no comments at all. Craig Cooke showed them to me to prove that we lost. I thought he was a sleazeball. I didn't trust him. He paid the press to overblow the event by saying there were 900 people there.

The following day, we listened to a cassette recording of the gig. It wasn't any different than the bootleg tapes of the big bands we used to follow. Gary and I determined it was Jeff Tate's fault because he sounded too gay at the beginning of *We Will Rock You.* He came out screaming with a high-pitched "c'mon c'mon," repeating it over and over. It was the only thing we had to pick on. Other than that we were great.

We had a band meeting in Gary's kitchen to discuss our future. I started screaming at Jeff after I played him the cassette. We decided that we were going to break up. It got nasty, and I told him, "Fuck off. I could have your job." I was just being a spoiled asshole. My dad would never fire anybody just because I told him to. Jeff Tate worked at the bakery for practically another year, and he got himself fired when he got caught stealing bread. At that point, Randy quit the band too. It was the end of summer, and almost the end of 70s. The 80s were just around the corner.

Gary Thompson, Adam Brenner, Jeff Tate, and Randy Nelson
Tyrant - The Final Battle – photo by Yetta Brenner

Backstage Kiss

On October 17, 1979, Judas Priest released a live album, and did a free concert at the Coliseum. I got backstage, and showed the guitar to KK Downing and Glenn Tipton. Rob Halford walked around the seating area, and started singing right next to me as I watched the sound check.

Judas Priest was a two-guitar team who I really liked. I watched them warm up in the dressing room. I was a huge fan. Glenn and KK wanted to get a Floyd Rose tremolo bar, so I rang up Floyd, and he came down. The Floyd Rose was a hit with rock stars.

Glenn Tipton had a massive cold sore on his upper lip. It was hard not to stare at it when I talked to him. KK Downing was very friendly. He invited me to come to the hotel and have a drink with him after the show. I went to the Edgewater Hotel and sat in a booth at the bar with KK, Rob Halford and the drummer, Dave Holland. Dave said, "I hate being a drummer; I'd much prefer to be a bass player. Far easier job. Nobody likes the drummer."

I talked to KK, whose name was Ken or Kenny, about his Flying V, and I told him, "I have a V. I also play in a band called Tyrant, and we play *Hell Bent for Leather*." He was drinking Crown Royal and 7UP. We talked for a while, and he said, "You're a good lad. I want to give you a leather jacket I have at home that doesn't fit me anymore. Did you know I'm the one who brought all the leather and studs to the band? Everybody thinks it's Rob, but I'm the one who started it. He's a half soaked knob-head. Call me, and I'll send you the jacket. I'm off to kip." He gave me his number in England, and went off to bed.

I actually called him a few times and got him on the phone, but he never did send me the jacket. KK left me sitting alone with Dave Holland and Rob Halford. They were talking to each other, and then Halford started to stare at me. The drummer looked at him, and shook his head in disapproval. I didn't realize what was going on, and Rob said, "I'm gonna go to my room now, do you..." and he paused. I thought, "He's hinting to invite me up and, why would this guy want to take me up to his room? He's not a guitar player." Dave Holland interrupted him. He was tired, and gave me a little sign to go towards the door, so I said goodnight and left.

At the time, it was not common knowledge Rob Halford was gay. Judas Priest did a photo layout in *Penthouse* magazine with *Pet of the Year*, Cheryl Rixon, dressed as a maid. The spread was entitled *What Rock and Roll Dreams are Maid Of*. It never crossed my mind that he was into boys. I think Halford wanted to pick me up. I never got to thank Dave Holland for literally saving my ass.

On November 21, 1979, Pat Travers opened for Blue Oyster Cult at the Coliseum. He was becoming really big, and they just had put out a live album called *Live! Go for What You Know*. We played a few of his songs in Tyrant. The second guitarist, Pat Thrall, was extremely interested in the Floyd Rose. When I met him he said. "Wow. I've been searching for something like this forever. Thank you," and he gave me a big hug.

Pat Thrall was extremely nice, but Pat Travers was mean and arrogant. Pat Travers entered the dressing room with Gail, the groupie I saw with Alex Lifeson at my first Rush concert. Pat Travers wore a Hawaiian shirt, and his nostrils were caked with cocaine. Little white rocks were falling out of his nose.

I was alone with the four guys from the Pat Travers Band in the dressing room. The drummer, Tommy Aldridge, was smoking hash from a metal pipe, and he passed it to me. I smoked it, and passed it on to the bass player, Mars Cowling, who only spoke French. I got really stoned; it wasn't just some ordinary weed from Seattle.

I asked Pat Thrall to show me something on the guitar. He tried to teach me a scale that was two frets below the blues scale. I couldn't get it. I saw where it was, but I couldn't do it; I was just too high from Tommy Aldridge's pipe. I remembered it when I came down.

Pat Thrall was really patient with me. It wasn't a major scale like Van Halen used or an extension of the blues scale like Rick Knotts taught me; it was a different place you could go to from there. Pat Thrall could use that tremolo bar like it was part of his hand. He could make it sound just like a slide guitar, and he used it to make the notes sing. He liked that it had a floating bridge; you could bend the string up in pitch as well as down. It truly was a revolutionary invention.

Pat Thrall wanted to use my guitar onstage, but he had to ask his boss, Pat Travers, first. Travers said, "Yeah I guess it will be alright but only if you make sure it's a hundred percent in tune, and you got to tune that fucking thing. So come here and tune it. Right here. Right now." Pat Travers and Mars Cowling huddled around me. I had to tune it up by ear, and Travers was pissed off, and skeptical.

I had to unlock the nut to tune it and relock it, two strings at a time. When I relocked it, there was a chance it could go sharp. It was always a balancing act to get all six strings in tune with each other. Pat Travers insisted, "Do it again; it's not right." I was really stoned, and Pat Travers made me so nervous I was shaking. It was real serious, and I was scared shitless.

It took me 10 minutes to tune it, but it seemed like an hour. I thought Pat Travers was going to hit me. He was such an asshole. Finally I got it tuned close enough to pitch, and Travers said, "Fine, but it better not go out of fucking tune on my stage or I'll smash it and come looking for you."

Pat Travers was a mean bastard, but I was a huge fan, and I loved Pat Thrall. He used my guitar on four or five songs. That guitar was becoming a star. Floyd sold another unit to Pat Thrall, and Pat Travers gave me a dirty look after the show.

When Jeff Beck came to town, I got backstage. He was not friendly at all. He had a mean streak. You could see it in his eyes, like everyone was in his way. He looked at my Floyd Rose like it was a joke. He gave me about a minute. He picked it up, looked at it, hit the bar a couple of times, and said he wasn't interested. Fat chance I could get him to show me how to play something.

I watched his show from the front row. Even though he was a prick, his music was amazing. That guy spoke so heavily with his guitar that it didn't matter how much of a jerk he was to me backstage. His music was a little jazzy, but it was rock enough to reach me. Gary and I covered his song *Space Boogie,* and Randy Nelson got Taurus bass pedals so we could do it correctly. Beck had a way of playing arpeggios in his leads like Eddie Van Halen. Most of Jeff Beck's playing was way over my head, but when he hit one note, it left me breathless.

On November 21, 1979, *The Return of KISS Tour* came to the Seattle Coliseum. Paul Stanley, Ace Frehley, and Gene Simmons went on KJR the day before the show and announced twenty times on air where they were staying; the Edgewater Hotel. Mike McCrea and I went into the hotel diner, and saw Gene Simmons sitting at the counter. We recognized him instantly even though no one ever saw a photograph of KISS without their makeup.

Gene was very nice. He immediately said hello, and starting asking us questions, quizzing us about bands we like, records we buy, and concerts we go to. I told him that I had a band and I was a guitar player. I mentioned the Floyd Rose, and he told me to ask for Tex, Ace's guitar roadie. When Gene went to pay for his breakfast, he opened his wallet, and 20 credit cards spilled out of it. Before we left, he gave us an address in New York City to send demo tapes to. It was a company called Glickman/Marks.

At the Coliseum, we went by the loading area, and asked for Tex. It worked. I got backstage, and when KISS entered we saw the whole band without the makeup. Ace Frehley was so skinny and cool. He was talking to Gail the super-groupie, and he said, *"You gotta see this guitar."* He picked up a Les Paul, and flipped a switch. Lights started flashing from inside of the guitar, and then he made this cackle of a laugh. He was really friendly.

Ace checked out my Floyd Rose guitar. I tried to show him that I could play by demonstrating the tremolo bar through an amplifier for a bit. The sound got the other guys in KISS to take notice that I was a badass guitar player and not just some little kid. It was really hard not to just blank out and stare at their faces, especially Paul Stanley. Seeing KISS without makeup was a really big deal. They had New York accents and wore boots with cool jackets.

Peter Criss walked right up to me to and said, "So Adam, tell me about this guitar?" He called me by my first name, I hadn't even introduced myself to him yet. I showed him the guitar and told him all about it. Then he asked, "Tell me about your band." I told him, "My drummer Gary hits his drums harder and louder than anyone I've ever seen." Peter Criss said, "It's not how hard you hit the drums that matters. What's important is the groove. Buddy Rich doesn't play hard, but he's one bad motherfucker. It's all in the wrist."

Watching Ace play the guitar for just a few minutes backstage was really captivating, He had his own dressing room with a rack of guitars in it. He just hit a few D chords and some Chuck Berry-type riff in the key of D. He then bent the middle string back and forth like the guy I saw at Bandwagon when I first started playing. He touched the tremolo bar a little bit. When he spoke, he sounded like Curly from *The Three Stooges*. He played my guitar for a few minutes, and handed it back to me. He wasn't interested because he didn't use tremolo bars. Paul Stanley took a quick look, and I watched him play a few chords before he handed it back to me. I called Floyd, and he came down and spoke to Tex and Ace, but I think KISS was a no sale.

Nobody cared about the support act, The Rockets. I watched KISS from the front row, and the guitars sounded amazing. They opened with *King of the Night Time World.* Seeing KISS that close in 1979 was watching them in their peak. Paul Stanley and Ace Frehley together were so rock and roll.

Paul came out and said, "I got a feeling we may have some people out there with a little rock and roll pneumonia, I think we better call out the doctor. You know what I'm talkin' about. *Calling Dr. Love.*" Ace slammed into the chords, and Gene Simmons sang like a giant. I watched him spit fire.

Ace sang *2,000 Man,* and did a ravaging five-minute guitar solo where he played the theme from the movie *Close Encounters of the Third Kind.* His pickups spit out smoke. He shot fireworks out of his guitar, and made a speaker explode. What Ace played was way simpler than Edward Van Halen, but it all had an outer space theme.

Kiss was a rock band where all four members sang lead on certain songs like The Beatles, but I always identified Paul Stanley as the lead singer. He screamed, "I'm gonna get you with my... Love Gun." Then Gene Simmons did a bass solo, and spat blood. It got all over us, and he flew into the air. After a drum solo and *Black Diamond,* everyone shouted, "We want KISS! We want KISS!" and they came out and played *Detroit Rock City*. Peter Criss sang *Beth,* and I think it made the whole audience cry.

Paul Stanley could captivate an audience when he spoke. He came back out and said, "You been doin' a lot of clappin' for us tonight. You give yourselves a round of applause. Seattle, I tell ya, all you got do is look around here, you sure got some good-looking girls in Seattle. We're taking some home with us tonight. We'll introduce 'em to the rock and roll national anthem. If these ones don't believe in rock and roll all the way up there, and all the way up in there. If you people don't believe in rock and roll, by God I know you do… Stand up and kick their asses, Rock and Roll All Nite and Party Every Day!"

Paul drove the crowd into a frenzy. After that last guitar riff, and all of the pyro and confetti, Paul Stanley said, "Seattle, we love you." I never felt a crowd more electrified. KISS put on a show like no other band on Earth. It was the same band like the giant poster I had in my bedroom. They were all really nice, especially Peter Criss and Gene Simmons. I never forgot how Peter Criss came up to me and called me by my first name. It was the last tour they would ever really do as a band; that rock band from New York whose record I stole from a shop in Crossroads. I had a feeling I'd cross paths with KISS again. It wasn't hard to tell that I was in the presence of greatness.

Barracuda

Gary and I continued on, and we eventually got another bass player, Brian West. He was 28, and he also got a job at the bakery. Brian was short like me, had long curly blond hair, and played a Rickenbacker bass all the way down to his knees. He had Taurus Pedals like Rush used. We came up with an original riff that McCrea called *The Future Song* and we worked on other original ideas too.

We auditioned a slew of bad lead singers. One guy came in with short hair and a southern drawl. He called himself Ray Jr., and he had an original called *Hitting the Bottle Again.* The lyrics went: I been hitting the bottle again, I've been drinking since half past ten, I passed out and I fell on the floor. Got up and starting drinking some more. I been hitting the bottle again.

I put some chords to it, but after a few rehearsals we gave up on him, as he couldn't figure out the words to Van Halen, and just sang nonsense. I think he was hitting the bottle.

Then we auditioned Scott Palmerton. He was into Bon Scott, but I was not really too familiar with AC/DC. I saw them open for Ted Nugent. They were just starting to get played all of the time on KISW by top Seattle DJ Steve Stayton. I remembered the records on Chris Jacobson's floor. They were scruffy guys with tattoos, and had a lead guitarist that dressed up like a schoolboy.

When Scott Palmerton came in, I had three guitar riffs that we made into original songs. I played a riff in E that he wrote lyrics to on the spot, and called it *Standing in the Lights.* I had two other riffs that became songs. One that he called *Wheels of Fire on Thunder Road* and another that was a slow heavy power ballad in drop D tuning.

We offered Scott Palmerton the gig. He didn't want to be in the band, but he agreed to record a three-song demo. We arranged through Johnny Boghosian to borrow an 8-track recorder from Roger Fisher's studio and we could mix the tapes on the big mixing desk.

We did the recording in my friend Casey Pratto's basement, because he had a big concrete room for drums. We also had crazy production ideas. For *Thunder Road*, I wanted an intro of a car screeching and a couple getting it on. I had Boghosian call Brenda Lane to come down to record a production scene. We set up microphones outdoors. Casey drove his car fast and screeched the brakes. We put the mics in the car while Brenda and me just talked a bit, and made out with the engine running. They couldn't hear anything on tape, and I made them keep doing more takes to try and get something. Brenda and I just wound up making out and we got nothing worth using as an intro, but it was sure fun trying.

When we finished the three songs with guitar overdubs and lead vocals, I couldn't wait to mix them at Roger's studio. When that day came, Mike Fisher and John Boghosian spent six hours setting up the board. It took ages to get ready. We mixed one song on the first day, and two songs the following day. I got to move the levers to get the special bits up so slightly, and I was over the moon. It was the first time I got to hear my music and my guitar blaring back at me through giant studio speakers. No matter how badly things were recorded, I thought everything sounded great in big studios.

Roger Fisher came in and listened to it after we finished. His comment was, "Well ya know, when you record and write originals you're competing with the Rolling Stones and Led Zeppelin. I don't know; you should really keep that in mind. Ol' Rog has gotta go now." Roger's critique took the wind out my sails. I knew it wasn't a major professional record like his big hit, *Barracuda,* but I was just starting out and it was my first demo.

Roger never encouraged me as a guitarist even though I was really eager to learn from him. I hung out at his house quite often. He had a room with more guitars in it than Bandstand East. There was a complete chrome Travis Bean guitar that weighed a ton. He had a double neck, and a dozen old Stratocasters and Telecasters. He had Ibanez guitars, and weird-shaped custom things. He had so many guitars, he couldn't possibly play them all.

Roger bragged about his huge accomplishments, and showed me a picture he'd taken of me with his expensive 35mm camera. He framed it, and displayed it in his assistant Juliana's office. Roger knew that I was a special guitar player, but he was never interested in what I had to play.

At the time, Roger Fisher had just broken up with Nancy Wilson, Heart's blonde female guitarist. His brother Mike Fisher was just about to break up with her sister Ann. Mike was interviewed in

Playboy Magazine, and he had an aura of 'I'm too important to talk to you.' He liked John Boghosian and took him seriously, but he never said more than a few words to me. Roger was about to be kicked out of Heart, but nobody knew that yet. He probably saw it coming.

I tried to get our demo to Steve Slaton at KISW, but he wasn't interested in any new local bands. I thought that if he heard it, maybe he'd like it and play it, so I called him up anonymously and told him we found an 1/4 inch reel-to-reel tape that says AC/DC on it. I said it had some unreleased material on it, so he told me to send it in. I wrote AC/DC on an unmarked box, and mailed it to KISW. We called him a few days later while he was on the air and he said, "That wasn't AC/DC; it was just some tape by some weird band." Since the demos were finished and Scott Palmerton didn't want to play live with us, Brian West moved to Hollywood and joined a band called London.

Gary and I wanted to start a new band with the twins from Shifter, Brad Young on lead vocals and Rod Young on bass. The whole thing was instigated by Mike McCrea, and we were having secret talks with the twins. Gary thought it was a good idea so we went for it. The new lineup was going to be our key to making it. They were Terry Young's brothers. Terry's band Rail & Company just changed their name to *Rail,*  and they were booked as opening act for 12 dates on the next Van Halen tour.

I got my driver's license when I turned 16, but I still didn't have a car. My dad would always loan me his after work, and I had to get it back by the time he had to leave. I was doing a lot of partying at Marion Moulton's, and I discovered how difficult drunk driving was. I was getting the spins, and had to stop the car and sleep it off even though I was only few miles from home.

At another party at Marion's, I took mushrooms, and got really paranoid. Cory Houston was there, and they had to talk me down and give me cocaine to snap me out of it. At 4:00 AM, I had to give Cory a ride home, and I pulled over and stopped on the side of the road. Cory asked me, "What do you want me to do?" and I said, "I want you to fuck me." We started making out, and she took off her bra and gave me a blowjob. I drove her home, and got back to my dad's at 7:00 AM. He was not happy; he'd been waiting two hours. I wanted to tell him, "But I just got a blowjob from Cory Houston," but I just kept it to myself. I dated Cory a few months later. I took her out to dinner and back to the condo. She let me tit fuck her on the couch in my daddy's garage. We never saw each other much after that, but she was one of those high school babes that you could never forget.

After that episode, my dad decided to get me a car. He arranged it through the same company that leased him bakery trucks. I picked a five-speed silver Toyota Celica with a hatchback that could hold all of my music gear. David Morris went with me to get it. He fell on the ground laughing because I didn't know how to drive a stick shift. It took me an hour to get it out of the parking lot after I finally worked out how to use a clutch. The next morning when I drove it to school, I dented the passenger side fender trying to park it.

The new band with the twins was rehearsed and ready. Brad and Rod Young could sing harmonies together like Van Halen. Brad Young had put down the guitar, and just became the lead singer. We rented the theater at Bellevue Community College for $75 to put on a concert that we promoted ourselves.

By now, we had crew. Besides David Morris as my occasional guitar roadie, there was John Boghosian - our preppy pothead sound engineer, Casey Pratto - a kid from Redmond with hair like mine. We could have been twins. We played an outdoor party on his dad's property. He was a semi-reckless driver with a blue Camaro that had a really loud engine. He got tons of speeding tickets, and always got his license suspended. We went out a lot in his car to gigs and parties.

There was Todd Clapp who was Gary's drum roadie. Todd was a stocky guy who liked to bench press. He was a high school wrestler, and he would always get so frustrated and angry that he turned bright red. There were others too, like Gary's best friend Darren Smith - the high school quarterback at Redmond High who drove Gary to Bandstand East when we first met. His only claim to fame was he had a smoking hot girlfriend named Shelley Morgan, and he shot a load that hit the ceiling when he fucked her. We were a rock and roll gang.

My dad gave David Morris, Casey Pratto, and John Boghosian part-time jobs at the bakery. He was always really nice to all my friends, and they could always eat for free. We all worked hard putting on this show at Bellevue Community College. The holidays had passed, and Heart with Roger Fisher had three sold out shows at the Coliseum for New Year's Eve 1980. I went to one of them and sat in the rafters.

The Bellevue Community College theater show was all ready to go. We had promoted this show using flyers and hand-written tickets. The opening act was Joker with Paul Passerelli. I hand drew flyers that read: Black Leather Productions Presents an Evening of Heavy Metal. TYRANT and special guest JOKER, Advance tickets available at Bandwagon Music, January 19, 1980 $2.50. Don't Miss It!!

TYRANT

We played our final rehearsal, and I had all my gear packed and ready. My Marshall amp and cabinet, the V and the Floyd Rose, my echoplex and pedal board, and I parked it in my driveway and went to sleep. The next day, when I got to the gig at BCC and unloaded my car, my V was missing. It was inside of my Celica when I packed it. I distinctly remember seeing it in the window of the hatchback, but the guitar was nowhere to be found. I was frantic. It had been stolen.

My perfect V that had been signed by Edward Van Halen with two PAF pickups worth $300 each, was gone. I felt like somebody ripped out a piece of my soul. I called Mike Lull on the phone crying, and he reassured me that he'd help me get another one. I did my gig with the Floyd Rose and McCrea's Les Paul.

The set list for the show included *Running Wild* by Judas Priest, *Natural Thing* by UFO, *Light Up the Sky* by Van Halen, *Coast to Coast* by Scorpions, *Stevie* by Pat Travers, *Hot and Ready* by UFO, *Three Mile Smile* by Aerosmith, *Lakeside Park* by Rush, *Virgin Killer* by Scorpions, *Space Boogie* by Jeff Beck, *Beyond the Realms of Death* by Judas Priest, and *We'll Burn the Sky* by Scorpions.

The gig sold out, and I did my best to not let my sadness show in my performance. We did our covers, and we were exciting. Playing with the twins was great. They were more like kids our age; the same height and had long hair. We played Van Halen songs, and we were cocky and badass. I still had my guitar with the Floyd Rose, but I was too hurt to have a good time.

After the show, I filed a police report, and my dad was able to claim $600 through insurance. I never got wind of who, how, or where my guitar was stolen, but my thoughts were it was an inside job from one of our gang. It's still a mystery to me to this very day. I still feel a connection to that guitar, wherever it may be. It's like a missing child.

A few weeks later, Mike Lull tracked down a similar V at a shop in Spokane. My dad gave me the $600 and we drove out one weekday morning. We drove 90 miles an hour both ways, and made the 600 mile round trip in about nine hours. I bought the guitar for $550, and left five minutes later.

Mike Lull set up the guitar just like my old V and his partner Ron Van Ryn sold me another PAF pickup for $300. I only got him to part with one PAF pickup. They're extremely rare. When we arrived back at the bakery, my dad didn't believe that we could possibly drive to Spokane and back so fast. He asked, "What did you do with the money?" Nothing Mike or I said really convinced him otherwise. My dad was funny that way.

Crashing Rush

I was still going to concerts and trying to meet guitarists. I went to the Paramount to see Al Di Meola, a jazz guitarist famous for playing blindingly fast guitar solos on an acoustic guitar. I got backstage, and I had to wait in a room upstairs, until after the show to see him. His roadie brought him upstairs and closed the door behind him. Di Meola looked at the guitar and said, "Sorry, I'm not interested in this. I only play Ovation acoustic guitars. I don't why they bothered to make you wait here for so long. Thanks anyway, now if you'll excuse me." He turned the handle, but the door was locked from the outside.

Al Di Meola turned the handle a few times, tried to shake the door, and got upset. He started banging on it, but nobody answered. He kept banging away, and after a few minutes, we both realized that he'd been pranked by his roadie. I said, "Since you're locked in here, you wanna show me some guitar tricks?" He said, "Guitar tricks? You've got to be kidding me. C'mon guys, open up the door!" Here was this 40-year-old, balding international jazz musician, who had no time for a 16-year-old heavy metal kid, banging on a door. He spent 20 minutes pounding, but they wouldn't let him out. He screamed out the window, "Help! Guys, help. It's not funny. C'mon guys. Somebody let me outta here." Finally, somebody came up and opened the door. As he ran down the stairs, I said, "Are you sure you don't wanna buy a Floyd Rose?"

When Rush came back on March 18, 1980, I got backstage by showing the Floyd Rose guitar to the roadie of the support act, .38 Special. I went to the show with my friend David Morris; we were still crazed Rush fanatics. I bought a few color 8X10 photos of Rush for $5 a print from a picture seller in the parking lot at school. I was dreaming about meeting Alex Lifeson, and hopefully, I'd get him to show me how to play some Rush riffs and let me play guitar for him.

I waited alone in .38 Special's dressing room for the band to arrive. They burst in like a gang of rodeo clowns. They had three guitar players, like Lynyrd Skynyrd . The lead guitarist, Jeff Carlisi, was the only one who checked out the Floyd Rose guitar. He picked it up and played some hillbilly guitar riff. He looked like Randy Nelson or Buck Dharma from Blue Oyster Cult. He wore a silk shirt with a gold chain razor blade, and had a strong smell of cheap cologne. He wasn't interested in the Floyd Rose. Neither was I in .38 Special. I had a bigger agenda; crashing Rush backstage.

I nervously went over to the Rush dressing rooms. Alex Lifeson had his own room. I got my courage up. I took a deep breath, knocked on the door twice, and opened the door. Alex was sitting in there alone playing a guitar. I spoke, "Excuse me Mr. Lifeson. I have this guitar with a locking tremolo unit that will not go out of tune. I'd like to show it to you, do you mind if I come in?" He looked at me kind of funny and allowed me to enter. I opened the case, and showed him the guitar.

I handed him the guitar and he hit the bar a few times, and gave me a look of 'so what?' I showed him that strings could go totally limp and snap right back again. He looked at me like I was a little punk, bothering him in his quiet time. I was so scared. I just froze.

I was dead silent, but in my head I was screaming, "Holy fuck. You're Alex Lifeson, I love you. You changed my life, I wanna know how play every riff you ever wrote note for note. Show me *Hemispheres*. Watch me play *Xanadu*. Teach me everything!" Alex Lifeson was right there, alone in a room with me, and I was terrified. I felt like a teenage intruder posing as a guitar salesman, invading his sacred backstage.

I said, "So would you be interested in getting one of these tremolo bars? I could call the guy who makes them and he could come down." He said, "No, that's okay, thanks." I quickly tried to ask him something about any Rush song I could think of. I wanted to say something as he handed it back to me, but I only mumbled. My tongue was tied. I put the guitar back in its case and thanked him for his time. As I picked up my guitar case, I accidently knocked over a glass when I turned towards the door.

I put the guitar back in .38 Special's dressing room. I had failed miserably. I walked out of the backstage to meet my friend David Morris, who only had a general admission ticket. He was on the balcony overlooking the backstage area while 38 Special was playing. I went up to the balcony to join him. We looked down, and saw Geddy Lee scratching his butt, talking to some guy.

David said, "Oh please, you got to let me use your pass. I got to meet Geddy. C'mon dude, I'll owe you for life." I gave him the pass and pleaded, "Don't do anything stupid; my guitar's still back there."

David Morris went backstage, and walked immediately into Neil Peart's dressing room. Neil was with his wife and their baby daughter. David was wearing a bootleg Rush T-shirt and Neil's wife made a comment about it. His recollection was, "Neil, look at this. You need to do something about this." David just sat down on the couch next to Neil and spoke, "So Neil, 2112. What possessed you to write that?" Neil's response was, "Who the fuck are you? Who let you get back here? Get the hell out of here. Security!" They threw David Morris out of the backstage and security took the pass away.

During Rush's show I had to convince the security guard to let me back to get my guitar. Luckily he remembered me, and I was able to get my guitar and drive home. The next day I was going to Canada to see Van Halen.

Rush – Seattle 1980

The Day Night Came Early

On March 19, 1980, Mike McCrea and I went to the first date of Van Halen's *World Invasion Party 'til Ya Die* tour. The opening act was Rail, and we got all the secret hotel details from Debbie Ward. It was in Victoria, British Columbia, and there was a direct ferry called the *Princess Marguerite* that went from Seattle to Victoria in four hours. Traveling to rock gigs was like going on vacation. I brought along my new V, and I was sure I could get Edward Van Halen to sign it.

We got a room at the Bayshore Inn. It was a fancy hotel, not like the motels they stayed in on the last tour. We were able to get backstage passes through Rail and their road crew. Terry Young of Rail was not allowed to wear his white fur boots. Van Halen made Rail follow all of these rules to open for them, and we stayed out of Rail's way. I watched Van Halen do a sound check from the barricade.

David Lee Roth had platinum white hair and used a microphone that was attached to a rope. He only used it at the first show in Victoria. The show was in a big hockey arena, and they played *And the Cradle Will Rock* for the sound check. Michael Anthony played a Wurlitzer electric piano that was being fed through a Marshall amp. The keyboard was housed in a big hollowed-out army surplus war bomb. They practiced the solo a few times, and when Eddie did the little quiet guitar part at the end of the solo, just before Roth sings "Have you seen Junior's grades?" it brought tears to my eyes. David Lee Roth wasn't at the sound check.

While Rail played, I sat on a small stairway backstage, just outside Edward Van Halen's tuning room. I listened to him warm up from through the closed door. When he came out, he saw me and he asked, "Why do you look so sad?" I told him, "Hey Eddie, do you remember my guitar, ya know, my V that you signed? It got stolen and I had to get another one, I brought it with me. It's back at the hotel, the same hotel you're staying at. Do think maybe you could sign it for me?" He told me, "Really? Aww fuck! Yeah, I'll sign it, call me at the hotel after the show."

I went out, and saw Van Halen's new show from the front row. They opened with a new guitar trick that started a song called *Romeo*

Delight. Another live guitar showstopper was called *Loss of Control*. They played a song called *Take Your Whiskey Home*, where Eddie and Dave came up front and played real quiet like a country duo. David Lee Roth stopped him, pointed towards me and said, "Hey Ed, wait a second. Look at this motherfucker's eyes." They started back up quiet and the band slammed in like a freight train.

They had a song called *Everybody Wants Some!!* Edward really made use of his Floyd Rose tremolo bar, which was on his main Frankenstein guitar. I took notice that the title was lifted by David Lee Roth from his own in-between song stage banter. He repeated the same rap every night on the last tour before *On Fire*. He could talk to crowd of 10,000 just like he was talking to an old friend or pretty girl.

He picked up a joint off the stage, sparked it up, and said, "I forgot what I was gonna tell ya." The audience went crazy, and he timed it just right and said, "It seems like everybody wants some. Everybody thinks about it. My grandma who's about 85, 86 years old, told me, Dave, it's better to wear it out than to rust it out. It seems like everybody's getting some, well I want some too. How about you?" Van Halen made a song out of it for this tour. I took it as another clue on how to write songs.

Whatever Roth said onstage was always geared up with a punch line to get the audience to cheer. Roth did his *'This is Joe'* rap about a card game with Alex and a shotgun he called Joe. He had this great way of telling a story. Another stage prop Roth came out with was a white furry acoustic guitar with mirrors on it that said *Diamond Dave* in big letters. He used it for the song *Ice Cream Man.* They did a blues song that wasn't on any album that featured Michael Anthony's high voice singing, "Bright lights, big city, but it's gone to my baby's head." It was really was just a blues jam. The sound of the hall was horrible, but the guitar amps always sounded big and huge from the front row, and that was only place I wanted to be. Right in front of Edward's amps. I would've put my face in the speaker cabinet if I could have.

Back at the Bayshore Hotel, Eddie ran to the elevator to avoid the crowd of girls and fans in the lobby. They weren't just partying in the hallways anymore. I rang his room using the alias Debbie gave me to reach him. He picked up the phone, and told me to come up. He signed my new V with a hotel pen. He was sad for me that I lost the other one with two PAF pickups, but he thought my new V was just as good. I asked him, "Did you sign any other guitars?" He looked at me apologetically and said, "I signed one in Japan." It was a little foolish of me to think I was the only one in the world who had a guitar signed by Edward Van Halen.

I asked him to autograph another hotel paper and then I asked, "How do you play *Romeo Delight*?" He showed me how to do the guitar tricks in that song, using tapping harmonics with his right hand. He showed me the guitar solo intro for his song *Fools* with its 6-fret spread and muted D string, and the way he bent the E string when he started off the song.

He showed me the guitar trick in *Loss of Control* - he did this strange rhythm, muting the neck with his left hand thumb. He taught me the solo part. It wasn't based on any scale, it was just crazy like music I used to hear in cartoons. He showed me how to play *And the Cradle Will Rock*. The main riff was just two string chords. He played the verse on the guitar as he played it on a piano, He stretched his hands across six frets. He wrote it on piano, but he said, "I've played piano for a while but my brother Al doesn't want to me to be a 'Jack of all Trades' so we only do guitar songs. But I write a lot of stuff on piano."

Eddie was not doing any drugs this time. But it was as if we just picked up the lesson where we left off in Tacoma. He showed me how he played *Whiskey*. It was simple but he had a way of making simple stuff sound really cool. He showed me how to play my favorite new song of his, *In a Simple Rhyme*. KISW got a pre-release copy of *Women and Children First*. They played the whole album and I taped it off the radio. It wasn't going to be released for another week and I already knew most of it. It blew him away. We didn't talk as much as last time, we just played. He said, "I don't have my travel guitar here or I'd string it up." I didn't mind just passing my V back and forth. It gave him a chance to watch me play.

Lightning struck twice. We were able to see a lot more shows on the tour and we planned on going to as many as we could get to. That was the last face-to-face guitar lesson I got from Eddie Van Halen, but their tour, everything and everyone around it was about to become a bigger education for me than I could ever hope for.

Back in the lobby we saw David Lee Roth and the lighting designer, Pete Angelus, picking up girls to take them upstairs. Girls usually came back down 20 minutes after they went up, looking disheveled and unhappy. I asked Pete Angelus to autograph the paper that Eddie signed. Pete Angelus was one of those guys that were always around the big bands. He looks like a rock star, had an important job with a rock star band so everybody thought he was a rock star, but nobody had the slightest clue who he was. He wore the latest Van Halen fashion trend - a pink army jumpsuit just like Edward. Pete signed my paper 'Light On.'

I put my hand on David Lee Roth's arm. It felt like I was touching gold. He was like a lion. It was the best he ever looked in his life. The very peak of his game. He signed my paper perfectly without even looking at it. He was a rock God. Girls would line up and get in fights to get his attention, just to be with him for five minutes. It was really easy to get laid at a Van Halen show. I got one of the girls hanging out in the lobby to come upstairs and have sex with me. She thought we worked with Van Halen because we were staying there. I completely loved rock and roll.

Two days later, we drove to the show in Medford at The Compton Arena. We also saw them in Eugene, Oregon at the Lane County Fairgrounds. It was in a cow hall with hay and horseshit on the floor. Van Halen usually played concrete arenas where the sound was washed by echo but this place had a real dead ambience. I told that to their soundman Townsend, after the show. "You did an excellent job on the sound tonight. That was the best sound at a VH show that I ever heard. Thanks." Townsend looked at me like, "Why the fuck is this kid talking to me?"

Paul Passerelli, the Joker singer, came along to Vancouver, Canada. When I told Edward that he was a singer and that he sounded like David Lee Roth, Edward's reply was, "Well he doesn't have Dave's body." Paul told him, "Thanks a lot." Outside of the venues, we'd only see them as they got back to the hotel or when they left for the show. Dave was sick with the flu (or hungover and on something) in Portland and his roadie Big Ed was carrying him to the lobby elevator. He was saying, "Dave's not well, let him through." I yelled at him, "Somebody give him a shot." Dave laughed, looked up at me and smiled. When Eddie got to the hotel he just dashed through the crowd, and went up to his room.

I'd always listen from outside when Eddie warmed up in the tuning room if I got backstage. I tried to keep myself hidden and out of the way. Rail usually hooked us up with passes and tickets. We always got in, and McCrea and I managed to follow Van Halen around for 10 shows on that tour. I didn't care about missing class; this was school.

The show had changed a little bit from the first show in Victoria. The mic on the rope and the furry acoustic weren't used after the first show. Dave's stage raps were evolving and he'd always screw up the lyrics or just not sing and look at the audience and say, "I forgot the fuckin' words!" to thunderous applause.

David Lee Roth was making it up as he went along. They did everything very fast, especially making records. I started to really watch how he operated. He had a slick way of repeating the same things every night but still making it seem spontaneous. There wasn't much acrobatics or dancing. That tour, he was a party host, and he bounced off Edward's guitar playing which carried the whole business as far as I saw. They took over radio stations and always made people laugh and smile with a routine that was pure Hollywood. All four of them had such a magic that everything they did at that point just worked. I'd seen Van Halen go from becoming an unknown band on the uprising to become the biggest band in rock.

Rail were local heroes when they opened for Van Halen at the two-sold-out shows at The Seattle Coliseum. We all thought they would go on to get a big deal and become huge from all of those big concerts and massive exposure. But after Van Halen did a show, everybody forgot who the opening acts were. All that time we spent on the road with Van Halen, we only watched Rail once or twice.

Van Halen stayed in the Seattle Hilton. After Edward got in the elevator and went to his room after the second Seattle show on April 5th, I went back home to my life. We rehearsed more and added new songs to the set. I tried to catch up with school and I wanted to really start playing shows with the band.

I worked out a new guitar solo with every trick I knew. We learned Van Halen's *Romeo Delight, Somebody Get Me a Doctor,* and *Runnin' with the Devil.* We also learned *Always Somewhere,* and *Another Piece of Meat* by Scorpions, *Green Manalishi* by Judas Priest, *Long Live Rock and Roll* by Rainbow, *Midnight Rendezvous* by The Babys, *Pack it Up (And Go)* by UFO, and *Touch Too Much* by AC/DC. We did some originals - *Where Were You* and *Out of Faze.* We did a show at Lake Washington High School on April 24, 1980, and played for over two hours.

Somehow, between Gary and the twins, we managed to book two shows in Eastern Washington for May 16 and 17. The first gig was just 30 miles east of Spokane in Coeur d'Alene, Idaho. It was our first band road trip, and we all went in separate cars. Mike McCrea rode with me in my Celica while Gary and Todd Clapp drove across together. The twins took their own car.

We stayed in a cheap motel, and thought we were rock stars. Gary would put on his sunglasses, and point his nose in the air. It was our first gig in a different state. We all crammed together in two rooms. Todd Clapp was getting bent out of shape because the rooms were small - only one big bed. He knew that he was the one who was going to sleep on the floor. It was big fun. The gig was in a hall, and it wasn't packed, but 80 people came to see us. The next gig was in a school. I got a speeding ticket going over 100 miles an hour on the Idaho state border freeway between Coeur d'Alene and Spokane on the way to the gig. I was lucky I didn't get arrested. It was a big fine, around $300, but I had six weeks to pay it.

After the gig we stayed overnight in the same Coeur d'Alene hotel we stayed in the previous night. On May 18, 1980, we all checked out of the hotel really early and left in our cars to make our way back home to Bellevue. It was a beautiful, sunny, Sunday morning.

I was driving slow, enjoying the drive. I did not want to get another speeding ticket. The other guys had left before us and we had no plan to convoy together or meet up anywhere. Mike McCrea was putting on cassette tapes, and we were talking about music like we always did. We were in no big hurry to get home.

It was around 9:00 or 10:00 in the morning and we noticed that a strange darkness started to appear in the form of a black swarm that was creeping up on the sun. At first we didn't think anything of it. Minute by minute, it started to get a little closer as the sky grew dark. It was ominous, like a glowing black and orange sunset, but it was way too early in the day to be night. Within an hour it was starting to become pitch black. We didn't think to turn on the AM radio. There was no FM radio reception in the mountains, and we were listening to Van Halen on cassette tapes. We just turned on the headlights and kept on going.

It was becoming too strange to think about what was actually happening. We thought that maybe the world was ending or an atomic bomb had blown off. It wasn't like rain clouds taking over the sun. It was obviously something completely different. Something catastrophic had happened, it was a pitch black day, despite only being around 11:00 AM.

All of sudden, what I thought was snow started to hit the windshield. At first just a few flakes and then more and more until it was like a blizzard. It was getting hard to see the road so we took the next exit off the freeway and pulled over into a parking lot just as soon as we saw one. We got out of the car, which was now covered in this dark grey dust like ash, like it was snow. Everywhere was covered in two inches of this stuff and more kept falling from the sky like black snow from Hell on Christmas Eve.

There were no cars passing by or streetlights on. It wasn't even noon. It was dead quiet except for this dark wind. Everything and everywhere was covered in this ash. We were still over 100 miles from home and it looked like we were on the surface of moon, leaving our footprints behind while the ash was starting to build up my on my hair. We got back in the car and I said, "What should we do now? I don't wanna die here in this parking lot".

McCrea said. "Maybe it's got something to do with that volcano Mount St. Helens that was in the newspapers recently. But that volcano is over 100 miles away." No one predicted what was going to happen if it erupted. I asked, "Are you sure it can affect us even though it's so far away?" We stopped a passing motorist and when we asked what happened he said, "The volcano erupted and the roads are going to be shut down so you better get moving if you don't want to be stuck here." We turned on the AM radio and got a signal. I was relieved that the world wasn't ending or Seattle wasn't blown off the map. I wanted to see my dad and Oggie again.

We drove about two hours very slowly on the motorway. We only got about 20 miles until we came to a police roadblock that forced us to drive off into a small town. We drove into the first hotel we saw and went into the lobby to get a room but the hotel was full. They said there was another hotel a mile away but it was probably sold out too. We didn't know what we were going to do and we went back in the parking lot and all of sudden we saw Gary, Todd Clapp, and the twins. They got there earlier and they got a room. It was just a strange coincidence that we all wound up at the same hotel.

Todd Clapp had managed to get a joint from somewhere and everybody spent the night talking shit until the ashes stopped falling from the sky. The next morning when the roads were cleared, Gary and I convoyed back together, and both our cars were covered with four inches of volcanic ash.

When we arrived in Redmond at Gary's dad's Chevron station, his father Wayne looked at our cars and said, "Holy shit!" He owned a small town main street gas station that did car repairs and he said he could clean it up to make sure the ash doesn't ruin the engine. He wanted me to drive it home, unload my gear that was in the back, and bring it back later. McCrea got a ride home from there and I drove the car back to the bakery. My dad and everyone else at the bakery

came outside to gawk at the car that was covered in inches of ash. My dad hugged me and said, "That must have been something. I'm glad you're okay. I love ya kiddo." Then I said, "I love you too Pops. By the way, I got a $300 speeding ticket."

The ash didn't come off unless you scraped it, and it was almost the same color as the car. I scraped off enough to fill a small garbage bag and saved it. Wayne got it cleaned up and changed the fluids, but it never ran the same after that.

We did a show at Lake Hills, and I threw an after party while my dad was working the night shift. I had the place to myself. Debbie Ward went into my bedroom, took her clothes off, and got in my bed. She was really cute and she had a large birthmark on her breast. She wanted me to fuck her. I sat down on the bed and told her "I love you Debbie but I just I can't because Mike McCrea is in love with you. It would kill him if I fucked you." So she said, "Go get Mike."

I noticed that the curtain was open in my room and anyone could see in if they climbed up on the rocks and went on the hill that was outside my window. I told McCrea, "Dude, go to my room because Debbie's in there and she's completely naked and ready to go. Now's your chance. Get in there."

He didn't want to go up. Gary and I had to drag him inside and we shut the door behind him. Then I got Gary and the other 20 people at the party to come outside and climb up the hill. We had a perfect view and we watched Mike McCrea fail miserably. She was really trying to get him to do something, but he was too scared. He stripped to his underwear and sat on the edge of the bed. She tried to pull him down to kiss her, but he kept sitting back up to talk. We were making play-by-play commentary from the hill. It went on for about 15 minutes before he looked out the window. When he realized that everybody was outside watching him, he shut the curtain. We were in hysterics.

Debbie didn't care. She was a good sport and she just wanted to get laid. She was a good friend and would always come see us play. Her boss John Bauer divorced his wife Ivy and married Debbie a few years later. They had a son named Jessie and they're still together. I always loved Debbie Ward.

Now that I had a car, I was picking up girls left and right. I met girls hanging out at 7-Eleven and fucked them in my car. Then I'd just leave them in a parking lot. I didn't have a girlfriend and some of my friends' girlfriends wound up fucking me. Shelly Morgan went after me when she broke up with Darren Smith. Casey Pratto's girlfriend Mellissa also slept with me and Casey beat me up when he found out. There were always fights in our little clique, and there was usually drama.

When my dad went on holiday, I met a beautiful 14-year old blonde girl at a convenience store in Kent, and I took her home. I kept her there and fucked her for three days. I was a terror around town with girls. If a girl had a crush on me and I didn't really like her, I would just be rude, but they still chased me all over town. I'd try to avoid some of the girls I already had sex with, with but they still stalked me. There were tons of parties and concerts to go to all the time. It was a brand new decade and Van Halen had taught me how to act like a rock star. Now I just had to become one.

Gary graduated from Redmond High School. His parents owned a lake house and we went water skiing during summer. I wasn't very good at it like Gary and his friends. Gary was a pro. He taught me how to get up on one ski. There was a raft in the middle of the lake that people sat on while they waited for someone to do a ski run. The good skiers could spray water on the raft people as they passed by. I tried to do it to but instead of spraying the people with water, I crashed into the dock at 30 mph. I got the wind knocked out of me. I thought I was sinking but the life vest saved me. They all jumped in to help. I was spitting up blood, but I survived. We had some good times at that lake, smoking pot on the boat, but we never stayed up there very long.

My dad wanted me to meet a woman that he was dating, He thought she looked like Elizabeth Taylor. She was around 40 and her name was Joan Zukin. He called her Joanie. She had a punk daughter who was two years older than me, Lisa Silverman. She changed her name from Lori Lampman to Lisa Silverman because they were hiding from her mother's previous husband. Joanie had been married several times before she met my father.

Miss Boat Show 1957 - Joan Herbert / Zukin / Lampman / Silverman / Brenner

He asked me if it was okay with me if he married her. I said, "I guess it's fine as long as she doesn't ask you to call the police if she catches me with marijuana." Joanie and my dad took me out to dinner and Joanie was drunk after three glasses of wine. I thought she was a lush, but if it made my dad happy, I was fine with it.

Joanie and Lisa moved into our condo and I had to let Lisa share my room. I hated that and so did the dog. Lisa tried to look like Siouxsie Sioux. I couldn't stand Lisa, she was gross, but she did have a few hot girlfriends. Punk girls are easy so I fucked a lot of her friends, but just the pretty ones. Lisa had a lot of ugly punk girlfriends. Her best friend, Kim Fastback, had a band called The Fastbacks. Later, she changed the name of the band to The Fartz. The drummer was a guy named Mike McKagan, who later changed his name to Duff, and switched to bass. I despised punk rockers.

Homegrown RockFest

Matthias Jabs playing my guitar at Seattle Center Coliseum

I had Mike Lull cut the shape of my Floyd Rose guitar to look less like a Fender Strat and more like a Gibson. We cut the curves out of the headstock into a sharp angled point like a weapon. We also sharpened the cutaways to look like devil horns and sawed off curved chunks on both sides of the bottom, so it could rest on my thigh like the V. It came to a point where the strap was attached. It was a perfect one-of-a-kind design.

When The Scorpions came to Seattle on May 28, 1980, I met Matthias Jabs outside his hotel, and I showed him the guitar. He put me on the guest list, and Matthias asked if he could play my guitar onstage. Backstage, all of the Scorpions band members spoke in German to each other. I was very excited to meet Michael Schenker's brother, Rudolf. I was allowed right into the band's dressing room and I watched the singer Klaus Meine, who did not have much hair, put some dark spray paint on his head to cover his bald spot.

Matthias was such a cool rock star. I adored him. I thought his solos were incredible. He wore a train engineer's cap and a ripped t-shirt. He was happy to show me some of his leads on my guitar and I got to play guitar for him. When he warmed up backstage he played Jeff Beck and Van Halen riffs. I let Matthias use my guitar and I watched him play it onstage for two songs from the seats to the right of the stage. I felt like a star in that audience, even though the only people who knew it was my guitar were my friends.

Journey had become popular when they got a new lead singer, Steve Perry. They had a big song on the radio that I played with Jake in Anthem, called *Wheel in the Sky*. They were headlining the Coliseum on June 3, 1980, and the opening act was The Babys, a group who had a song we covered called *Midnight Rendezvous*.

Mike McCrea and I went down early to try and hustle our way in. We had met two guys wearing colored jumpsuits from the Babys road crew. We thought they might have been in the band because they looked like rock stars. One of them saw that I had a guitar case and he said, "Hi. I'm Kim Turner, I work for The Babys. Do you want to be Wally Stocker's (The Babys guitarist) roadie for the night and tune his guitars? All you have to do is a couple of guitar changes? I'll pay you $75." I said, "Fuck yeah!" and took the job.

I met The Babys when they arrived in the dressing room. They were all English and reserved, except for the American keyboard player Jonathan Cain. The next year he replaced Journey keyboardist Gregg Rolie. The drummer Tony Brock and the singer John Waite really shone, but Wally Stocker was too stock. He wasn't a guitar hero. I wanted to meet Journey's guitarist Neal Schon.

Before the Babys went on, I could see Sherry Secord, a girl that I had dated, in the front row. She was screaming my name to get her attention but I ignored her on purpose. I was pot friends with her younger brother Shane. Sherry stalked me for a while. She was pretty but very clingy. She would do anything I wanted but she wouldn't let me take her shirt off.

I did the Babys guitar change. It was only once. It seemed like a big deal at the time but it was nothing. I got paid in cash. Wally Stocker was not interested in the Floyd Rose but Neal Schon was. Over in the Journey dressing room before their show, I showed Neal the guitar and he flipped out. I plugged it in to his warm up amp and starting blasting some lead guitar. Steve Perry came up and put his arm around me. He was laughing and smiling, and he said, "Hey Neal, where'd you find this kid? Man, that kid can play guitar. This little kid is gonna make it big someday." Neal Schon had me call Floyd, and Neal gave me his phone number in Mill Valley California. He said he knew a bass player that was my age I might be good with. I left the Journey concert feeling like I might have a chance of playing these big concerts myself one

day. I was just 16 but I already got paid to be a guitar roadie for a big band at the Coliseum, and two of my guitar idols played my guitar onstage. I just needed to get myself there.

The band was not really moving as fast as I wanted it to. Now that Gary had graduated high school, life was becoming serious. We had to do something to make it quick, or he was going to have to get a job.

His parents wanted him to work at the gas station. I was just about to start my senior year of high school and I was a stoner on a mission to graduate.

Tyrant with the twins wasn't working out. The twins were not really part of our clique, and I was starting to look for other options. Brad Young wanted to stop playing music altogether and get a job. Rod Young wanted to go to college. We weren't close friends and Brad Young was not really comfortable being a lead singer. I listened once more to Rob Halford sing, "Tyrant, the hideous destructor, every band shall fall." Gary and I decided it was time to retire the band name.

Roger Fisher had just been fired from Heart but he didn't talk much about it. I was at his house and he asked me, "What do you think about you and Gary playing with Ol' Rog?" I thought it was a great idea. He came over to Gary's basement and we jammed for a few hours, playing new riffs that he wrote and stuff like *Barracuda*. He brought in a Marshall combo amplifier, and an old wood grain Fender Strat that Mike Lull had rebuilt with him.

Roger, Gary and I played without a bass player. Roger wanted to be the lead singer and he did an interview with Patrick MacDonald that came in out in the Seattle Times. He announced in the article "I'm starting a new project with Adam Brenner 16, and Jerry Thompson 17." It was in every home in the greater Seattle area. Gary was devastated. He was afraid all of our friends would tease him and start calling him Jerry. He was right. Everyone did for about two weeks.

Roger came to the basement and played with us two more times. It was obvious we didn't have any chemistry or anything in common musically. We played whatever he asked of us, and he improvised singing through the PA. He sounded like a bad Neil Young. Roger had had a rough time since he stopped working with Ann Wilson and Heart. It chipped away at his confidence. He said, "When we first got together and Ann found her voice, my guitar playing soared and the group blossomed. We started playing big gigs in Canada, and everybody fell in love."

On the third rehearsal, Roger took his amp home. Outside, before he got in his Jaguar sports car parked in Gary's parent's driveway, he said to us, "I'm not really starting a band with you guys. You're just helping out Ol' Rog until he figures out what he's gonna do."

Gary and I looked at each other like, "What the fuck did he just say?" We could already tell it wasn't going to work out with Roger and we felt bad for him. He left his guitar behind and said he would get it at the next rehearsal but he never came back. After a few months, McCrea took it home and rewired it. He routed in a DiMarzio pickup, and painted it with purple bicycle paint. Then he routed a hole in the edge, moved the input jack, removed the pickguard, and glued in two fake pickups. He destroyed that poor guitar trying to do what Edward Van Halen did. It was an abomination.

On November 14, 1980, I entered a talent show at Lake Washington High School. They called it *The Homegrown Rockfest.* The flyer read - The cadle *(sic)* will rock… with ultra-violent tunes. Expected rock groups are Adam Brenner, Spectre, Crystal, and Bad Reputation. All profits will go to the purchase of a new stage curtain for the drama department. Tickets $2.00. It was my very first solo show.

I put together a 10 minute guitar performance that started with an acoustic bit into something clean sounding on a Fender Stratocaster for an instrumental version of the Led Zeppelin song, *Hots on for Nowhere.* I played it on the Marshall's second channel to get a clean sound. I switched guitars to the first channel with the V plugged into a separate cable. For the next song, I did a slightly louder instrumental Rush medley that ended with the echoplex feeding back on itself. I went back behind the amps and quickly took off the dressy black suit. Underneath my clothes, I was wearing a rock and roll outfit of purple spandex pants and a ripped shirt. I came back out with my new Floyd Rose guitar. I plugged into the second Marshall head and switched off the first one so there was no dead air between the guitar changes. Then I did my guitar solo I played at shows with Tyrant. Gary was pumping dry ice into a fog machine that was connected to a Marshall cabinet with no speakers. At the end of the solo I took off the guitar and smashed it into the empty speaker hole on the dummy cab with smoke coming out and knocked all of the amps over on to the ground. I walked offstage while the amps were still screaming feedback at full volume. It was legendary.

We pulled off the talent show exactly according to plan, but I broke the newly cut headstock of the Floyd Rose guitar. Mike Lull replaced it with a vintage Telecaster neck that was at the shop for $250 and reinstalled the Floyd Rose into the new guitar neck.

I talked to the girl next door to Gary's house while I was unloading gear. She was a cheerleader with centerfold potential. She was moving stuff into her own place. I drove her to her new apartment and like always, it started with a kiss and we ended up fucking. We got caught in the act by her boyfriend who came in to her bedroom through a sliding glass door.

He burst in and said, "What are you doing? Oh shit! Who the fuck are you?" I got out of bed and as I went for my clothes, the guy punched me in the face four times. I fell down to the ground, then he kicked me in the nose, and I heard a crunch. He started crying and he said to the girl, "Why did you do this to me? Why? I thought you loved me," and he ran back out the sliding glass door. I was all curled up on the floor, a naked bloody mess. She cleaned me up and sucked me off. Gary had been after the girl next door for his whole life. He was very proud of me, so I thought it was worth getting clocked by an angry jock.

The next day, my face was swollen with two black eyes, a broken nose, and a fat lip. I was living in David Morris' basement since Joanie and her daughter Lisa moved into my dad's condo and Gary's next door neighbor came over to David Morris' house and pity fucked me. Girls weren't really a problem. Only their boyfriends were, but girls were becoming an unstoppable addiction.

Our soundman, John Boghosian, had moved into a big house on a big hill in Juanita, near Kirkland. His roommate was a 30-year-old, beer-drinking, drug-dealing, fat bastard with a southern accent, named Tex. They had a driveway half-a-mile long so it was very private. Tex called every girl he saw 'Funbuns.'

We had small parties on weekends, and 200 people showed up. Cars would line up and down the streets. The cops came once, but it took them an hour to get up the driveway because it was blocked with cars. Cocaine was becoming a very big thing. It was as easy to buy as pot. Everybody would run off into little rooms, talk about solving the world's problems, and drive away into the sunrise. It only lasted a summer before Johnny moved out, but we did some damage and lost a few brain cells.

There was a new, all-ages rock club in the Northgate shopping center called Mr. Bills. I used to go there with my friend Casey. We'd buy cocaine from Tex and go up there and meet girls. Casey got so many speeding tickets that his license got suspended. And since he looked like me, he'd give them my name and my details. We were both hoodlums. He had me try to steal a car stereo from a truck at his job at Bellevue Honda. He left the truck unlocked so I could do it but I couldn't get the stereo out so I put a bunch of paper garbage in the truck and tried to set it on fire. I was a really shitty vandal.

One time we got pulled over when I screamed at a cop, "Give him the book occifer." We were driving on the other side of the bridge and he chased us all the way to Seattle and cited Casey because I wasn't wearing a seatbelt. Casey screamed at the cop while has writing him up, "Hey, what's with the light show?" It was a good thing we never got searched. We were asking for trouble, and it's amazing we didn't get arrested for the shit we used to pull. But we were young and dumb, and we didn't give a fuck.

Technical Knockout

On January 9, 1981, I went with Casey Pratto to Mr. Bills, and the band that was playing was TKO. Only the singer, and psychotic looking tall blond guitarist were still in the band from when I saw them at the Seattle Paramount. They opened with a memorable song that had a cool guitar riff called *Into The Night*. TKO's new bass player, Evan Sheeley, was losing his hair. The drummer, Bill Durham, looked fat. There was another guitar player named Greg Morlan that was just in the background. The singer Brad Sinsel sounded just like Roger Daltrey from The Who, and he pranced around the stage like Mick Jagger.

After the show the tall guitarist, Tony Bortko, said to me, "Hey kid, come over here. I want to talk to you." He seemed to know who I was but I didn't know him. He asked me, "Do you want to play guitar in TKO? We're playing here tomorrow night. Come back with your guitar and you can play a song with us and see if you like it. Don't say anything to the other guys, okay?"

I went to Mr. Bills the next night and got onstage. The singer said, "We got a young guitar player here. Alright. Give it up for," and leans over off the mic and whispered, "What's your name again?," I spoke in his ear and he shouted, "Adam Brenner." Then I started playing a guitar solo and did the first chords to *You Really Got Me*. The band followed behind me and I shredded as fast as I could. During the quiet break the singer put his arm around me and spoke to the audience, "So whadda ya think? Make some noise!" The crowd responded with a roar. That was my audition for TKO.

I told Gary about it and we decided that it would be good thing for me to do. TKO had gone on tour doing big shows and they might help me get to another level. I thought the drummer sucked, and I swore I'd get Gary in the band, just as soon as I had the power to make it happen. I met with Tony at Brad Sinsel's studio apartment on Queen Anne Hill in downtown Seattle. TKO had upcoming shows booked in bars around Seattle, including a big headline concert at The Showbox on 1st Avenue. They gave me a long list of songs to learn.

The singer Brad Sinsel was into groups like MC5, David Bowie, and Iggy Pop. He didn't know much about heavy metal groups like Scorpions, or Judas Priest. He was from a generation of rockers that grew up before I did. Tony Bortko was just plain weird. He had a lost soul look in his eyes. He said he lived in Seattle with his Uncle Dick. He didn't talk much. When Tony did speak, Brad usually cut him off or rolled his eyes. Tony reminded me a bit of my brother David. They wore the same type of clothes, which became fashionable when Seattle created grunge, but I thought Tony looked like a bum off the street.

Tony had been playing guitar for many years, and he was a songwriter. I loved the guitar riff he wrote for *Into the Night*. He had a real keen sense of guitar melody. If nothing else, playing in a group with a second guitar player could be educational, even though I thought it didn't look right. Tony was over a foot taller than me.

Brad's apartment was small but posh. He had a large black-and-white paper Japanese umbrella against the wall. Next to it was a framed newspaper article from a show he played in Texas, with his picture in front of the headline '80,000 People Beat the Heat.' He also had a poster sized, framed black-and-white photograph taken of him onstage, holding a microphone. It was a profile shot, and he looked a lot like Iggy Pop. Brad talked like a rock star. As far as I was concerned, he was a rock star.

Brad said he knew Chris Jacobson. He used to play with him in a cross-dressing theater troupe called *Ze Whiz Kids and Ze Fabulous Pickle Sisters*. Brad showed me an old promo shot that looked like eight clowns with a couple of guitars, all dressed up like Elton John. I couldn't recognize which one was Chris. On March 14, 1974, they opened for The New York Dolls at the Moore Theatre.

TKO toured with Kinks and got booed for eight weeks straight. They supported Cheap Trick right after *Live at Budokan* came out. TKO played in Enoshima, Kanagawa, at *Japan Jam* along with Heart, Firefall and The Beach Boys. Brad joked about Brian Wilson who was at his all-time low. He showed me photo albums with pictures of TKO playing big stages. He wore a white vest, red pants, and played a Les Paul Special onstage. He played the Palladium in New York City, wore an open yellow long sleeve shirt with a black T-shirt underneath, and black leather pants. He met Debbie Harry of Blondie, and he said, "She came backstage and started eating our catering. She had really bad skin."

Brad and his girlfriend Nina talked endlessly about the music business and they loved to drop names. He said, "John Bauer wants to be my personal manager." TKO opened Texxas Jam, at The Cotton Bowl in Dallas. It was put on by Louis Messina of Pace Concerts, and rock manager David Krebs of Leber-Krebs. Krebs wanted to duplicate California Jam II, the show he put on with his acts Aerosmith and Ted Nugent that was televised on ABC, and he put on three major festivals in 1979 - Texxas Jam, The CaliFFornia World Music Festival, and one in Cleveland called The World Series of Rock.

Texxas Jam had the lineup of Walter Egan, TKO, Sammy Hagar, Journey, Head East, Van Halen, Heart, Blue Oyster Cult, Ted Nugent, Aerosmith, and Frank Marino & Mahogany Rush closed the show. The festival was hosted by Cheech & Chong who did skits between the bands while they changed sets. The crowd swelled to nearly 100,000 in the 108-degree heat.

Brad started TKO by joining a reformed version of a band called Mojo Hand with guitarist Rick Pierce from Ze Whiz Kids. Along with drummer Daryl Siguenza, bassist Mark Seidenverg and Brad's friend from his hometown of Yakima, Tony Bortko, they formed TKO. They got a deal with Heart's management who got them a record deal on Infinity Records, a subsidiary of the major label MCA.

After touring America, Brad and Tony fired the drummer and the bass player. They hired two guys they grew up with, from a Yakima band called *Water Closet* - Evan Sheeley and Bill Durham. TKO's debut album *Let it Roll* sold 150,000 copies in the USA, but TKO lost their deal when Infinity Records went out of business after losing millions on *Pope John Paul II Sings at the Festival of Sacrosong*. Infinity pressed over a million albums and 99% got returned. The label folded and got absorbed by MCA. Rick Pierce quit the band, Heart's management dropped TKO, and Brad Sinsel was left with the challenge of picking up the pieces of his career.

Brad knew a record producer, Rick Keefer. He was the engineer on Heart's number one smash hit *Barracuda,* as well as the new album *Dog & Butterfly.* Keefer was the studio engineer on *Let it Roll,* TKO's first album with Heart's producer Mike Flicker. The studio had just relocated from Seattle to Hawaii. Brad said, "Rick really wants to make a record with me just as soon as I've got enough songs to make a full album."

Tony was 30 and Brad was just a few years younger. I had just turned 17, and I wasn't quite sure that I was old enough to play in bars yet. They said it didn't matter, so I learned the songs in their set and rehearsed with the band. The drummer Bill Durham played really wimpy compared to Gary. I wasn't thrilled about sharing the stage with another guitarist, but I thought it was worth the compromise to be in this band, so I gave it my best shot.

We played *I'm Eighteen* by Alice Cooper, *Wild in the Streets* by Garland Jefferys, *The Jean Genie* and *Suffragette City* by David Bowie, *My Generation* by the Who, *Rock and Roll Star* by The Byrds. We did the TKO songs, *Come a Day, Let it Roll,* and the new one, - *Into the Night*. They did *Summertime Blues, Born to Be Wild, Louie Louie, Wild Thing, and Dirty Water* by The Standells. I was a teenage dreamer, playing with older guys. I tried to Van Halenize these cover songs like Edward Van Halen transformed the covers he recorded.

We also played songs that were more my style. We learned a ton of AC/DC songs. *Dirty Deeds Done Dirt Cheap, Sin City, Dog Eat Dog, Shot Down in Flames, You Shook Me All Night Long,* and *Highway to Hell.* We played *Marseilles* by Angel City, *Doctor Doctor* by UFO, and *Day Tripper* by The Beatles. Songs like these were standards, and we had to play three one-hour sets in bars.

We rehearsed a couple of times and played some taverns with tiny stages and dirty floors that smelled like stale beer. I got to do a guitar solo in the show and Brad introduced me. "Ladies and Gentleman, this man here is our newest band member. The 17-year-old monster on lead guitar. From Bellevue, Washington. Make some noise for Adam Brenner." I did a four-minute mix of Van Halen style solos, Rush type guitar riffs, and dive bomb noises with the Floyd Rose. I turned my Marshall up to 10 and used my echoplex. I got everybody's attention.

Brad was very protective of me with Tony and the other band members. He kept me dreaming about the music business and it all sounded so glamorous to me. It kept my mind off the fact that I was playing in some smelly bar. Older guys like Bill Durham were trying to pick on me, but Brad always had my back. I hated Bill's style of drumming. I thought he sucked, and I wanted to get Gary Thompson to join TKO. Bill probably sensed it, or maybe he didn't. He smelled bad and he was always drunk. Brad made sure that Bill couldn't get close to me offstage.

These bar gigs were nothing like the big concerts I got backstage to with the big trucks, huge PA systems, and Anvil road cases with bands names spray painted on the side. TKO only had one big road case which was six feet long, to protect a giant lighted TKO sign that went underneath the drum riser. They also had a road manager, a fat guy in his 30s that had something to do with wrestlers in Seattle. He drove the equipment to gigs in a rental truck and his name was Dan Revisto.

Brad Sinsel knew a lot about glam rock and got me into learning about it. He liked to drink alcohol every day. I only drank at parties and I rarely drank beer. Once in a while, Brad would take a hit off of my joint. We didn't need to like the same high; we both loved music and wanted to combine what we liked. He was a real lead singer, the best one I got to work with since Jake, and he loved the way that I played my guitar.

We shot a promotional band photo with Lynn DeBonn, a photographer from the local Seattle music and arts magazine, *The Rocket*. We went into Thunder Oak Studios for one day and recorded *Born to Be Wild, Rock and Roll Star, Day Tripper, Into the Night* and a rough original riff I had called *Comin' for You*.

We did a few more bar gigs and then we did The Showbox. The opening act was a band with big hair from Portland, Oregon called Movie Star. I could see the whole band watching me sound check. The guitar player introduced himself, "Hi, I'm Tommy Thayer." He was 21 years old. Movie Star had a singer named Julian who looked like Robin Zander from Cheap Trick. They were more power pop than metal. They were nice guys, but I wasn't impressed.

The Showbox was the first time I had played in a really big concert hall with real stage lights. Brad and I walked around in big circles on the stage. There was a spotlight that shone on me during my guitar solo and the band played and sounded really good. I dressed up in black leather pants, a T-shirt with no sleeves, and white Capezio dance shoes like David Lee Roth wore onstage.

Tommy Thayer and the drummer Jaime St. James stuck around to watch the whole show. They came right up to me after the last song and said, "That was amazing." They had never seen anyone play a Floyd Rose before, and I made all of these scary bomb noises on it. I really made an impression. They drove back to Portland talking about the little kid guitar wizard they just saw named Adam Brenner.

We left the Showbox and I went to Nina and Brad's apartment with Tony Bortko. Brad was drinking and I could see he was getting annoyed with Tony. I was smoking pot through a silver pipe, sitting on the floor, listening to them argue. I was dead silent, watching the Japanese umbrella spin as I stared at it. All of sudden Tony says in his deep voice "I'm gonna tell him." He turned to me and spoke.

"I have to tell you something. I'm gay. My Uncle Dick is not really my uncle. I'm going blind in one eye and I'm dying. I'm quitting the band and I asked you to join so you could replace me."

Brad was furious at Tony and said, "Why did you say that. You've freaked him out." I was silent. I couldn't believe what I'd heard. I just looked away and kept staring at the umbrella until I got dizzy. Nina and Brad were yelling at Tony and then Tony got up and left. Brad said, "Well, it looks like you got your wish, we're now a one-guitar band." Brad knew I was a one-guitar gunslinger like Eddie Van Halen and he knew I was good enough. I turned to him and said, "While we're at it, I got this really good drummer we should check out."

Brad told Evan on the phone that Tony quit and Gary Thompson was the new drummer. Evan was in. We set about rehearsing and Gary's first gig was in a few weeks at Mr. Bills. We quickly put together a new set and upgraded and *Van Halenized* all the songs. We did a song from the first TKO album called *Ain't No Way to Be* and I grinded up the guitar part and we added a drum and guitar intro like Eddie & Alex Van Halen. Gary thought it was cool that Brad wrote the song about Nina when she told him to take out the garbage. We beefed up *Let it Roll, Into the Night*, and the best cover songs. We had a killer set.

For the Mr. Bills gig, I wore black leather pants, and a black and white striped arm sock like the junkies wore to cover their arms. I also wore a white shirt that had purple streaks that I bought from Baby & Company, a trendy, overpriced, new wave clothing store on 1st Avenue. The concert was packed and we went down like a storm. The band was a million times heavier with Gary on drums. He pounded his new black-and-yellow Ludwig drum kit that went with the colors on the big TKO sign under the drum riser. We slayed the audience at Mr. Bills.

David Morris was my roadie for that gig. The dressing room was behind the stage and I wanted to go out to my car and smoke a joint after the show. David opened the backstage door, and I walked down the small flight of stairs. I noticed there was a crowd of 50 girls waiting for me. It was mayhem, I felt so Hollywood, like I was David Cassidy or Leif Garret. I didn't know there were so many girls at that show. David immediately acted like he was Van Halen security saying, "Move along, move along, excuse me," while he was dragging me slowly through a mob of teenage girls that all wanted a piece of me. The girls grabbed at my clothes and tried to touch me or pet my hair. It was surreal. We got to the exit and walked out to the car and I smoked a joint and thought, "Wow, this must be what it's like to be a Beatle."

After we smoked the joint David went back in to pack up the gear and told me to stay in the car. I waited about five minutes, and I started to think why the fuck did I let that bastard drag me out here to sit alone when I was being mobbed by all those girls? I walked back in to the venue but all the girls had disappeared.

We went about creating original songs to eventually record on an album. John Boghosian set up Gary's mixing desk and microphones all over the basement. We needed songs to send to Rick Keefer at Sea-West Studios in Hawaii, so first, we took the songs from the demo we did with Scott Palmerton and rewrote them. We pretty much kept the guitar arrangements the same while Brad wrote new lyrics, changed the phrasing, and came up with a different vocal melody.

Thunder Road became *End of the Line*. Brad might have written those words about Tony Bortko. *Standing in the Lights* turned to *Schoolgirl*, and Brad morphed the power ballad into *Without You*. Now we had four songs to record, along with *Into the Night*, but we needed at least six or seven more. I brought home the amp and blasted it on 10 in the living room for the dog. I was working on a melodic mid-tempo riff and my dad said, "What are you playing? Jesus Christ. That could be a hit." When my dad told me that, I knew I had changed his mind. Playing guitar was not going to be just a hobby that I gave up like stamp collecting.

I had a new idea that featured the Floyd Rose. I based it around *Everybody Wants Some,* with jungle drums and tremolo bar at the intro, that went into a Led Zeppelin influenced guitar riff against a *Kashmir* type drum beat. It had a melodic pre-solo before a ripping lead break. Brad Sinsel came up with lyrics about a heavy metal kid that takes it from the basement to the Coliseum stage and then on to New York before crashing up his car, called – *"So This is Rock and Roll."*

I had just been rear-ended in an auto accident on the new Eastside Bridge, which was being repaired on the direction towards Seattle. There were speed bumps, and it was reduced to one lane. I was driving home a punk rock girl named Josie that was a friend of my stepsister. It was 7:00 in the morning, I'd been doing cocaine, drinking vodka and fucking her all night in my daddy's garage. I had half the bottle of Vodka still in the car but I wasn't drunk when I drove her back. I saw a car creeping up on me fast in the rear view mirror. It didn't slow down and hit me straight in the back of my silver Celica.

The other car flipped and rolled over with his wheels spinning in the air. We got out unhurt and checked on the other car. The driver was stunned but ok, just a few cuts and bruises. He smashed my car to the tune of over $2,000. He was a 19-year-old drunk driver without insurance, named Craig Leake. The cops came and took a report. He didn't even get arrested for being drunk but he got cited for it. As the tow truck came to get us, I saw the bottle of vodka in the backseat of my crumpled Toyota. My dad was pissed but I still took advantage of the situation and had the body shop paint my car black.

Brad Sinsel always had a few beers at rehearsals. He constantly picked on Evan behind his back. He'd go upstairs and play the piano in Gary's house and sing, "Hello, my name is Evan, toot toot toot, I've been going bald since I was seven, doot doot doot." Sinsel loved to talk about the trouble he caused in Japan by getting drunk at a record company dinner. He got way too drunk, tried to fuck the daughter of a promoter named Mr. Udo, and insulted everyone about Hiroshima.

Sinsel constantly complained about his ex-manager, Ken Kinnear. Brad would only say, "He won't take my phone calls." I think he drunk-dialed him one too many times. He'd only say dribs and drabs of what happened to the old TKO that I saw at The Paramount. He persistently made fun of Tony Bortko and brother-in-law's friend, drummer Darryl Siguenza. Brad called him Brown Boy. If Brad was sober, he spoke nice about his former guitarist Rick Pierce, but when he was drunk, he'd rip on him, saying, "He's a toad."

Sinsel could keep drinking without passing out but he'd become completely irrational and say things like, "Gimme the keys." He didn't drive. Evan usually picked him up and drove to rehearsal. Brad loved alcohol and he raided any swill that was at my dad's place when he came over. Thanks to my stepmother Joanie, the house was always stocked with wine, booze, and beer. I think he took his inspiration towards drunken behavior from Iggy Pop, but Sinsel was always really careful not to cop to where his influences, or certain lyric lines he wrote, came from directly.

I added an ascending guitar riff while Evan did a descending bass riff to my mid-tempo song in A. Now we had a chorus. Sinsel wrote the lyric 'All I wanna do is talk to you' to my riff. I think Nina caught him chatting up some girl. He borrowed a little bit from Eric Burdon and tried to cover his tracks through song with his problems at home. He hadn't broken up with her quite yet when he penned *Without You*, the power ballad we redid from my demo, but he had a premonition.

Gary came up with a drum beat we could drone over for a verse. We connected the two parts with a short bridge that went to E. We added a half time part in the middle to '*take it down*' so Brad could talk over it like David Lee Roth. I added a chord solo that I thought was like a Pete Townshend riff. The song went back into a double chorus, the second half increasing in tempo a bit, and there was nowhere to go from there. The song had no guitar solo, but we made it so I could shred over the long fade while Brad scatted.

We had a bit of a break from writing with a road trip when Dan Revisto booked us to play a two-night stand at a bar in Missoula, Montana. The venue looked like a 1950s malt shop. The audience of 20 looked like they came straight from a farm and had no interest in the band. By the second set, Brad got really drunk and said in the mic, "Fuck off you bunch of redneck sheepfuckers. I'll fuck your daughter." There was only about 20 people and they just wanted to dance. We couldn't play the gig seriously. It was a joke, the venue said we were way too loud, fired us, and they cancelled the second night. We went back to the basement and wrote a song about it called *Run Outta Town*. I used the V and put together a Scorpions-type verse with a Van-Halen-style chorus.

We needed a fast opening song, so I brought in a sound check riff that I came up with on the V. The guitars that I played had a direct impact on the ideas that came out of me. This was a UFO/Van Halen mashup with a typical riff like I would play. I put in a droning power chord chorus and a solo rhythm similar to *Light Up the Sky*. Brad wrote lyrics about a runaway who gets taken in by all of the seedy glamour in the bad part of town. He called it *Danger City*.

That was enough good songs to send to Rick Keefer. After a few weeks we heard back. Keefer liked it. He arranged to record us in Hawaii for a month in the summer, as soon as I graduated high school. I had been scamming my way through school for 12 years, and I was not going to let one American Government teacher stop me from getting a diploma. I crammed, did the work, and passed the class. At BEST my guidance counselor named PT Espinoza, a Hispanic former drug addict who wrote in my yearbook, "I've learned a lot from you this year. I am really proud of you having worked and bullshit your way through school." PT helped me to file enough bullshit self-taught classes to give me enough school credits to graduate. They didn't have a yearbook

Adam Brenner

147

photo so someone took a picture of me getting into my car and they used that.

Brad Sinsel came to my graduation with my father and Joanie. Mom and Dick didn't come. I could hear Brad scream when they said my name. I got a big round of applause as I walked up to collect my diploma in my purple gown. My graduation cap was falling in my face as I took my diploma.

There was no Senior Keg. That tradition died with the class of '79. There was a Senior Ball that I went to instead. It was just a DJ dance in a fancy hotel ballroom. I brought a gram of coke and the party was uneventful and boring. I just walked around and kept to myself. I didn't know too many people from the class of '81 at Lake Washington High School. I had basically skipped school for most of the 12th grade but one class. All my close friends went to other schools or had already graduated. As a graduation present, my dad bought me the ticket to Hawaii. Evan and Gary bought their own tickets. The studio owner Rick Keefer paid for Brad's plane ticket and a vacation house for us to stay in. Dan Revisto had the Marshalls and the drums shipped over by cargo. The band all flew over on the same plane. Gary Thompson and I we were about to record our very first album.

Honolulu Danger City

Heavy Metal Kids – Gary Thompson and Adam Brenner

It was the summer of 1981, and the weather in Seattle was rainy and grey. Right when we got off the plane, Hawaii had blue sky and smelled like orchids, just like when I went there with my father. Rick Keefer's wife, Donna, met the band at Honolulu airport and got us the use of a van for the month we were recording. The studio was a two-hour drive from Waikiki on the north shore of Oahu, in a small town called Haleiwa. It's where all the surfers went to catch eight-foot waves. We stayed in a weather beaten three-bedroom jungle house that was surrounded by palm trees and black rocks. Brad and Evan each took a bedroom. Gary and I shared one.

Sea-West Studios was a 30-minute drive from the jungle house. The studio had an outdoor hot tub and a huge yard surrounded by palm trees. The main recording room was not huge like I imagined, but a den-sized room with carpeting and a high ceiling. The control room was much smaller, but inside was a gold 32-channel Dean Jensen mixing desk with 1,000 knobs and switches. The studio had an MCI 24-track tape recorder, and EMT echo plate, an Ampex ATR-100 mastering two track tape machine, two huge racks of outboard gear, 10 different digital delay units, UERI parametric EQs, compressors, limiters, and Altec/Mastering Lab 604-E studio monitors. Sea-West had a substantially larger than normal array of instruments, amps, and keyboards.

At first, I thought Rick Keefer was a nerd. He had thin red hair and thick glasses. He only wore aloha shirts with khaki shorts, and flip flops. He was Jewish, and a big fan of Brenner Brothers Bakery. Sea-West Studios used to be a big Seattle recording studio, and Rick Keefer had a long Seattle history.

Rick Asher Keefer was from Portland, and he used to be a bass player in a band during the early 1960s. He took out a loan to buy a Fender Jaguar guitar that he still had in the studio. He also had a '59 Fender Precision bass, a Coral sitar, and a Martin acoustic guitar.

His band supported The Kingsmen and Paul Revere and The Raiders. In 1965, he collected recording equipment, took recording classes, and got the studio bug. He gave up playing to get into recording full time, and got a low-paying job at a studio in Vancouver, Washington called Ripcord.

At Ripcord Studios, Rick learned about the music business and how to operate a studio from Gene Breeden, who owned the studio and put out records by country and western artists. The studio was featured in an article in *Billboard*, the most influential American national music industry trade paper. Rick also learned about high-tech recording gear and how studios made money from record companies by bringing in artists and signing them to production deals.

In the late 60s, Rick Keefer wanted to fly solo, and he thought Seattle had a wide open market for a recording studio. There was only one in town at the time called Kaye Smith that was half-owned by the actor Danny Kaye. That same company owned most of the radio stations in town including KISW and KJR. Rick convinced another one of studio engineers from Ripcord, Bob Holden, to come to Seattle to invest his time. Together, they built Sea-West Recording Studios in a building Rick rented on 85th and Greenwood.

In the summer of '69, Rick Keefer traveled to Germany to take advantage of the weak Deutschmark, and bought eight Neuman microphones for $200 apiece - they normally cost a grand each. Rick made deals with companies and he sold shares in the studio to partners. He bought the new studio gear with borrowed money and he and Bob Holden built the place from scratch.

A woman came into the studio to pitch her brother's demo tape in 1974. Rick listened to the demo and told her, "Sorry but he can't sing. That's the worst demo tape I've ever heard in my life. There is no chance he'll ever be able to make a record." Then he pulled out a bottle of wine and they drank it and listened again. He still thought it was bad, and he asked her out to dinner. They fell in love, got married, and within a year, Donna Alexa Keefer was running the studio. After a few years, Sea-West was a big enough success that Rick eventually bought his partners out.

After having a hand in recording Johnny Mathis, Bachman-Turner Overdrive, Foghat, Bob Seger & The Silver Bullet Band, Wendy Waldman, Bell & James, and two albums by Heart that took years of studio time, the Keefers had enough money to relocate the studio to Hawaii in 1979. Rick said he did it for his health. The weather was a lot better than rainy, grey Seattle. He shipped over all the studio gear and the mixing desk by boat and built a studio in a pre-existing house.

Rick still had connections with record companies and producers after he moved to the remote location of Hawaii. He got Marvin Gaye, Stephen Stills, Jim Nabors, Kidd Afrika, Japanese and local Hawaiian recording acts as clients. *Billboard* did an article on Sea-West that came out on November 1, 1980. I got there in July 1981.

Rick had a Porsche 911, and we followed him with the van into the small town of Haleiwa to discuss the recording and go to dinner. There was a pink stone theater in the center of town, called The Haleiwa Theater. They had local bands play occasionally and we went in, spoke to them and arranged a show for TKO. We did a pre-production meeting at the studio where we talked about the songs and played them acoustically while Rick made comments about ideas he had, suggesting certain minor changes that made sense. We were all excited about recording. Keefer wanted to make a hit record that could get on the radio. He thought that we still needed to write another song. The next day we set up in the studio and started the sessions.

Rick hired a local kid, Gaylord Holomali, who was training to be a studio engineer, to work on the TKO album project. The drums were in the front room, and the guitar was so loud through my 50-watt Marshall that the speaker cabinet had to be buried in a back room that he used for tape storage. They baffled it with everything he had in the studio but he could still hear the bleed slightly on the drum track. We decided to record the guitar live with the drums for the basic tracks. Sinsel sang a scratch vocal from an isolated booth while the band played. Evan's bass amp was in the toilet, but it had a really nice ambience in there. I loved it, when I looked through the glass doors and saw all the red lights lit up like Christmas on the 24-track when we were recording. It made me think, "What I'm doing right this very second is gonna live forever."

We started with *Danger City* and it only took a few hours to get the sounds right and the headphones sounding big with echo plate. We got the first track down very quickly; it took only two takes. We had a great second take but screwed up the ending and Rick said, "No problem, that was real good. I want to keep that. Just take it from the last chorus where you screwed up and start again, I'll splice it." We did the right finish and Rick took a razor blade and cut the two-inch master. He joined the two takes together, and when we heard it back we couldn't tell where he made the splice.

I wanted to do as much as I could in this studio. Van Halen would cut most of their guitar tracks live including the solos and the whole recording experience would be over in a day. I wanted to overdub all the solos like Led Zeppelin records and that was what Keefer wanted to do too. That way I could get the solos perfect.

The next track we did was *Into the Night*. Keefer had an idea for a backwards echo effect on the drum intro. He turned the tape over and did it right after we finished the basic track. I did all the basic tracks with my V, live with Gary. Keefer was a stickler for tuning, and we spent a lot time tuning and retuning between takes. We tuned down to a D flat like Van Halen did so it was even more difficult to make my guitar sound in tune. Nothing could be considered a master take if it wasn't perfectly in tune, and it had to be a master to make it on the record.

We did the basic tracks for *Run Outta Town, Schoolgirl, All I Wanna Do,* and *End of the Line* all on the same day. During the breaks between songs Gary and I would go out and smoke joints of the amazing Hawaiian pot that Donna arranged for us.

Rick would only work around six hours in the studio before Donna would come get him and tell him he had to stop for the day. When we worked on a part for more than 10 minutes, Gaylord would usually run the board and tape deck while Rick would go in the kitchen and read *Billboard*. I really was anxious to keep working in the studio but it was okay to take a break. I was in Hawaii and I used to love going there with my father. The waves in the Northshore Beach were insanely huge and guitar parts were buzzing in my mind.

So This is Rock and Roll was a bit more difficult to get down; my Marshall head was stacked on a piano with a long speaker cable going to the storage room. My cables always got tangled and it became a mess. The Marshall head crashed to the ground a few times during takes. The Floyd Rose was a bitch to get in tune. Every time we tuned it and locked it, the pitch would change on the strobe tuner. It took some work, but we eventually nailed it.

Without You was done to a click track so we could put in acoustic and 12-string guitars at the front. I worked out a harmony solo that I wanted to do overdubs on, and build it up like Brian May of Queen. The guitar track I played during the basic take was meant to be a scratch and removed later but it was so good, Rick decided to keep it. We got that done in one take like we did *Run Outta Town*. The song was a heartbreak power ballad in 3/4 time. Brad did a real emotional vocal on it. He'd just broken up with Nina who he was with for years.

Keefer would make us take a day or two off, so we went into town. Brad and Evan went to bars to meet girls. Gary and I were too young to get in. We went to the beach and hung out at the jungle house at night while the older guys went out to bars in Korean Town, the seedy nightlife area of the Northshore. Brad had met some girl named Delilah that he came back raving about. He went out, got really drunk on Primo Beer, and he met this girl. He said, "I think she's an exotic dancer. Either that or a prostitute, and she's coming over."

After a huge delay, Delilah showed up in a beat-up car. She was everything Brad said she was. Delilah was a 35-year-old stripper with pancake makeup. She was wearing a belly dancer outfit like *I Dream of Jeannie.* She had fake boobs and bad skin.

Evan had met some blonde girl in her twenties and was staring out his window like a sad puppy dog for three hours waiting for her. We all thought he was going to get stood up and he looked so upset, but she eventually came, and he perked up. Both Evan and Brad got laid that night. Those girls hung around for most of the time we were there in Hawaii. Gary and I were teenagers in paradise with nowhere to go to meet girls. We had no chance. We'd have to go into Honolulu, danger city.

Back in the studio, we moved on to doing some bass fixes and then guitar overdubs. We put the Marshall into the main room and Rick had me double the rhythm guitar parts; it sounded huge. We did everything really fast, usually in one or two takes after a practice run. I played from inside the control room, which looked like a cross between a spaceship and a Hawaiian Tiki hut. We used a long cord, and Rick liked to watch me and make sure my guitar was in perfect tune. We had to make sure the playback was really loud as the two sliding glass doors were no match for the awesome sheer power of my electric guitars through my 50-watt Marshall amp.

When I did a really special guitar track, or a track with a really good sound, Rick would put a gold star on the track sheet like the ones teachers put on school kids papers. He'd give the individual tracks funny names like Stereo Power V, Super RK Flange, or Adam 'Dive Bomb' solo. He was a studio wizard like Brad said he was. We had a blast doing guitar tracks and he was really impressed on how quickly I got master takes.

I worked out a new song on the V that was kind of *Schenker,* kind of *Somebody Get Me a Doctor.* I played it to Brad, he'd been having drunken episodes with Delilah while I was doing my guitar tracks. He called it *Working Girl,* and he wrote it about her. He had the idea for a verse: 'From the start, I knew she'd been around, But I was lookin' for action. She came from Korean Town, so skilled in satisfaction.' It was perfect. He came up with a chorus: 'She was a working girl from the streets to my lonely heart. Work it out, my working girl, guaranteed to tear you apart. Work it out.' The song had no solo; just a chord break in the middle and the whole song was three minutes long. Rick Keefer loved it and we set up the drums again. We rehearsed it for a few hours, recorded basic tracks live as a band, and did a guitar overdub.

For *All I Wanna Do,* I had some ideas I wanted to do using feedback, so I played from the main recording room and used headphones. Rick had an idea to take off the tape and turn it around and record an echo using his effects. Then he flipped the tape back around and the echo became backwards, going from silent to loud. It was a really cool effect and it gave the song a different texture.

For the guitar sound on *So This is Rock and Roll,* Rick used the exact same flange effect that he used on Heart's *Barracuda.* I played the Floyd from outside the control room to get feedback so I could get nasty-sounding squeaks and screams from the tremolo bar. Rick couldn't believe that I could handle the volume. He was terrified every time he left the control room that I might hit a chord and damage his hearing. He was careful to make sure I didn't play anything until he was safe, back in his control room with both of the glass doors shut.

We did the acoustic guitars for *Without You,* and Rick had me sit on a stool in the main room, and he placed all of these expensive German microphones around a Martin acoustic guitar that belonged to the studio. He also had a Coral sitar, which was a 12-string guitar with little strings below it that resonated like a sitar. English guitarists like Brian Jones and Jimmy Page used it on their records. Edward Van Halen used one in the guitar solo of *Ain't Talkin' 'bout Love.* Building guitar tracks was so much fun. I loved working with Rick Keefer in that studio. I wanted to make a thousand songs.

One night they had a party and Rick had cocaine. Donna made Piña Coladas and some strange cocktail with Belladonna. The band hung out in the hot tub, then we went inside and listened to some of the tracks in the studio. It was coming along. Making records was fabulous at Sea-West Studios.

Donna was great and Brad said she was a knockout when she married Rick, but she was now in her 30s and overweight. Brad said she got drunk one night in Seattle at a party at the old Sea-West when they recorded *Let it Roll* and she sort of hit on him telling him, "Rick and I really like you." But Brad could stretch the truth, and Donna was not a knockout anymore. She was a homemaker who gained a few pounds after she got married, and ran the business of the studio. She had two Boxer show dogs that she took to dog shows named Sabra and Irving, She arranged all of our travel details, cooked for us, and got us weed. I thought was Donna was awesome.

Rick told us stories about Marvin Gaye, who recorded his last album, *Love Man,* for Motown at Sea-West Studios in Hawaii. "Marvin had a shoebox that was loaded with all kinds of drugs. Pills and potions, weed, and huge bags of cocaine, it was all in Marvin's shoebox. He carried it with him everywhere he went and especially when he recorded." He only did vocals and mixing at Sea-West. Marvin Gaye's depression and cocaine addiction was so severe that he wanted to scrap the whole album after listening to a mix in Rick's control room. Rick loved to talk about Marvin.

"Marvin was out of his mind crazy most of the time and he did a whole ounce of cocaine at once in an attempt to kill himself. Marvin carried a gun and knives to the studio with him and I was terrified at times, it was a nightmare, but when he sang he was brilliant. He always did perfect takes and he knew exactly what he wanted to get and did it in one take. But all of the drugs in Marvin's shoebox couldn't put him back together again. He always said, 'I'm an artist, I must have drugs,' and he was always high. But, when Marvin was in a clear mind, he was a very sweet guy."

Donna talked about Stephen Stills, who recorded the Crosby, Stills, & Nash album *Daylight Again* at Sea-West. Donna said, "Stephen was really fussy about everything. Every little detail, he wanted candles in the studio, or he wouldn't sing, so I went out and got him some. Then he said they were the wrong color. I had to get all of these fancy foods and special tea shipped over from California. The president of Atlantic Records, Ahmet Ertegun, came to the studio. There were problems with Stephen Stills' vocals. It was just supposed to be him and Graham Nash making the record, but after Ahmet came to studio, David Crosby came to Hawaii. When the three of them sang together, it was magic." The album went platinum, and Rick had gold and platinum RIAA records on the studio wall from *Daylight Again.* The walls also had platinum records from Heart, some gold records from Japanese and Hawaiian acts, and a lot of Ampex Gold Reel awards.

Donna and Rick talked to me about the music business, record companies, A&R men, hit records, and *Billboard*. They were going to get us a record deal. There were contracts issued, drawn up by Rick's lawyer in LA, Bernie Fishbach. The whole band signed a production deal with Rick and Donna who were Sea-West Productions. Brad Sinsel and I also signed a separate publishing agreement as the songwriters. I didn't care about the contract. We all signed it, and that was the first contract I ever signed.

We had a gig booked for the Haleiwa Theater and we took the gear from the studio and set up for the show. There were about six other bands on the bill. They tried to make it a mini Woodstock. Most of the acts were local Hawaiian singers with ukuleles or old hippies singing the blues. There were not dogs chasing chickens that were running across the dirt floor of the theater as Sinsel described in interviews. It

was a really nice old theater and it had a little Hawaiian history. When we went on, most of the locals got scared and ran outside.

Bill Hale, a local photographer, loaned me some Marshalls. He had a gold Les Paul that looked like Chris Jacobson's guitar but slightly shinier. Bill Hale took Hawaiian pictures and became a famous rock photographer, shooting Metallica and Ritchie Blackmore. The Haleiwa gig was good, but it was a small-town affair, and there were no girls there my age. Rick came out and watched. He could see we were a strong live act. And my guitar was loud.

For the last big full day of guitar overdubs we did guitar solos. I played from the control room and tuning was not an issue because I could control the pitch with my vibrato. Rick got a huge guitar sound that he used all of his toys on. We started with *Into the Night* and I got the Floyd in tune: close enough for rock and roll. I started with a pre-solo octave melody that Tony had written while vibrating the tremolo bar up and down in pitch just ever so slightly. I started the solo with a screeching dive bomb, followed by tricks on the bar way up on the high strings. I used finger harmonics holding the second fret and tapping at the fourteenth fret and I ended it with a screaming descending double harmonic while the springs of the wang bar crackled. I got it in the first take. It got a gold star.

All of the solos went quick, and Rick usually kept two takes. We spent some time getting the double lead harmonies on *Without You.* I played slide guitar in *Schoolgirl,* and Rick came up with an effect that made my guitar sound like a Hammond organ. I did the theme that was in the movie *Rollerball, Bach's Toccata and Fugue in D minor* but I played it A. Rick laughed and called it *Phantom of the Opera.* We added it in as an intro to *End of the Line,* which had a whipping tremolo bar solo in it.

Brad would only do lead vocals for a few hours a day, and we were not allowed in the room while he did his vocal tracks. Gary and I went to the back door of the studio and listened from outside as he did his takes. Brad was awesome, he even sounded amazing acapella.

Rick could set up a sound or an effect within 5 or 10 minutes and he'd always try to explain to me what he was doing as he put cables in and out of the mixing console. He said "It takes some guys hours or even days just to get sounds, like Heart. Geez, Heart's producer Mike Flicker spent three days on a five-second guitar riff, all at the bargain rate of $300 an hour."

TKO's deal with Keefer was that he would get paid for the studio time after we got signed to a label. He said this record we were making was cheap and would cost between to $40,000 to $50,000. He wrote down all of his hours on a time sheet. Rick had invested his time and studio time, a month at a vacation home, a rental van, one plane ticket for Brad, recording tape, a few grams of cocaine, and some chicken dinners. He was all in for less than $3,000.

After the solos were done I stayed behind at the jungle house. I was there alone with Delilah and Evan's blonde girl. Over the weeks, I flirted with them and they got a little nasty. They poked me and said, "Ha ha ha, Adam can't get laid." I ran out of the house and they both chased me outside, and I tripped on a rock and fell in the grass. The girls jumped on me and started fawning, petting my hair and trying to kiss me. My fear-instincts took over. I hadn't even talked with a girl the whole trip. I thought it was a set up. I got scared, pushed them off of me, and ran back inside. I asked the blonde later if they were serious and she said, "Yeah, Delilah and I were bored and we thought it would've been fun if we both fucked you, but you ran away."

Gary and I wanted to do a production sequence for *Danger City*. Rick gave us a portable recorder and we went into Korean Town and recorded sounds for *Danger City*. It was just a small tourist town so we only got mumblings from a bunch of shoppers and store owners. One old Hawaiian lady was selling flower leis and we recorded her saying, "Lei for one dollar, lei for one dollar." Rick thought it was hilarious, put it through his toys to beef up the sound. He put a repeat echo of the traffic we recorded and fed it back into itself until it created feedback. Then we faded it out. Now we had an ending for the album and Rick flew it on to the master at the end of *Danger City*.

On the last day of recording I did some final things, like a 12 string Coral sitar part in the bridge of *Run Outta Town* and a couple of fixes of things that bothered me from the rough mix work tapes he let us take home. Gary and I took the van into Waikiki and I made him take me to Ala Moana shopping center where my dad once took me to get food at Li's Chinese kitchen. We cruised the strip, I knew this town. We wound up at a rock bar with cover bands and I got up and jammed. I picked up a skinny Asian girl in a pink satin dress, got her in the back of the van and started making out with her. She didn't want to have sex in the van, she wanted me to come home with her. We kept making out and when we got up to leave, She asked me, "Did you...?" and she stopped herself mid-sentence and reached behind her dress to feel that her ass was wet. I came all over her. She got out of the van and went back to the club with a huge wet stain on her pink satin dress.

159

Keefer thought all the songs we recorded were enough to get a record deal. He was going to mix it and send us a cassette when we got home. Evan, Gary and I left, Brad stayed behind in Hawaii to finish a few things. We didn't go home with a tape. When Brad came home he didn't have one either. We got it the mail a few weeks later. I was drooling by the mailbox, every day for two weeks waiting for it.

Gary wasn't happy with the drum sound Keefer got, but I was in love with the guitar parts. It was all I could hear. Keefer had done something electronically to beef up the snare drum that Gary thought sounded synthetic. I thought that it sounded a thousand times better than any tape we ever made in the basement. The vocals sounded great. Brad did an awesome job on every song. It was the first real professional recording I ever did and I thought it was amazing. The guitars were raw and dirty. Now we just had to wait for Rick Keefer to send it out to his music business friends in Los Angeles and get us a record deal.

Susie Wimberly & Debbie Ward on stage with TKO

The End Zone

Our new tape with Keefer got a big hype around town. After we lived with the mixes a few weeks, Gary and John Boghosian still thought the sound was muddy. Keefer added all kinds of electronic drum slaps and percussion after we left. The guitar leads were not as loud as I wanted them to be, but I knew everything I played so I could hear it even if it wasn't on top of the mix.

I thought the band image needed some help, mainly because of bass player Evan Sheeley, I wanted to tell Evan that he should wear a hat. Brad got really nervous and said, "No, you can't say anything about his bald spot. He's really sensitive about it. Don't do it. He doesn't think he's bald. He'll freak out." Nobody had ever confronted Evan about his lack of hair before. I nominated myself for the job.

Evan started losing his hair around his senior year when Brad grew up and went to school with him in Yakima. At the time, it was a real sore subject for Evan and a constant source of comedy material for Brad's amusement. Despite Brad's warning, I walked over to Evan and said, "Hey man, have you ever thought about wearing a hat?" Evan asked, "Why, what for?" I said, "Umm, because you're bald. You certainly don't have a big hairdo." He looked back at his refection in the window and said, "What do you mean, I'm not bald." Brad was right; Evan was in complete denial.

The band did a photo session with Lynn DeBonn, the Seattle photographer who shot a promo photo of the band when I first joined TKO. Evan wore a black leather jacket, black leather pants, mirror sunglasses, and black leather cap. He looked like Rob Halford. When Brad first saw Evan's new outfit he said, "Don't you think he looks a little bit like a gay biker?," however, it was a big improvement from the jumpsuits that he used to wear on stage. I thought he looked like a badass motherfucker. He stopped posing on stage and just stood mean, like a cold statue with a scowl. The band had its image.

TKO's first gig post-Hawaii was at Lake Hills, which was now called The Palace, on September 19. We were headlining Metal Fest '81, along with eight other groups. My former singer Jeff Tate was in two of the bands, Babylon and The Mob. He started playing keyboards and had a new look. He wore a skinny tie and thin sunglasses. For his set with The Mob he just wore grey sweatpants. We talked before my show. Jeff was a little pretentious. He said, "I hate heavy metal bands with opera singers. They are so cliché. I'm doing these kids a favor in The Mob by playing with them. How's your Aunt Yetta?" I apologized, "Sorry for being such a dick in Gary's kitchen after the Battle of the Bands. We really had some fun times. Yetta's just as wild as ever."

There were so many kids I went to school with playing at Metalfest, they could have used our yearbook as the program. Everybody was in a big hurry to get something going on with music. We all graduated high school so it was high time to do or die. I was confident that I was on the road to glory. My first album with TKO was recorded and we were the headliners. We had an after party at my dad's condo.

I threw a few parties when my dad went away with Joanie on weekends. Lisa Silverman moved out to a squat downtown with her punk rock girlfriends. I had the house to myself and I took a couple of cases of beer from the bakery. I charged $3 a head just to let people inside. One night I made over $200. I could've made more, but the cops came and shut it down.

Terry, the manager of The End Zone, a new pinball joint that opened up in downtown Kirkland, located in an old carpeting warehouse, asked me if my band TKO was interested in doing a concert. The place was certainly big enough for it. I arranged two shows for October 9 and 10. Brad wasn't too keen on letting me handle booking a show, but I let him deal with the money, and Gary and I took care of the rest. Money was never an issue with Gary and me; it was always just about playing rock and roll. It was the most important thing in the world.

John Bogohosian worked it out with Terry to bring in Mike Fisher's studio mixing desk, effects rack, and a huge PA. We recorded all of the shows. The opening act was Culprit, a new band formed our by first bassist, Scott Earl. Their lead singer was Jeff L'Heureux, a stoner buddy of mine from Juanita.

L'Heureux lived with his girlfriend at her parents' house. Her brother Tony was a coke dealer. I spent more than a few nights hanging out at Jeff's place. He got a job at the bakery, and he became one of my best friends. Culprit did a cover of *Radar Love* by Golden Earring and an original song called *Guilty as Charged*. L'Heureux got arrested for breaking into a house and did six months in juvy.

The End Zone shows were such a success that they wanted to do two more shows, two weeks later. The opening act was the cover band from MetalFest, The Mob, with my former best friend Chris DeGarmo and Mike Wilton on guitar, Eddie Jackson who played with us in junior high on bass, a drummer named Scott Rockenfield on drums, and Jeff Tate. They played *The Mob Rules* by Black Sabbath and named their band after it. They also played *Wrathchild* by Iron Maiden, who had a guitar player that looked like KK Downing. I thought Maiden was a poor man's Judas Priest.

I caught up with Chris DeGarmo. We went out to my car and smoked a bowl. He'd been kicked out of Joker and replaced by a guy who had a PA system. He started a band called Tempest with Mark Welling on drums, who we went to school with. Then Welling quit and joined Babylon with Jeff Tate.

DeGarmo formed Crossfire and changed the name to The Mob when he was able to convince Jeff Tate to sing at a few gigs. We talked about high school and girls and he told me he fucked Jil Rivet when he went to Interlake. I was really impressed. We didn't talk about Rick Balch or the Led Zeppelin concert. I played DeGarmo the songs I recorded in Hawaii from the cassette deck of my car. He was really impressed and kind of jealous, but I was more envious of him that he got to sleep with Jil Rivet.

Chris was always really likeable and popular at school. He wanted to make originals, but Jeff Tate hated singing songs like Judas Priest and Iron Maiden, it was difficult for Chris to get Jeff to commit to anything. Jeff Tate was in two other bands, Myth and Babylon. Both were progressive keyboard bands, which Chris and I hated. Putting a band together was dirty business. Singers were always a problem, even when you had one. Brad Sinsel was becoming a little difficult for me as well.

The gig on October 23 was fine. Brad went out drinking after the show. When Brad showed up at The End Zone the following day, he'd been on an all-night drinking binge and hadn't slept. He was so trashed that I thought he wasn't going to be able to do the show. He was passed out for most of the opening act but he woke up and started drinking again, and by the time we got on stage he could barely walk.

We made it through the first two songs, *Into the Night* and *So This is Rock and Roll.* Brad slurred the words, did his Jagger dance, and stared with a glazed look in his eyes at the packed crowd and the kids in the front of the stage. For the third song, *Run Outta Town,* I had a guitar change, and Brad disappeared from stage and returned all energetic like he took a hit of coke, but I never saw Brad take drugs. By the time we got to *All I Wanna Do,* Brad was wobbling on the stage to try to keep himself from falling over.

He didn't even sing the song, He just kept saying, "Take it down," so the band played really quiet behind him as he proceeded to go on a drunken tirade that went on for about 20 minutes. The band sounded really good through this massive PA that Mike Fisher brought in. John Boghosian was doing the sound and making big echo bombs with the drums.

Brad went on to talk, "This band has been around the world, and my manager, he will not take my phone calls, he does not like me." Then Evan chimed in, "He does not like me either." Brad went on and on for another 10 minutes. I tried to come up to him and get him to sing the song and he told me, "Back off or I'll punch you in the nose." I had already had my nose broken at least once, and I didn't want another. The kids in the front were loving it, and I could hear one of them say, "Yeah, punch him in the nose." Brad carried on talking, and sang for ten seconds, "I said oh yeah," and tried to get the audience to respond back with an, "Oh yeah!" But there was a serious lack of communication, and the audience stayed dormant. Brad got frustrated; he started to do something strange up at the front of the stage. I was behind him by my amps, and couldn't see what he was doing.

As I moved back towards the side of the stage, I could see Brad fooling around with his zipper. He unbuttoned his jeans, pulled his dick out, and flashed the kids at the front of the stage. When the song was finished, Gary and I walked off stage, looked at each other, and wondered if we just blew our whole career. It was really bad. The next day the kids that were on the front had started calling him Bad Brad Sinsel. That show became legendary, but Gary and I still thought it sucked. Brad wasn't Jim Morrison and I couldn't stand it when he was drunk. It wasn't that funny anymore. He moved in with Tara Whitney, an overweight princess with pancake makeup who he knew from Yakima. He bragged that her family was rich and her mother had the hots for him too. Tara supported Brad, and he spent her money on booze and got drunk every day.

On November 4, 1981, Def Leppard played to a sold out crowd at the Moore Theatre on their *High & Dry* tour. They were incredible. There were as tight and professional as all of the older groups they supported. Steve Clark played a Les Paul guitar slung down below knees. Joe Elliott sang like a stud. He screamed at the crowd, "*Let it rock, Let it roll, Let it go!*" and got everyone on their feet for the entire show. During *High & Dry,* he shouted, "Seattle, get your hands in the air. We want you to do some singing on this one. It's the title track from our new album..." and whole theater chanted, "Saturday Night!, Saturday Night!" It was a Wednesday. Ten days later I'd get my shot to play the Moore Theatre. We were opening for Shooting Star.

We got booked for two big shows. We did a show in the Portland Paramount on November 13 and in Seattle on November 14 at the 1,400 capacity Moore Theatre opening for the band Shooting Star. I loved playing those theaters. They had big stages, balcony seats, and dressing rooms with mirrors. I always thought theaters were the best place play a rock show. They have spotlights and just have a feeling of *show biz* attached to them. Playing the Moore was a milestone for me. There were some great photographs from that show. Someone gave me a 11" x 14" glossy photo of me during my solo with the spotlight on me and the TKO sign behind me. It looked so good it could have been a poster.

Brad was starting to attract kids from all over Seattle that were my age and younger as fans. They were coming to meet us like I would try to meet Van Halen. They loved *Bad Brad Sinsel*. Some of the kids that were at the Moore show were Layne Staley and Jerry Cantrell who grew up to form Alice in Chains, and Stone Gossard and Mike McCready who started Pearl Jam. After that show, Stone went home and took my riff from *Schoolgirl*, and turned into a song called *Thru Fade Away* that appeared on the album with his band, Mother Love Bone.

Rick Keefer didn't have any news about a record deal. He said he had sent out tapes to people that he namedropped in LA who worked at labels. He was still waiting to hear back. He pressed up a 45 rpm single of *Give Into the Night* with *Danger City* on the B-side. Keefer had Brad changed the title because a New York City singer, Benny Mardones, had a song on the charts, called *Into the Night.* I took our single to KISW and called Steve Slaton endlessly until he played it. They only played it once. I didn't understand how you got records played on the radio; it was lot more involved than just taking a song down to the local station like I saw in all the movies about Elvis and Buddy Holly.

I saw a movie called *Bird,* about the jazz musician Charlie Parker. I wanted to play smoky little places in Paris and stay in little dive hotels. That to me was what it was to be a musician. With all of Brad's and Keefer's talk about 'the industry,' I still had no idea how a band could crack into the big time. We waited to hear something from Keefer but any news that Brad got must have been bad, so he kept it to himself. I think every label had passed on TKO because it was a sophomore album from a group that didn't go gold the first time around.

Keefer went to meetings in Japan about TKO while he was there, trying to get new clients for the studio. Rick said, "I went to a meeting with four Japanese record executives at Sony Records in Tokyo. The head of the company shook my hand very formally. We all sat down and one assistant talked in bad English, 'So Wik Keefa, you have some new music to listen?' I pulled out your TKO cassette and said, 'Yes. I have this great new hard rock album from a band out of Seattle called, TKO. They have a new lead guitarist and they just...,' the Sony president put his hand up, waved to his assistant, whispered in his ear, and the assistant said, "TKO? Prease reave. You must go now, right now, prease reave. They had security escort me out of the building. I've never been so embarrassed in my whole life."

Whatever Brad Sinsel did at a record company dinner in 1979 got his band blacklisted. Rick was humiliated but he still wanted to get a deal for that record somewhere. The weeks turned to months and we never heard anything, but we still never gave up hope. TKO did a video shoot for a local access program, *Rocking You,* hosted by Craig Cooke, named after Rail & Company's first original song. We brought our gear into a TV studio somewhere downtown. The band was interviewed by Craig Cooke and we lip sync'd to *Working Girl* and *Into the Night.*

After the video interview, Brad had made a deal with Craig Cooke for TKO to be represented by Unicam. We got booked and we played a few taverns. We played a one-night-stand at The Detour in Renton and The Slammer in Auburn. We played three nights at The Town Cryer in Redmond. We did three nights at The Buffalo Tavern in Ballard opening for Geffen Records recording artists Berlin. We did an outdoor show at Seattle International Raceway where they held drag races. We played Rat City Rock, two nights at Popeye's in Olympia, and four nights in Gasoline Alley in Bremerton. It was a busy month, but the band was going nowhere.

When the lease was up on my Celica, my dad turned it back in. I managed to get a car loan for $5,000 to buy a white 1974 Alfa Romeo Spider Convertible with around 80,000 miles on it. I bought it at Eastside Motors in Bellevue. I took it for a test drive with the top down and I loved it. The next day after we did the paperwork, I drove it off the lot. The car broke down and died at the side of the road, less than an hour after I got it. I had to have it towed backed to the dealer and the Middle Eastern salesman said, "Sorry, we can't take it back. You have to take it to a repair shop. The engine needs to be replaced and it has to be fixed under the warranty." I had to pay a $500 deductible. I thought that the car would be a chick magnet but I bought a lemon. Once it got fixed, I was off to the races.

The band was playing but things were not happening fast enough. I wondered if TKO was ever going to get a record deal. TKO left Unicam, and Gary started working at his dad's gas station. I worked the night shift at the bakery for a while. I earned enough money to rent a tiny one-bedroom house on Lake Sammamish for the summer of '82.

I didn't work as hard as the other bakers; I didn't have to. I was the boss's son and it was the night shift so I could get away with anything. One night I went off with two teenage girls who were cruising by in the parking lot at 1:00 AM. I was smoking a cigarette at the loading door, they stopped so I starting talking to them. They said they hadn't heard of my band TKO, but I kind of thought they did. They looked like two girls I'd seen before at a gig. I got in their car and we went to one of their parents' houses, and I fucked both of them for two hours. I got a ride back to the bakery just before my

Uncle Itsey arrived at 4:00 in the morning, and I clocked out at 8:00 AM for a full eight hours. That was my first threesome.

I read an ad in *Billboard* that said – 'Major Recording Act looking for a lead guitarist. Must be at least 21 years old, at least six feet tall, can sing, and have recording and touring experience.' It said to send a photo, a tape of my guitar playing, and contact details. I mailed it to an address in Los Angeles. It didn't say what group it was for. I took the photo I had from the Moore Theatre and the TKO cassette, wrote a letter saying I was 22 and six feet tall, and popped it in the mailbox.

I spent the night with Brenda Lane. She was between boyfriends and she had broken out in chicken pox or hives, but I got her to come over to sleep with me anyway. She had just left the next morning and

the phone rang. I picked up and a guy with a New York accent said, "Hi, is this Adam? My name is Eric Carr and I'm the drummer in the rock band KISS. We're looking for a new guitarist to replace Ace Frehley. My girlfriend Bambi (pictured) and I loved your tape and your photo looks real cool. Can you come to SIR Studios in Hollywood next week and audition? KISS won't pay for the plane ticket or hotel but you should find a way to get here and try out. You need to learn *Firehouse, Detroit Rock City, Black Diamond,* and *Calling Dr. Love,* okay? Oh yeah, one more thing, you have to sing one of them." I took down all of the info I needed on where, when, and what to bring. When I hung up the phone I couldn't believe it. I was going to audition for KISS. I called my dad and told him about it, I also told him that I needed a plane ticket to Los Angeles and money for a hotel, taxis, and food.

I called Gary and McCrea and told them. They couldn't believe it either. I started working on learning the KISS songs immediately. I went to Gary's basement and practiced. He had *Alive II* which *Calling*

Dr. Love was on. I didn't even have a stereo anymore. I listened to music in my car. They watched and coached me as I worked on the four songs. Mike McCrea told me that I should wear heels, but that only gave me an inch or so at best. "What are you gonna do about singing?" McCrea asked. I was scared to death of singing lead. "Maybe I'll try and sing *Rock and Roll All Night.* "

I wrote down the words and practiced singing it through the PA. It wasn't so bad but it wasn't so good either. I wasn't comfortable with a microphone singing anything but background shouting. I sounded like a little kid, but got my courage up and practiced. It got around town that I was going to audition for KISS. Everybody thought I was going to get the gig, so I started dreaming. I imagined getting my picture in People Magazine. Then I started thinking about how KIS had a big anti-drug policy. Gene Simmons even warned us as kids at the Edgewater Hotel, "Don't ever use drugs or alcohol." I thought about what life would be like being the guitar player in a big band like that. I wondered, "It must be like a prison. How would I be able to hide smoking pot?"

I wasn't 21 and six feet tall. I was 18 and 5'7". I wasn't so sure I was going to get the job but I was going to give it my best shot. I practiced those songs day and night. I learned every solo note for note. I played every lick, shake, and squeak that Ace Frehley made on the live and studio albums, and I had fun learning them. If nothing else, I was going to play those songs with KISS.

The week went by fast and my stepmother Joanie took me to the airport. I was really late getting to the plane. I ran down the jetway with my V case in my hand, but the pilot had already closed the doors and was backing up. I looked at him and begged him to come back, but he just shrugged his hands in the air and kept backing up. I missed my plane but I was able to get on another flight a few hours later. My audition wasn't until the next day.

When I got to LA, I took a taxi to the Tropicana Hotel, checked in to a cheap room, and I was in Hollywood. I went to the pool and later that night I went to the Starwood, a club where Van Halen used to play. Hollywood was scary to me. This was the first time I had been on my own so far from home and the Tropicana Hotel was a shithole. The Starwood was really crowded and there were so many people out in the streets. I was a little intimidated by West Hollywood in 1982. I wished I had a friend.

The next morning, I got up, took a shower, and put on a white blazer. I looked at my white boots. I didn't want to wear them. I decided to just go short and just be me. I put on my Capezios, I could walk better in flat shoes. I ate breakfast downstairs at a place called Dukes. I took a taxi to SIR studios and was buzzed inside. SIR had an old west motif, it looked an attraction at Knott's Berry Farm. There were three small rehearsal rooms and a large soundstage. Framed posters of the Rolling Stones and KISS adorned the walls.

I was about 45 minutes early for the audition. I went into an empty rehearsal room, sat on the floor, and started tuning my Floyd Rose. It took me 30 minutes. I waited by the door of the soundstage and listened to KISS auditioning another guitar player. His leads were not so good. They weren't like Ace's solos at all. I watched the guy come out with a guitar case. He was really tall and ugly with frizzy brown hair. A minute later, Eric Carr introduced himself. We walked to the vending machine, and he was short, like me. He was wearing sweatpants and white tank top. He got a candy bar and said, "Are you ready?" Then he brought me into the soundstage.

As I walked in, I saw Gene Simmons wearing his bass. Gene was leaning against a case next to his Ampeg SVT amp. When he shook my hand he was a foot taller than me. Paul Stanley was sitting on a couch. I introduced myself, and told Gene that I had met him before in Seattle. I had to look up at Paul Stanley too. They were nice, but not warm like Eric Carr was. Gene was wearing a black button down shirt with a black leather jacket, dark blue jeans and cowboy boots. Paul was wearing a blazer and blue suede boots that looked really expensive. They had already auditioned six guitarists that day and nearly 40 others previously. My audition was the last one of the day.

They told me to plug into a Marshall amp with one cabinet. The amp didn't sound like my Marshall, it had no grind at all. I asked for another amp. I plugged into another and it wasn't much better so that was the best sound I was gonna get. I tuned up my V and we started up.

Paul Stanley sang facing me, Gene stood to my right to watch me. Eric Carr counted us off, and I started the intro to *Detroit Rock*

City. Paul Stanley followed me and Gene came in like thunder. It sounded really heavy playing with Gene Simmons on bass. He was a lot louder and had a much heavier sound than any bassist that I had ever played with before. When the drums came in and we hit those first two chords it sounded huge. Eric Carr played it really fast compared to how it sounded on the records with Peter Criss. It was really energetic. I watched Paul sing and I looked at my guitar neck and tried not to make eye contact and just watch them, watching me.

I had the KISS songs down pat. I didn't make one mistake. I wasn't sure if the double lead I did with Paul was perfect but I did it just like Ace did on the Alive II album. After *Detroit Rock City,* I asked, "What's next?" Gene said, *"Calling Dr. Love,"* I was psyched. I felt a little connection with Gene on how he was watching me. I really liked playing that song because it reminded me of AC/DC with those massive guitar chords at the intro. I said, "I'll start it." I cranked out the power chords and Paul Stanley followed me. I didn't sing background vocals but when they all sang together it sounded great. I did my own lead work in there at the end. It ended with a big crash.

I wanted to scream but I kept my cool. I was still a huge fan. I pictured them in my mind from the record jacket for *KISS Alive!* and from seeing them in concert in Seattle. I felt like the whole world stopped turning for a moment. It was just me in a room in Hollywood, playing lead guitar with KISS.

We did *Black Diamond.* Paul sang and played the intro while Gene and Eric sang perfect background harmony. Eric Carr sang the rest of the song. It was a very lyrical Ace Frehley solo, and I had that solo dead on. We only hit the ending about four times before we sped up, instead of the 9 or 10 times before it speeds up into a big crash like on *KISS Alive!.*

I had *Firehouse* down as well. Paul sang it, and I did the solos perfectly. I wanted to play with KISS all day long. After we finished that they asked me about vocals and I said, "I didn't learn how to sing any of the four songs. How about *Rock and Roll All Nite?*"

Paul said, "That's okay; you don't need to sing. Why don't you play us a guitar solo." I switched to the Floyd Rose and did the solo I was doing at TKO gigs. Paul was watching me closely and nodding his head up and down. All eyes were on me as I played every trick in the book. After I finished my guitar solo, Paul thanked me for coming and shook my hand.

I went over to Gene and thanked him, and I asked him, "So what do you think my chances are?" He looked at me and said with a slight grin, "Well, for one thing, I think Paul would get jealous because you're too good looking, and maybe you're a little too old." I was the youngest guitarist to ever audition for KISS.

I left the soundstage and Eric Carr walked me out. I asked him what he thought and he said, "You're too short, I can only get away with being short because I sit behind a drum kit. And we're looking for somebody that can sing. You're younger than you said you were, but you played really good. You should keep it up. You're great. Thanks for coming all the way from Seattle." He smiled and gave me a hug. As I left SIR, Eric laughed and told me, "If we change our minds, I'll call ya."

I went back to Seattle knowing I didn't get the job in KISS, but for a brief moment I was part of their world. I loved the fact that I got to play guitar for them. I didn't care so much about not getting the job, but I still felt rejected. I wasn't ready for Hollywood and I wanted to go back home to my dog Oggie. I didn't want to worry about smoking pot. I wouldn't have quit pot for any job. Not even KISS.

MetalFest II

On Sunday August 22, 1982, we played MetalFest II, an all-day show at Lake Hills. TKO co-headlined with Culprit. They were becoming very popular by playing a lot of shows around town. Culprit had recorded a song called *Players* for a national compilation album called *US Metal Vol. II,* released on Mike Varney's Shrapnel Records. They wanted to release the TKO album, but Keefer wanted a major label, and Shrapnel didn't pay advances. Mike Varney was discovering young unknown hotshot metal guitarists and releasing instrumental records. Culprit recorded a full album called *Guilty as Charged* and released it through Shrapnel the following year. The other bands on the bill at MetalFest II were Overlord from Seattle, Myth with Jeff Tate, Hazard Luck, Kidskin, and Realms.

After the summer was over, the three-month lease on my lake house was up. I moved back in with my dad and Joanie, and her daughter Lisa. I worked the ovens at the bakery and I got burned by a hot pecan that jumped off the pan when I flipped the pastry buns. I was always getting burned on my arms from the oven. Baking was a dangerous job. One of my friends nearly lost a finger in the bread slicer. My cousin Alan drove a bakery truck off a six-foot cliff in the parking lot. David Morris and I saw Alan Brenner passed out in his car in the bakery parking lot one morning. We woke him up, and Alan had no idea how he got there. It was his drunken instinct to just get to the bakery.

Def Leppard came to The End Zone in their tour bus. They weren't going to play; they were just going to meet kids. The tour bus pulled up, and four of them got out. One of the guitarists, Pete Willis, was so tiny. He was eight inches shorter than me. I asked the singer, Joe Elliott, "Where's Steve Clark?" He was one of my guitar heroes. Joe said, "He's in the bus sleeping mate." It was 4:00 in the afternoon. Steve Clark was the only one I wanted to meet. I was really into them, and they were not much older than me, playing all over the world opening for AC/DC, UFO, and Judas Priest. They were also being managed by Leber-Krebs. The guys from Def Leppard walked around The End Zone for 10 minutes and left. Most kids didn't care that some English rock band came to The End Zone in a tour bus. They just continued playing *Asteroids* and pinball. Steve Clark never got off the bus.

By now, most of the local bands who started out playing covers were writing originals and recording in local studios. I saw Chris DeGarmo hanging out at The End Zone. He had a beat-up Ford Pinto, and he played me a four-song tape of song demo he made. He was pretty excited about it. It was very progressive. The guitars sounded good, and there were lots of high screams like Judas Priest. Jeff Tate was the singer, and they recorded it at some studio in Redmond called Triad. DeGarmo said that Tate was now singing full-time in the keyboard band Myth.

Brad and I had been writing a few new songs. One was called *Kingdom Come,* about his world that was imploding. It had a really good guitar solo, and we recorded more basement demos. I had some Rush-type power chords for a mid-tempo song. Brad wrote lyrics and called it *I Wanna Fight.* He was starting to become bitter and negative. His life reflected his lyrics, but he was much too arrogant to ever admit that TKO was going nowhere. It had been over a year since we recorded our album, and it got passed on by every major label Rick Keefer sent it to.

Brad's solution to our band problems was to bring in a second guitar player. He was back in touch with Rick Pierce. They had been working on some songs and writing together. Playing with another guitarist was something I really did not want to do in TKO. We voted on it, and I lost three to one. Gary thought it would sound better to have another guitarist, and he thought Rick Pierce was a stud. I was still into Van Halen. That was the formula. We didn't stick to our guns. I hated being stuck in Seattle; I wanted the world. I believed in our record but it was Brad Sinsel's band, so I agreed to give it a shot with Rick Pierce.

Rick Keefer wanted to cut two new songs and try another round at getting a record deal. He flew to Seattle, and booked a local 24-track studio downtown. We did *I Wanna Fight,* and the cover song *Wild in the Street*, a song we used to play when I first joined the band. I did two rhythm guitar tracks on *I Wanna Fight,* and all the guitar solos. Rick Pierce did a rhythm track, but Keefer buried it when he mixed it in Hawaii. For *Wild in the Street*, Rick Pierce did the solo, but that song didn't really have a lead; just a melodic middle that Brad sang over. Pierce did some leads at the end during the fade. Recording had a different vibe. I really felt like I had to fight to get my guitar a chance to shine. Rick Pierce was an average guitarist. We had no connection musically, but Gary really liked him. I started to feel like I was getting pushed out of TKO. It was only a matter of time.

I started to spend more of my time doing drugs with David Morris. I was at David's house, and we took mushrooms. Some guy on television was screaming, "John Belushi's dead and we're all gonna be there soon." Then there was a banging on the front door, and David's brother answered it. It was two police officers. They asked if there was a disturbance, then they just walked in and waved their flashlights around the dark room. They took a look at us and said, "Well you two keep it down. We don't want have to come back here," and they walked out the door. After they left I said to David, "Did that really just happen?" It was like our paranoia summoned them to our front door. I started to think about atomic bombs and wars and police. At that moment it came to me, "I have to make a record someday about the end of the world."

David Morris had a friend he grew up with, Timmy McAuliffe, whose parents owned a landscaping business. Timmy was always drunk or wasted, and not very smart. He kept a bank card in his wallet, and he wrote his PIN number on the back of the card. David Morris stole Timmy McAuliffe's wallet, and took out the $200 that was in the account. We buried the wallet in the new freeway that was being constructed in Redmond. The next day, David felt guilty, and went looking for the wallet but it was impossible to find where we buried it. They paved the road, and now 200,000 cars a day drive over Timmy McAuliffe's wallet on the 520 Freeway.

I was still getting into trouble with girls, mainly because I was going through so many of them. I had a few stalkers. Some girls would send me three-page love letters or draw portraits and tape them to my front door. I was picking up girls all over town. I was starting to get a bad reputation for sleeping around, but it was not so easy to say no. It was usually hello-to-sex in seven minutes.

Brad did an interview in *The Rocket*, a local music and arts newspaper. There was a picture of the new lineup with Rick Pierce. He talked about TKO's future. Keefer started shopping the TKO album to record labels with the two new songs on it, and gave the album a title - *In Your Face.* I was never told about the album title. I hated it. Brad said it was Keefer's idea. TKO was a boxing term that stood for 'technical knockout'. The title *In Your Face* didn't connect to me. I thought it sounded too much like a punk band. This was going to be that album's last shot, but I had doubts that anything was ever going to happen with that record.

The Last Party

I went to visit Chris Jacobson, who was working as a projectionist in a porno theater in downtown Seattle. He suggested that I should go to Los Angeles, and check out the scene there for a week. He said I could stay with his ex-bandmate, Eldon Hoke, who had some punk band called The Mentors. I drove alone to Hollywood in my Alfa Romeo. I was used to making long drives. It was just a straight 1,000-mile shot down I-5. I loved driving with the ragtop down on the winding roads through the California Shasta Mountains.

I stopped in Oakland to visit my Uncle Sam, and I called up the guitarist of Journey, Neal Schon. He was on a break from touring. He remembered me, and I asked him about the bass player he told me about when I met him in Seattle. He suggested I come visit him, and gave me directions to his house.

Neal Schon lived in the hills in Mill Valley in a really secluded house surrounded by lush green hills. He had huge glass windows with an endless view. There was a copy of *Billboard* that just came out that week. Journey had a special feature where their record company, concert promoters, and everybody they did business with bought ads congratulating the members of Journey and their manager, Herbie Herbert. Journey's album, *Escape,* was certified nine times platinum in the USA. Neal Schon was the biggest guitarist in the music industry that week. I was at his house, and we were just hanging out.

Like Eddie Van Halen, Neal said his major guitar influence was Eric Clapton. He also liked Jimi Hendrix. Neal said when he was 15, he played with Santana. Carlos Santana took him on as his protégé. Neal reminded me of Dave Pierce, the bread slicer who gave me my first guitar. The bay area bands like War, Tower of Power, Sly & The Family Stone, and Santana owned the 70s. Neal emerged as the most successful guitarist to rise out of that scene.

We talked, played guitars, and he made me a sandwich. Neal called the bass player that he knew, and he came over to Neal's house. The kid's name was Dan Levitan. He had long hair and zits. He was my age. We jammed a little bit, then we all went to see a band playing called 415. The singer was an unknown kid with major charisma. His name was Eric Martin. Talk was the Journey's manager was going to sign them.

I spent that night at Dan's house. I gave Dan my TKO tape, and showed him the new riffs I'd been working on. I told him about the band with Brad Sinsel, and that I wasn't sure what the future held. TKO was on a downward spiral. We only had one upcoming gig at Lake Hills and nothing else. Dan was interested in coming to Seattle. I took his number, and drove to Hollywood to meet Chris Jacobson's friend.

When I got to Hollywood, I stopped at Famous Amos on Sunset to buy some cookies, and called Eldon Hoke from a payphone. I got directions to a dilapidated house on a street off of Fairfax. Eldon called himself *El Duce*. He lived with Steve Broy, who played in his band, The Mentors. They were a punk band who wore black hoods like executioners or the Ku Klux Klan. There were beer cans everywhere, and the house was a mess. There wasn't even a couch in the living room. I was told to put my sleeping bag on the floor behind some boxes, and they'd clear a space for me.

I didn't know anyone in Hollywood, so I went to see a band play at Whisky-a-Go-Go. They were called Ratt. The guitar player was named Mark Toriegn, and he wore the exact same outfit with overalls as Eddie Van Halen. He had a guitar with black and white stripes on it, he had the same curly brown hair, and he would point at the audience and make an 'O' face, just like Eddie Van Halen. I was beginning to understand what Eddie was really talking about when he said don't copy him. I thought it was a joke. Later he got fired from Ratt, and changed the spelling of his name to Marq Torien. He started a band called BulletBoys, put down the guitar, dyed his hair blond, and became a singer copying David Lee Roth in their music videos.

I spent the night on the floor at The Mentors' house, and when I opened my eyes in the morning, I saw a cockroach staring at me. I looked around. and there were cockroaches everywhere. The place was infested. I couldn't handle it. I didn't want to stay with these guys, so I drove back towards Seattle that afternoon. I stopped in San Francisco on the way back to see Dan Levitan, and he asked me if I wanted to go see a couple of new thrash metal bands at the Old Waldorf, a club owned by concert promoter Bill Graham.

On October 18, 1982, Dan and I went to see Lääz Rockit and a new group that was creating a buzz in the thrash scene called Metallica. There were hardly any girls at the show. Dan knew a girl named Toni Isabella. Toni worked for Bill Graham, and she totally hooked us up. We got in for free and we sat in the VIP section. I'd never seen a thrash metal band, so I didn't know what to expect. The first band was Metallica. They started with a normal crash build up like any rock band, then they went into a song called *Hit the Lights.* They played so fast that I thought it was a joke. The guitarist, Dave Mustaine, had really long hair, and played with his face in his guitar neck. He played so many notes during every guitar solo that it sounded like gibberish to me. The singer, James Hetfield, played a V, and a nonstop barrage of barre chords. They spent a lot of time tuning up between songs, and the audience loved them.

Lääz Rockit played a song called *Fire in the Hole.* They had rock and roll hair, but they wore jeans, T-shirts, and basketball sneakers. Their songs were not as fast as Metallica, but they were still too fast for me. This was the dawn of a new music scene, with no girls allowed. Both bands didn't change from their street clothes when they played. I always thought that was disrespectful to the art of being onstage.

On Saturday October 23, 1982, TKO did a gig at Lake Hills. We threw a midnight afterparty in the recreation center by the swimming pool of my dad's condominium complex. The party started late, and about 80 people showed up. Brad Sinsel was there as was my usual crowd of friends, and there were ton of girls there. There were people with cases of beer, and it was a typical Bellevue party.

A guy that I didn't like, Vic Carr, showed up at my party. He was the type of guy who was always getting in trouble for breaking into houses, and he was rumored to be the cause of giving some girls VD. He wasn't in our group of friends, but David Morris had known him since grade school. He had a case of beer, and he was already drunk when he got to our party. He came with another guy named Terry Martin. They didn't come to my gig. They'd been to some other parties earlier, and ended up at my pool room because my party started late.

There were these three young girls whowere drinking beer. Heather Jarvis, 18, Dawn Dennis, 17 - who called herself Kathy, and Kelli Knapp who was also 17. I knew Kelli from school, and we hung out at Moss Bay Days in Kirkland when I played there. She was a really cute flat-chested blonde with a beauty mark on her face, and I always had a crush on her. I did some coke with her at the party, but I didn't see her leave. Vic Carr offered to give the three girls a ride home. Kelli sat in the front seat, and the other two girls sat in the back with Terry Martin in Vic's beat-up '71 Dodge Charger.

Next to our condo, there was a Park & Ride, a public 500-car parking lot for commuters to park their cars and catch a bus into downtown Seattle. It was completely empty at 5:00 AM that Sunday morning. Vic decided to show off in front of the girls, and he drove into the Park & Ride and started doing donuts, screeching his tires while driving around in a circle, burning rubber.

A nearby policeman heard the screeches. He turned on his cop lights and drove into the Park & Ride. Vic didn't stop. He raced out of the parking lot towards the 520 Freeway while the police car chased him. Vic sped down the hill past the entrance to my dad's condo, ran a stoplight, and tried to drive towards Bellevue. He was about 200 meters, and missed the turn in the road. The car crashed into a ditch, and flipped over into another embankment.

The car got crushed like a tin can. Vic was killed. Kelli, Dawn, and Heather died within minutes.

Terry Martin recalled it to an assembly at Ballard High School. "We started off the night by hitting three or four parties. Vic Carr had been drinking beer and I had been drinking beer and smoking pot. As the partying wore on I became hungry. We grabbed a few women, hopped into Vic's car and took off. I was in the backseat behind Vic and he drove into a parking lot to do some driving stunts including squirrelling and brodies. When Vic hit a curb, that's when I told him to cool it so we planned a mellow split. But then we saw the flashing lights of a police car. It scared the hell out of people as drunk and high as we were. Vic hit the gas, hit the wood and went go, and I knew we were going too fast to make the corner coming up. The car left the road, jumped over an embankment and plowed into another. All of the windows sort of exploded, and I saw the right hand door move a foot-and-half, maybe two-feet inward. The wrecked car smelled of gasoline and I screamed for help. When I opened my eyes everything was pitch black. My first thought was this must be Hell. Then I saw a little light and thought, 'My God, I'm alive.' I called out to others but I didn't hear any of them. The policeman poked his head into the wreckage and squeezed the hell out my hand and said, 'We'll get you out of here.' At that time I felt wanted. They took me to Overlake Hospital. They wouldn't tell me what happened to my friends but I guessed their fate since I was the only one being treated in the emergency room. I got a broken leg, broken ribs, and torn diaphragm. I don't know why my life was saved but all of this resulted from one substance, alcohol."

The coroner's autopsy report showed that Vic Carr had taken psilocybin mushrooms.

Terrence Martin went on to lecture the kids at Ballard High School on the dangers of drunk driving. "I'm not saying don't go out and party because many of you will. Just don't drive when you party."

The day after the party, I was awakened around noon by Oggie barking. Joanie told me that the police were at the door. They told me about the accident. I had no idea that it happened. I was asked if I supplied or gave Vic Carr any alcohol at my party.

I was shocked when I learned that Kelli Knapp was killed. The examiners found pot and cocaine in Heather and Kelli's blood and determined they were legally drunk. I felt so bad for the parents. Nobody liked Vic Carr. Only David Morris knew Terry Martin. A liquor store owner from Redmond got charged for selling alcohol to minors, and the city fined him $500. That was the worst car accident in Bellevue's history. It was the last party I had at my dad's condo.

In a move that I never saw coming, Gary, Evan and Rick Pierce formed a new band with Floyd Rose called Q5. Floyd made a deal with Dennis Berardi of Kramer Guitars, and was now a millionaire from his invention. The singer for Q5 was Scott Palmerton, who did my first demo tape. I didn't know it, but that gig at Lake Hills was to be the last time I was going to be in a band with Gary Thompson.

911 is Disconnected

TKO had fallen apart. It was now just Brad Sinsel and me. We weren't sure what the next move was. I took the time to send my Floyd Rose guitar away to Mike Lull's Guitar Works to get painted. I had it done in black and white stripes, with the stripes starting out thin at the bottom, getting bigger as they went up the guitar. It wasn't at all like Edward Van Halen's stripes. This was a brand new design that came out perfectly. I called it the Zebra.

On November 20, 1982, I went to see a concert by a punk singer named Billy Idol at the Hippodrome, a hotel ballroom in downtown Seattle. I was completely blown away by the guitarist, Steve Stevens. He was dressed in black leather, had hair to the sky, and played guitar with his teeth. He even played behind his back. He could make sounds I'd never heard before. Billy Idol and his band had this New York, new wave, new romantic image, but they weren't punk rock. The bass player was Phil Feit, who was solid as a rock. They had a keyboardist, Judy Dozier. She looked really sexy onstage. The drummer was a bit of a wacko; his name was Gregg Gerson. He came out from the backstage door, and came right up to me and asked, "So dude, what did you think of the sound?" Then he whispered, "Hey man, do you know where I can get something?" Billy Idol came out, and took photos with the fans. He was wearing a long black fur coat. I spoke to guitarist Steve Stevens.

BILLY IDOL BAND

He was just standing by the backstage door, so I approached him and asked him about his effects. He said, "You should check out the English guitarist from Siouxsie and the Banshees, John McGeoch. He's really good." There was a lot more going on in the world than I was aware of.

I told Sinsel about the bass player in Mill Valley, Dan Levitan, and he told me, "I got a better idea." He found a new drummer, Mike Alexich, the boyfriend of rock photographer Lynn DeBonn. Mike knew a keyboard player named Greg Umphries, who changed his name to Gregg Fox, and Brad wanted keyboards since Rick Keefer added them to our album. Brad also wanted to use the former lead singer and guitarist of Striker, Scott Rosburg, who also played guitar and sang lead in The Roger Fisher Group. I saw them rehearse Roger's new hit (or so he thought), *Real Love,* off The Roger Fisher Group's solo album. It didn't compete with the Rolling Stones and Led Zeppelin, so Roger's band broke up. Scott Rosburg hooked up with TKO, and Rosburg was willing to switch to bass. He briefly played bass for Randy Hansen, so I was keen to give it a go.

We rehearsed in this old barn in Kent called The Barn. Susie Wimberly was hanging around at the time. She had an apartment, and I went to sleep over on her couch. She started hitting on me, and I was hesitant to sleep with her because I didn't want things to be strange later. She said it wouldn't affect our friendship, so I fucked her. She also taught me to spoon. Two days later, she started dating Brad Sinsel. I never told Brad that I fucked Susie. She just ignored it like it never happened, but she was hanging around all of the time. It got a little strange for a while. She'd wink at me sometimes, and we shared a secret. I didn't mind at all.

I helped Greg Umphries get a job at the bakery. After we stopped rehearsing at The Barn, we started rehearsing in a downtown theater. Lynn DeBonn organized a photo shoot for the new TKO lineup. I was at home getting ready, picking out clothes to wear. We organized a little private jam at the bakery with Jeff L'Heureux for the following day, and I already brought our gear over. It was going to be Bakery Jam, and my cousin Alan was going to play drums.

My stepsister Lisa Silverman had just come back from three months in London. She was living in a punk rock squat. Lisa was eating out of garbage cans. She caught hepatitis C, flew back home to Seattle, and took over my bedroom. I knew Lisa was shooting up drugs. Lisa's skin was yellow from jaundice, and she complained that the color of her shit was white. I couldn't fucking stand her. I had just finished my makeup for the photo session, was all dressed up, and camera ready.

I had 30 minutes to kill, so I sat on my bed and lit up a joint. Lisa started bitching when I wouldn't pass it. She was always bitching and never shut up, so I said, "Lisa, you are a disgusting bitch. I wouldn't pass it to you in a zillion years. You're a fucking walking disease. Do you really think I wanna catch white shit syndrome from you? Fuck off, I hate you. You're a cunt, now get out of my room!" and I threw a pillow at her. She said, "Fuck you," picked up a drinking glass, and chucked it straight at my head with all of her might. The glass slammed against my face and broke into pieces.

The glass hit me in my left temple, shattered, and sliced open an inch-and-a-half cut next to my eye. I felt a warm river of blood, as it streamed down my face. I looked down at the sleeve of my dressy white shirt I was wearing for my photo session. Blood spread instantly down my sleeve and the front of my shirt. I was bleeding on everything. Lisa said, "Are you alright? Oh my God, I didn't mean to do that, are you OK?" I said, "Do I look like I'm fucking okay?"

It was a pretty severe head cut. I had a Polaroid camera in my room, and I screamed at her, "Take my fucking picture, I have a photo session today and I want my photo taken." Then Lisa said, "No way, you're crazy. You're bleeding really badly, I need to call 911." Blood was rushing down my face, and I said, "911 is disconnected. Just take the fucking photo." She took the picture, and ran out of the room. I held a white towel up to my head that quickly became red, and waited for the image to appear in the Polaroid picture.

I was starting to get dizzy from losing blood, and I went downstairs. She must have called 911 because an ambulance came in about three minutes, but Lisa had left the house in case the police came. I went outside and raised my hands and screamed, "Yarrowood. You want blood? You got it. Here I am!"

I was all dressed up in my blood-soaked stage clothes. The neighbors were staring at the spectacle while my blood trailed down the driveway. The medics helped me into the back of the ambulance, and I shouted, "That's all folks, the show is over. Elvis has left the building. Thank you, goodnight!"

Joanie met me at the hospital. I showed her the Polaroid, and she wouldn't give it back to me. Her daughter nearly killed me. I got stitched up, and Joanie took me home. All the blood that got in the bedroom had been cleaned up so my father didn't know how badly I'd been cut. When my father asked me what happened, I said, "The bitch cut me with a glass and tried to kill me." Joanie chimed in and said, "Well you did call her the C-word."

I had so many stitches I looked like Frankenstein's Monster. The next day, my head swelled up like I was the Elephant Man. It looked like there was a baseball in the side of my head. Joanie was in denial that her daughter really hurt me. My dad didn't know what really happened, and he assumed that I did something to Lisa. No report was ever filed.

We had that private gig at the bakery, and I took acid for the first and only time with Jeff L'Heureux. Joanie showed up, and my head was so big that my hair couldn't cover it. She looked at me sadly, and I wondered if I was going to look like a mongoloid for the rest of my life. I didn't play that night. My head felt like a water balloon. I didn't like LSD. Maybe it was my head, but it was just a bad trip.

When the swelling finally went down, the scar was huge. The nerve of my left eyebrow was severed and left paralyzed. Joanie took me to a plastic surgeon who said he could fix the scar, but it might change the shape of my face. He suggested surgery. In a month, I was pretty much healed, and my hair covered it anyway, but my left eyebrow was dead for life.

The latest version of TKO with Brad, Scott, and Gregg was different. They all sang together in three-part harmony. They could harmonize really well together on *Run Outta Town.* Playing with a keyboardist was fine. Most of the time, he tried to mimic an electric guitar. We rehearsed in the Eagles Auditorium, and did a few shows around town.

Greg Umphries got caught stealing bread from the bakery, and my dad had to fire him. I could never understand why Greg, or Jeff Tate, never asked me to get them a bag of food. I could always take anything from the bakery that I wanted, and I would never let a friend go hungry, even if I hated them. It's in my Brenner DNA.

Scott Rosburg left the group. His final show was at Astor Park, and Brad Sinsel had me call up the bassist from Mill Valley, Dan Levitan. He came up to Seattle to rehearse with us for our next show at Lake Hills. Dan and I became fast friends. He stayed with me at my dad's place, and we worked on some new music ideas. I showed him a riff that he thought was cool. I was building up my arsenal of future songs, and I dreamed about making a solo album.

After the Lake Hills gig, Dan Levitan went back home to Mill Valley. Keefer had allowed Mike Varney to put out *End of the Line* on *US Metal Volume IV*, which was coming out in six months. A group called Steeler with a Swedish guitarist, Yngwie Malmsteen, was on the same album. Dan Levitan also knew Mike Varney. I was encouraged to make an instrumental guitar album, but I didn't like those guitarists who were coming out with records on Shrapnel. I didn't want to be that. I couldn't play like the prodigies, and everything they did was way too classical. I wanted to play fun rock and roll like Van Halen. It was getting to the point where I was just going to have to start singing myself.

US Metal IV- cartoon me on the far left

Through the bakery, I got contacted to play lead guitar for a group called Rockin' Horse. They were a group of three teenage brothers who traveled in a Winnebago recreational vehicle with their parents and their 18–year-old sister. They had about four weeks of gigs booked, starting with a three-night stand in a bar about 200 miles from Seattle. We didn't rehearse; they just gave me a list of songs to learn. It was all soft rock and Top 40. They wanted a harder edge, so they had me sing two songs: *You've Got Another Thing Coming* by Judas Priest and *Hurts So Good* by John Cougar Mellencamp. I thought that it might be good practice on learning how to sing. I was way too loud for these soft rock brothers, I had to put my amp volume on two.

Their father was the manager. The daughter and the mother just went along as they traveled. The daughter came into my motel room after the first show in an empty bar with about 20 people. I smoked a joint, and we starting making out. When I tried to fuck her, she chickened out and left.

The next night, there were a few more people. There was a redhead girl playing pool. The only time people paid attention to the band was when I sang. The room became electric. I talked to the redhead after the sets, and I got her to come with me back to the motel. She had some crystal meth that looked like a chunk of amber soap. I told her I didn't want to put it up my nose. So, she said I could smoke it on the end of a cigarette. I took a puff. It didn't really do much to me, and I fucked her.

The next day, I told the daughter about it like it was no big deal. After the show the father said, "I think this is not working out. You did drugs." I said, "I didn't even do a line." He said, "Well you smoked it." I told him, "I only took one puff." They took me home the next morning, and when they dropped me off, the daughter said goodbye to me as I was getting my guitars out of the trailer behind the Winnebago. I turned around and stuck my tongue in her mouth, slammed her against the U-Haul trailer, and felt her up. I convinced the father to pay me for a full week. I said, "Sorry it didn't work out, it's probably for the best. And by the way, I fucked your daughter on Friday night. You might wanna have her checked out by a doctor."

No Quarter

John Boghosian had just driven his AMC Pacer to Hollywood. He got an apartment he shared with a keyboard player, Jeremy Roberts. I drove down to California, and moved in with them. John got hired as a tape operator for A&M Studios. His place was on Hillside and LaBrea. They rented a 2-bedroom flat in Hollywood for $600 a month. I only had to pay $150 a month plus phone, and electric, but I had to sleep on a mattress on the living room floor.

Hollywood was full of rockers who wore lipstick and makeup. Big hair rock bands were playing every night at Gazzarri's, Whisky-a-Go-Go, the Roxy, and the Troubadour. The Rainbow Bar & Grill was always the best place to pick up girls, but you had to be 21 to get in. John and I went out on the Sunset Strip, and we drove my car, since AMC Pacers were a chick repellant. There were hundreds of flyers on the street for a band called Motley Crue. Paul Passerelli played me their tape and said, "They're the best new band in the world," but I didn't think they were as good as Van Halen. Motley's bass player was sitting at the bar of the Troubadour. He said he was from Seattle, and he called himself Nikki Sixx.

I recognized the singer of the band Ratt, and there was his guitar player; a tall guy named Robbin. Another guy bouncing around the bar was Carlos Cavazo; he just looked like he was in a band. It was a parade of budding rock stars, and I didn't know any of them. A guy came up to me, tapped me on the shoulder, and said, "You're Adam Brenner. I saw you play at The Showbox with TKO. My band opened for you. We were called Movie Star. Do you remember me? My name is Tommy Thayer."

Tommy had a band that was playing around Hollywood called Black 'N Blue. His whole band came down from Portland to chase their dreams in Hollywood. They were living in an old white house on Martel Street, 100 meters away from where I was staying on Hillside and LaBrea. I drove Tommy back home and he introduced me to his band. The singer, Jaime St. James, used to play drums in Movie Star. The bass player was Patrick Young. His brother Steve, who they called Bird, came to Hollywood as a roadie. They had a soundman, Kenny Nardone, who everybody called Shaker. The drummer was

189

Pete Holmes, who was called Owl, the second guitarist, Jef Warner, went by Woop. Tommy Thayer's nickname was *Bison*, but everyone usually called him Tommy.

Black 'N Blue were managed by Garo Tashjian, the 60-year-old owner of a pizza restaurant called Garo's. He had a really strong accent. Tommy took me to Garo's restaurant and they fed us pizza. Garo quizzed me a little bit. I was the new kid in town. I gave him a copy of my TKO tape. Tommy had spread a few around town as well. I wanted to join a band like Black 'N Blue. We searched for a rock band in Hollywood who needed a guitar player, but every band in town already had one.

Tommy took me out to gigs, We went to see Ratt at the Troubadour. He introduced me to guitarist Robbin Crosby, and said, "They call him King." Robbin was six foot four. I'd seen this band before with Mark Toreign, the Eddie clone. They were a band that was going through guitarists like water but they already had a guy that stuck by them, Warren DeMartini. They had a Hollywood vibe about them, but they weren't fun like Van Halen; they posed. Gigs at the Troubadour were awesome, and the place had a big Hollywood history.

Black 'N Blue were playing at the Troubadour a few weeks later. Garo paid for a full-page color ad in *BAM*, the local LA music newspaper. Garo was paying the rent on the Martel house, and Tommy's band was one of the top new rock bands in Hollywood.

When I saw Tommy's band for the first time, I was blown away. They had this badass descending guitar riff for a song called *Violent Kid*. Another really good song was called *Hold On to 18*. They were fun, and they dressed in flashy spandex, bandanas, and black leather. They were completely Hollywood. I became a fan of what they were doing instantly.

Woop and I kind of gravitated to each other. He reminded me of KK Downing. He looked like a fun, cool rock and roller. We became drug buddies. When Woop and I partied, we went wild. We had the same taste in music, drugs, and women.

There was a drug dealer living in an apartment complex directly across the street from the Black 'N Blue house. He introduced himself to me: "My name is Ray but I'm a hellion, dammit I tell ya, I'm a hellion." Ray Bressler was a short blond guy from Ohio, and he had constant cocaine parties at his apartment. Woop and I would hang out until the sun came up for many a night. Tommy Thayer did drugs occasionally, but he always went home around 2:00 or 3:00 AM, leaving Woop and me to stumble back in at 8:00 in the morning with cigarette breath and cocaine eyes.

I was high and couldn't sleep so I went walking on Hollywood Blvd. about 4:00 in the morning, and I saw this girl that I thought was wearing a nurse's outfit. As she got closer, I saw she was just a 19-year-old redhead in a white hoodie. I said, "Hello," and she stopped and asked me, "Do you do cocaine?" We went back to my apartment and did a line. John was working an all-night session at A&M. I started to hit on her. She made me chase her around John's bed until we were dizzy and out of breath. She flirted with me, we started kissing, and then I fucked her. It lasted about two minutes, and she said, "That's it?"

It wasn't so easy to get laid in Hollywood at first. All of the really cute girls wouldn't even talk to you unless you were mega-rich, drove a supercar, and had a house in Hollywood Hills. I went to see a beauty contest at Gazzarri's. The old man, Bill Gazzarri, would hire these girls as waitresses, and he'd get them to blow him. You'd always see these old guys like Bill, or a guy named Fig, walking into the Rainbow, with four super-hot Hollywood gold diggers. There was a full house of rock sluts making the scene at the Rainbow, but I could only hang out in the parking lot.

A bodyguard who looked like Kenny Rogers got out of a white limousine. He looked around like he was in the Secret Service, and then opened the door. Prince got out, wearing a long purple jacket, and made this big entrance into the Rainbow in front of me and the 10 other kids who weren't old enough to get in. Then David Lee Roth rode in on a Harley. He went in the Rainbow, and 20 minutes later he left with Prince on the back of his bike. Then Jack Nicholson stumbled right into me, and practically knocked me over. He was wasted, coming out of On the Rox, a private club above the Roxy that John Belushi used to cut loose at.

After a while of being around Hollywood, getting laid was no problem. All the girls who didn't get scooped up inside would check you out in the parking lot, and if you could strike up a conversation at 2:00 AM, they would go home with you. There was always action at the Rainbow, seven nights a week. There was always a rock star at the Rainbow, whether it was John Entwistle from The Who, Chris Squire from Yes, or Ronnie James Dio, or Ozzy Osbourne, or all four, it was always jumping.

One night, I picked up a girl with big curly brown hair. She told me she saw my photo and heard my tape. Her name was Bambi, and she dated Eric Carr from KISS. We were an item for about a week, and she told me stories about New York City. There was a whole rock and roll scene in the clubs that I didn't have a clue existed. She knew about my audition for KISS. I didn't get the gig, but I got the girl.

I met a girl named Athena Bass outside the Rainbow. We hit it off, and I took her back home with me. When I drove her back home to the Valley the next morning, I met her brother, Tommy Lee. He played drums for Motley Crue. They had just played the Santa Monica Civic Auditorium, and got signed to Elektra Records. Tommy had only one tattoo, of Mighty Mouse, on his shoulder. We sat on the floor in front of the TV, and he told me, "Dude, it's my dream to play my drums upside down in a concert." He was just a California version of the guys I grew up with. He didn't have a problem that I fucked his sister. Tommy Lee and I chatted for over an hour. I was sure he was going to make that dream of his come true someday.

John Boghosian was the assistant engineer for a month-long session for Fleetwood Mac guitarist, Lindsey Buckingham. Lindsey was making a solo album, and usually had John work constant 18-hour sessions. Occasionally, John would let me come by the studio. I asked him if we could get some spec time and cut a song. Lindsey did a mountain of coke at A&M. I thought I was really high when I met him, because I was smiling a lot, but Johnny reassured me, "No, he really liked you."

They were shooting a lot of videos on the A&M Soundstage. I went to a shoot for the Tubes while they were filming *She's a Beauty.* They were filming a kid on an electric wheelchair decorated to look like he was on a carnival ride. The kid was Alexis Arquette, and he tried to set me up with his sister, Rosanna, who was only there chaperoning her kid brother. She was wearing a baseball cap, but she still looked really pretty. Toto wrote a song about her, and her brother told me, "She wants to be a movie star."

The director had everyone at the shoot stand around as heads in the background for a shot in front of a sign that said, Ride the Beauty. Rosanna Arquette smiled at me but we didn't speak, and I was too shy to try. Alexis was a nice kid. He grew up to be a drag queen. It was really good to see videos being made, but it was mostly waiting around for an hour for something that lasted 10 seconds.

Just up the street on Hillside they were shooting a movie with Richard Gere, filming at a big gate by a vacant mansion where Errol Flynn used to live. Hollywood was continually changing, but you could still catch glimpses of Old Hollywood if you knew where to look. Sting and The Police were shooting *Wrapped Around Your Finger* at A&M. John and I watched Sting run around the set of 1,000 white candles. Sting was very approachable. I talked to him about the chords of his song *Every Breath You Take*. John Boghosian was a huge Police fan; they were his favorite band. He got to work with Sting and The Police as a tape operator when they did stuff at A&M. I really wanted to make a video, but they looked very expensive to make, and I had to make a record first. I loved wasting time at A&M when John worked there. It's where Charlie Chaplin made all of his movies.

John Boghosian was able to get some studio time for me one night at A&M. We couldn't do anything more than record some guitar tracks and have me to try to sing over them. We didn't even have an amp. I plugged into the board, and started playing an idea I had for my *end of the world* album. It was just three chords going up in D minor like Pink Floyd's *The Wall*. I tried my first attempt at singing and just repeated, "Destroy them all, before they destroy us." We never made a mix or anything. John shelved it at A&M somewhere, and we never took the tape. It wasn't very good. It was just an idea that would eventually resurface in 2002 on an album called *Third World Roar*.

Black 'N Blue's manager Garo was interested in helping me. He wanted me to get together and start a band with his son Peter. I went to their house and we tried to make a demo tape, but Peter couldn't sing. I was an unstoppable guitarist, and I only could play with accomplished musicians. It was a little hard for me to face Garo. I didn't want to tell him that I thought his son sucked, so I avoided him like the plague. Garo was getting a lot of things done for Black 'N Blue but he wasn't a real rock manager. He was a guy with a pizza shop who invested some money in the group, but he meant business. It wasn't instantaneous, but Tommy always shared good news of something big that was coming up.

I was at the Martel house, playing my Floyd Rose guitar, the Zebra. I told Tommy, "I want to try being a lead singer and start my own band. Finding a group to hitch on in Hollywood is just too difficult. I can't even find a group to audition for. What do you think I should do?" I made some squealing dive bomb noise on my guitar and Tommy said, "I think you should call your band Adam Bomb."

On September 18, 1983, Tommy Thayer and I were over at my apartment, hanging around watching television with John Boghosian. We turned on MTV. There just happened to be a special news report. The rock group KISS were being interviewed by JJ Jackson for the first time without makeup. As we watched KISS unmask, I told him about my audition for KISS. He thought that was monumental. "Bro, you played *Detroit Rock City* and *Firehouse* with KISS. That's amazing!! Imagine that, playing with KISS. They should've picked you." I lit up and joint and said, "I was too young, too short, and I love to smoke pot. You're tall enough. You should've auditioned." He said, "Nah, I'm not good enough. I'm still trying to catch up to you."

Tommy Thayer considered himself a songwriter more than the guitar hero type. He was nice; everyone liked him, and he never really got too wasted if he went out or partied. He was always up in the morning, showered and fresh. Woop was a bit more notorious. We'd stay at Ray's until dawn and clean him out. We did it so often, I think his bandmates were wanting him to cool out. Woop was the type that would just say, "Fuck 'em," and carry on partying. He never missed rehearsals or important stuff. Tommy and Jaime always did the meetings. I'd occasionally go with Woop to Garo's restaurant, still up from the night before. Garo could tell when we were up to no good. Even though I wasn't in the band, he'd give us a lecture, and call me son.

Woop and I must have kept Ray in rent money for six months. We were inseparable for a while. Every night we were going out in Hollywood, causing trouble, and having no fear. He'd dress up in women's clothes or come out of a room stark naked just to make a boring party fun. For a few weeks, he was seeing a waif named Sherry who lived in Ray's building. I wound up partying with her one night, and we ended up fucking on her couch. Woop had a key, and he came over the next day. He saw us on the couch, said, "Aww fuck," and left.

I felt horrible, but it happened. I went next door to Martel Hell and told Woop I was sorry. He was pissed enough to hit me, and I would've let him, but he just told me to leave before he did something we'd both regret. I went back home, depressed and hungover. I slept for about six hours, and woke up to a phone call. It was Woop. He said, "I can't stay mad at you. I love you too much. Fuck that bitch, I was gonna dump her anyway. Let's go party."

Out of all my emerging rock star buddies in Tinseltown, Woop was my favorite guy to hang out with. He was like a Hollywood rock god on a non-stop party train. And when he played rhythm guitar on his black Gibson Thunderbird, his right arm was like a jackhammer. When they made Woop, they broke the mold.

I went to a lot of Black 'N Blue's gigs, and sometimes I'd play guitar in the backstage room while they were on stage. I was in their dressing room at the Hollywood Palace playing loud through a practice amp, and some guy opened the door, looked at me and said, "Sorry, I thought you were George Lynch." I wanted to be in a band so bad, my guitar screamed. At the time I was trying to teach myself how to be a singer. I sat in the car with top up and cranked Def Leppard's *Photograph*. I put in on repeat and tried to scream along. I must have sounded like a sick cat on its ninth life. I used to do it for hours trying to hit those notes. I wasn't going to win any karaoke contests, but I was getting a lot closer to finding my voice.

After staying in Hollywood for a while and watching Black 'N Blue play the clubs, I gave up on joining a band. I figured I needed a plan B, and that was to start singing and eliminate the problem of looking for a band or a singer. I thought I could ask Rick Keefer if he would make a record with me. I would be the lead vocalist, write the songs, and play all of the instruments. I could get somebody to make an MTV music video; something all of the big groups did at that time. If I could get it together myself, then I wouldn't need a band to get a record deal. It was a vague plan.

Jeremy moved out and I took over his room. I went out walking on Hollywood Blvd. with John Boghosian. There was a disco called the Seven Seas close to the apartment. It had an entry fee, so we didn't go in. I saw two guys that looked greasy. One of them came up to me and said, "Hey man. Do you got a quarter?" His name was Jeff Isbell. "No, I don't have a fucking quarter. Do I look rich?" Then the other guy says, "Hey dude, what's your trip? Are you a rocker or something?" We started talking. Isabell pulled out a pipe with some weed, I took a hit, and John and I invited them over to our flat to smoke a joint. Jeff Isbell had stringy unwashed black hair, dirty clothes, and wore a nose ring. The other guy was a slick hustler who talked a lot, with a spiky haircut and a big nose. His name was Nick Panicci. They were both about my age, maybe a little older.

We all walked back to our place and sat on the mattress in the living room. Jeremy took his piano and most of the furniture, so there wasn't much there. We passed around Jeff's pot pipe, and I played a bit of guitar for them. Nick picked up my acoustic guitar, and started playing the chords to *All the Young Dudes* by Mott the Hopple. He passed the guitar to Jeff Isbell. He really couldn't play the guitar very well. He could only play a couple of chords, and he had no sense of rhythm. I don't think he'd been playing guitar for more than a year.

Panicci suggested that Jeff and I talk about music. I was into Van Halen and guitar heroes. Jeff mentioned some group I'd never heard of called Hanoi Rocks.

Isbell said he made leather studded bracelets, so I asked him to make me a white one  that was six inches long. He said it would cost $20. I didn't know if I could trust him, but I gave him the $20, and they left. After a few days passed, Jeff came by with the finished bracelet. It looked like an armguard that Jonathan E wore in *Rollerball* - A white leather band with 50 spike studs riveted to it. He signed it with black marker on the back 'IZY' with circle around the Z. It was a lethal weapon.

I let Jeff spend the night. He didn't say it, but he was homeless. I felt bad for him, and Jeff and Nick were always at the apartment after that. Nick was from Hollywood, and he still slept at his parent's house. They stayed at Hillside with us for about six weeks. They didn't pay rent. They were street hustlers.

Nick sat on the mattress on the floor in the living room, chopping coke with a razor blade on a plate. He said, "I rarely do cocaine with my friends." He snorted a line and kept chopping, clinking the blade on the platter. Then he finished it, and said, "You can lick the plate." I didn't.

Nick could be a real asshole. Jeff was a little on the gross side too. Nick said, "Isbell jacked off all time when you guys weren't there and he just wiped his cum all over your sheets." They just took over the place having parties, and bringing people over that we didn't know. Jeff had a friend named Bill Bailey, from his hometown in Lafayette, Indiana, who came over a few times. He was alright, but most of the people they invited over were Hollywood street trash.

I was always a little afraid of getting stuff stolen while they lived there. I had to put a lock on my room, and I kept everything that was valuable in John's room. Nick took my unemployment check from the mailbox, and he wouldn't give it to me. I got so mad, that I kicked a dent in his beat-up GTO.

Casey Pratto came down to LA to visit and wound up staying with us. He told Nick that I kicked his car, and I when I finally got the check back, I had to give Panicci $200. Somehow, Nick managed to move into my place rent-free, and hustled me into giving him money. He was the best con artist I'd ever seen.

The lease on the apartment was up, and it was in Jeremy's name, so John, Casey, and I moved into an apartment building on Poinsettia Street, just 50 meters from the Black 'N Blue house. We let Nick Panicci and Jeff Isbell stay at the Hillside apartment and squat there. Nick let Bill move in, and when Nick moved out a week later, Bill and Jeff stayed there for two more weeks. Nick said that before he left, Bill and Jeff were working on a song idea in the living room, and they asked for him for help with some chords. He said the song was called *Paradise City*.

After we got settled in Poinsetta, I contacted Keefer and said, "I'd like to return to Hawaii and give singing a shot. I could play the bass myself, and what do you think about using a drum computer instead of a drummer?" John Boghosian had been getting into the Human League. They used only digital instruments. I thought heavy guitar with computer drums was an innovative idea. I did not have any complete songs or a demo. I hadn't even sung before except for the one time at A&M, a few times in Gary's basement, and my three-day stint with Rockin' Horse. Keefer was game to give it a go. He said. "I tell you what, if you buy the plane ticket, I'll let you sleep on the studio floor. I have time open in about six weeks. Come for a week and I'll record you. Write a hit."

I stayed in Hollywood for another month with John Boghosian and Casey Pratto on Poinsettia. Casey got a job working for Gil Turner, a liquor store owner who was rumored to like young boys. Casey looked inside my black zipper notebook and teased me about lyrics for songs I was trying to write. "Play me 'Ode to a Punk'," and then he'd laugh in my face. They were pretty bad. I had no idea what to write about. I had never written lyrics before. Now that I was on my own, writing a good song, not just a good guitar riff, was going to be a challenge. I remembered a quote of Keith Richards from 1978, "I feel like all the songs in the world are just floating around. It's just a matter of like an antenna, of whatever you pick up. A whole song just appears from nowhere in five minutes."

I picked up a rock magazine, flipped through it, and saw an interview with Keith, and I read, "As long as you turn the set on and put your finger in the air, if there's any songs out there, they'll come through you." I wanted to write a song in the spirit of Keith Richards. I put my finger in the air but nothing happened. I had to figure out how to turn on the set.

I was walking home from Hollywood Blvd., as I used to walk around the streets and try and think about lyrics. I was walking back past LaBrea, and I saw this guy get out of a black BMW. He picked up a cat that was nearly dead off the street and he asked me, "Is this your cat?" I said, "Aren't you Michael McDonald?" The singer for the Doobie Brothers had just run over and killed somebody's black cat.

Tommy Thayer took me to see the band WASP at the Troubadour. It was beyond capacity. They had this giant sign behind the drummer that spat out flames. When they fired it up, the heat in the room increased by 20 degrees. The singer also threw raw meat into the crowd. I saw Blackie Lawless from WASP at a house party in the Valley, playing John Lennon's *Imagine* on a piano. He said, "Everybody thinks I can just throw raw meat and scream. Nobody knows I can do this stuff." He was 20 years older than everybody else at the party.

I went to a party in the Ratt apartment on Franklin they called Ratt Mansion West. The singer, Stephen Pearcy, came up to me and said, "You're the dude with that tape." They were trying to a make a pro tape like the TKO cassette that Tommy Thayer gave them. Everybody that heard it loved it, but I still couldn't get in a band. I hoped for something more than living with a bunch of guys my age in a Hollywood apartment, picking up girls and doing drugs, but those parties were crazy fun.

Miles Copeland, the manager of The Police, threw a Rainbow afterparty at his house in the Hills. We followed him home, but he wouldn't let us in. When he opened his gate, I asked, "How do you get to meet bigwigs in this town?" He said, "I don't know. Become a bigwig." He let 25 people into his house, and closed the gate behind me. I was with Casey Pratto, and he wanted to jump the gate. Some girl he was chatting up was in there, so we scaled the wall and snuck in. When Miles Copeland saw me he said, "Oh, it's the bigwig. How did you get in here?"

A girl I met at the Rainbow took me to a coke party in a hotel suite on Robertson Blvd. Actor Paul Sorvino was sitting on a stool, and there were only a few people there. I started talking to a guy with huge blond hair and rhinestone earrings, Bruce Johannesson. He was a guitar player in a band called Sarge. He was charming, had a Brooklyn accent, and he was really funny. We went out on the Strip, and did coke together. He loved Cheap Trick. He lived in the Valley with his mother. We hung out a lot. We had the same dreams.

Shape of the World

On the set of my Shape of the World music video

I went back to Seattle, and worked at the bakery for a month so I could get enough money to get a plane ticket to Honolulu. I was watching a show about The Marx Brothers. I remembered my father taking me to see their films as a kid. In one segment, I heard Groucho say, "Hey what's the shape of the world?" And Chico answered, "I dunno, but it's better with a brother like you." It made me cry.

I decided to write a song called *Shape of the World*. It was my statement. "I wanna play in a rock and roll band, I wanna live in rock and roll land, and I don't care about the shape of the world anymore." Metal kids were starting to appreciate the Rolling Stones at that time, and I wanted to make a song that had the spirit of Keith Richards, so I wrote, 'I won't fade away, and if my teeth fell outta my mouth, I wouldn't change a day.' The rest I just wrote about myself; a stray dog who wants to play guitar real loud and pick up girls. I had some power chords and a cool melody to go with it. That was all I had. I went to Honolulu with my two guitars, a 50-watt Marshall amp, and a fire in my gut.

Donna picked me up and drove me to the studio. When I got there, they had a bag of pot waiting for me. I told Rick that I wanted to call myself Adam Bomb, and he said, "That's perfect. It pretty much sums you up." Rick liked *Shape of the World*, and thought it was a clever title. He'd written down some song titles for me like *Radio Active* and *Russian Roulette*. I played him the instrumental riff that McCrea called *The Future Song*. I thought it could be good for *Russian Roulette*. Another song title he had was *Prime Evil*. He made this eerie sounding four-minute bed of bubbling synthesizer that sounded like *muzak from hell*. That was our pre-production meeting.

The next day, Keefer set about making the first song - *Shape of the World*. I didn't have a Marshall cabinet, so I had to plug my amp head into Rick's Fender Princeton. It had one 14-inch speaker. When I flicked the switch, smoke starting coming out of the back of the Princeton. We plugged the speaker directly into the back of the Marshall head and it worked. It sounded really bright and punchy. He was really pleased with the guitar sound and he called it Punchy Princeton, but I fried Rick's amp.

Keefer had an MXR drum computer. It was a new technology. The only other drum computer at the time was called the LinnDrum, and Rick preferred the MXR. After spending around an hour figuring out how to use it, we started programming the arrangement, and writing the drum parts. We had a basic track to work on in about three hours. We laughed about how easy it was to use the computer rather than deal with a drummer. Once the computer knew the song it never made a mistake. We called the MXR unit 'Gary in a Box.' We broke for lunch, then did guitars. Donna always cooked really good food, and I loved Hawaiian pot.

I blasted power chords through my V and the Princeton. I also did an overdub track direct into the board to get a really clean shimmery guitar sound. The guitar tracks were all done very quickly. I added the bass, using Rick's 1959 Fender Precision. I didn't really know how to play bass. I used a pick, and played it like a guitar. Rick suggested, "Use a soft touch and just try and play what a bass player would play."

We had our first music track, and Rick said, "Let's try doing a vocal." He set up a vocal mic in the front room so I could face the control room. We went in the office, and Rick typed up the lyrics on carbon paper so I could have a copy. He set up a black music stand and got a headphone mix. He placed a Neuman microphone on a giant boom stand with a pop shield - a circle of pantyhose nylon that you sing in front of to stop the air from popping when you sing a word with the letter 'P' in it. I saw the red lights come on the 24-track and went for it.

I started singing and Rick stopped after about a minute. He needed to put on a second pop shield for when I sang the words *proud* and *play*. We tried again a couple of times to warm up. Then I started to scream really hard. My head pounded in agony, right after I spat out a vocal line. It was painful. After about three or four times going through it, Rick told me to come in and hear it.

I listened to the playback. To me, hearing my own voice was more painful than the headaches that I got from singing. Rick said, "That sounds believable. This will work. You sound like a kid that wants to play in a rock and roll band. Let's break for the night. Get some sleep and we'll do it when you're fresh, first thing tomorrow." I was relieved that Rick thought my voice could make it on a record. I wasn't so sure that I was going to get away with singing on tape but Rick gave me a glimmer of hope. I smoked a joint, and fell asleep on the foam baffles he used to muffle my amps on the last session I did with TKO.

On day two, we started again with the vocals. I sang, and Rick was right; I had more energy. After the first pass, Rick said, "That was a really good 'Yeah!' Nice scream, I'm gonna keep that. I want you to do the whole song over again." Little by little, we started getting lines he liked. We got the verses good, and then went on to the chorus. After every take, I fell down on the ground, my head throbbing. Rick would always ask, "Are you alright?" and I'd always say, "I'm fine. No problem." I'd take a hit off a joint or a cigarette, and carry on. After an hour-and-a-half, we'd finished my first master lead vocal. Rick even gave it a gold star.

We started to work on *Russian Roulette*. I had no lyrics yet, so we recorded an arrangement that made sense. Intro, verse, bridge, chorus, repeat, a guitar solo, double chorus, and then an outro that we could fade out. I just had an idea where I could say *Russian Roulette*. Rick had the production idea to put a gunshot right after I said it. The drum track took around two hours to create. I did rhythm guitar tracks on the V and the Zebra. Rick loved the new paint job on my Floyd Rose guitar. I laid down the bass, doing an ascending bass line while the guitar chords went down, and we had our second song created. I just needed to do a guitar solo, write some lyrics for it, and sing over it.

I went into the office to think about lyrics. I thought about guns, and I was staring at the TV set. I thought about a trailer I saw for a movie called *Videodrome,* where a gun came out of a TV screen. Then I thought about gambling, and I had my concept. I wrote the words to it in about 30 minutes, and showed Rick. He made a few minor word changes, and he typed it out. He said, "We'll do the vocals in the morning."

On day three, we went through the same routine. It was painful to sing, but the headaches were worth it. Rick really liked the song, and after we finished the vocal track, Rick asked Donna to come into the studio and listen. He thought we should have a female voice during the outro. We put Donna on the mic, and she said, "Your game is over."

After lunch, we set up to do guitar solos. Rick pulled out a little surprise. He had bought three grams of cocaine. We took a line, and I did the solo on *Russian Roulette.* I used the tremolo bar, and got it in a couple of takes. Creating a little harmony part for the B section of the solo was easy for me. Rick added the gunshot after the chorus and after Donna's little cameo. I added a low note synth pad to sound like a Taurus pedal. Our first track was in the can.

I used the V on the solo for *Shape of the World.* I had a melodic solo that I had worked out in my head. I got it in one take, and I asked if I could do a harmony to the second half of the solo. He patched in another track, and I got that in one take too. We kept getting high, and I asked Rick if we could record an instrumental guitar track without drums. I had this eerie demonic piece I used to play in the lake house. When Casey Pratto heard it he would freak out, go into convulsions, and ask me to play it again. I wanted a clean guitar sound. Rick got me his huge, shimmery, direct-through-the-board guitar sound that he used all of his toys on.

The piece was about two minutes long, and had these illusory, sinister-sounding guitar chords. I overdubbed a tapping harmonic that gave it a percussive feel like a drum. Then I overdubbed a dark phasing synth bass droning over the track with Rick's Synclavier - an $8,000 keyboard sampler. Rick asked, "What do you wanna call it?" We had been talking about my bar mitzvah earlier, and I said, "How about Israel." I went outside and looked at the stars. I loved recording in Hawaii. Rick poured a few drinks, we talked a little more, and he went to bed. I wished upon a shooting star, and stared at the universe.

On day four, we started late. We listened to Rick's *muzak from hell* track. Rick had a hangover, so he didn't want to program another drum track. I suggested that we put a slow drum beat with only kick and snare over the whole four minutes with no changes. That was no problem. I came up with power chords, E to G, which copied the phrasing of the three syllables in the title – *Prime Evil.* I held a B chord for eight bars to sing some sort of verse over. Then I added some clean demonic chords, and Rick made them echo in time with the beat. I thought it needed some heavy octaves, so I did a low string ascending guitar line that Rick thought sounded Russian. He patched the effect we used on the TKO album on the little guitar intro to *End of the Line.*

We filled the four minutes. I played a Zebra track making high screaming dive bombs and simmering explosions with the strings completely flattened against the pickup. I did a few squeaks by pressing the E string against the pickup. All of the music tracks were finished. I just needed to write some lyrics, and sing on *Prime Evil.*

Rick had some cocaine left, and we did some lines and went about writing the words. He mentioned something about Carthage and Babylon. I thought it sounded like World War III. I talked about atomic bombs turning everything to sand, and the guys who pushed the buttons that could set them off, bursting in air like *The Star-Spangled Banner.* We summed it up, and I condensed the words until it sort of made sense.

We did the vocals in about 20 minutes. I did some 'whoas' and sang the words *Prime Evil* over the power chords. I sang the verses so hard I though my head was going to explode. I fell on the ground, and Rick said, "We got it." The recording was done.

The next day, Rick set it up to mix. He had torn out all of the cables from the patch bay on the mixing board, and started to show me all of his special mixing tricks. He was monitoring everything very quietly, changing speakers from his tiny AM radio-style Auratone speakers to his Yamaha monitors. After about two hours he had finished *Russian Roulette*. Donna and I came in to listen. We broke for lunch, he started on *Shape of the World*, and mixed that in about two hours. He did *Prime Evil* in an hour and *Israel* took about 15 minutes.

Rick edited the ¼-inch reel-to-reel starting with *Shape of the World, Russian Roulette, Prime Evil*, and ended with *Israel*. He made 10 cassette copies with Sea-West stickers on them for me to take to Hollywood. I spent the whole day listening to it on a Sony Walkman. I was on cloud nine. I treasured it. There was no better feeling on Earth than that first time, listening back to the music that I created after it was properly recorded. It was all me. Hawaii was the most beautiful place in the world to make a record. I was on my way to somewhere. Like all dreamers, I was aiming for the top, but whatever my target was going to be, I'd find it when I hit it. On the seventh day, Rick drove me to Honolulu, and I flew back to Seattle. The recording session worked. I was now a solo artist and a lead singer. Not just a lead guitarist. Adam Bomb was born.

When I got back to Seattle, I went over to play my tape for Jeff L'Heureux. He was impressed, and thought I sounded like Alice Cooper. He was really proud of me. Culprit had just put out a complete album on Shrapnel. They were playing lots of gigs around the Seattle area.

Jeff Tate changed his name to Geoff, and joined Chris DeGarmo's band as a full-time member. They changed their name from The Mob to Queensryche, after their song *Queen of the Reich*. They got a massive two-page article in The Seattle Times and KISW was playing two of their songs on heavy rotation. They played a Rising Star Concert at the Paramount opening for Zebra. There was an A&R guy who saw them from EMI Records, and they got a record contract. Everyone in Seattle was blown away. It was like they had won the lottery. I thought bands had to leave Seattle to get a record deal, but that one came to them like a fairy tale.

After a few days back home, I drove back to Hollywood and went about my mission. Right when I got there, I went out and got a copy of *BAM* from the bar at the Troubadour. An ad caught my eye, like it was calling me – 'Belladonna Productions Looking For Music Acts to Share the Cost in Making a Music Video.' I called the number, and set up an appointment to meet Tony Schiff, whose company it was.

Tony was an Australian filmmaker who resembled John Landis. I played him the song *Shape of the World,* and he thought it was perfect. He sat behind his desk, and asked, "How much money do you have?" I answered, "None. I'm only 20 years old." I left the tape and went home. He said he would think about it. He called me right as I got home, and said, "I really like your song, I think there is something there. I'm gonna put up all of the money to do the shoot. I want to film it on a rooftop in downtown LA. Can you come by tomorrow so we can discuss it?"

I hung up the phone and smiled. My vague plan had panned out as if it was calculated. I was going to make a music video.

At the meeting, Tony Schiff told me his idea. "I want to make a making of a music video - inside a music video. I want to shoot you on a rooftop downtown on 16mm color film. I'll get a bunch of extras and you can interact with them while we shoot you playing guitar and singing on the rooftop. We'll cut to shots showing us filming you. What do you think?" It sounded fine as long as he was paying for it. I told him, "I want to have a wall of Marshall cabinets behind me and I think I can get my friends in Black 'N Blue to loan me their heads and cabs if you can pick them up and drop them off."

The deal was that I had to sign a contract saying I would pay Belladonna Productions $15,000 if I ever got a major label recording contract. It sounded fair to me. He said it was going to cost a lot of money to hire the location and equipment. He got most of the crew and the extras for free.

The video shoot took place on the roof of a skyscraper next to the Eastern Columbia Building. Rick Keefer had sent Tony a ¼-inch reel-to-reel tape of the song for the playback. Black 'N Blue loaned me all their Marshalls cabinets and heads. They sent along Steve Hermann, a hometown friend who was staying at the Black 'N Blue house. Everybody called him Stiv. They sent him along to make sure I didn't destroy their Marshalls, or set them on fire. We had to get there at 8:00 in the morning.

We arrived at the location, and they started filming me as I walked into the set. There were around 20 extras and 10 people in the film crew. It looked just like a big movie set you'd see filming around Hollywood. It was a perfect sunny day without a cloud in the sky. They had already begun shooting behind the scenes. There was a mass of film equipment; dolly tracks, reflectors, lights, and two film cameras. There were two makeup artists. You can see Stiv to my left on the first shot of the video. I wore a Zebra jacket, and my white boots to the shoot. I brought along yellow leather pants, a red leather vest, pink motorcycle jacket and my white studded wristband that Jeff Isbell made. I only brought one guitar, the Zebra.

There was no script. I just had to wing it. I suggested that I start off by climbing a fire escape and appearing for the first lyrics at the edge of the building, without a guitar, while I walked along the edge. They set up the dolly track, and we shot it. The song was really loud so it made it exciting. I sang and played along to the playback a couple of times from the corner of the building, and I suggested that they take a close-up of my wristband for the two power chords after the first vocal line.

For the next shot, he wanted to shoot the extras spilling through a door onto the roof, falling down and fighting. I didn't really talk too much to the extras. They stared at me a lot. It was a little strange. I felt they were wondering, "Who the fuck is this guy, and why did I agree to do this for free?" I only knew one of the girls; I asked her to come down and be in it. She had a punk haircut, and her name was Annie.

They set up the dolly in the center of the roof and had me walk through the crowd. The girls were sitting on the film gear while I strutted through the crowd of extras. I did my little walk, and we got that shot. For the guitar solo, I had a plan. I had them set up all the Marshalls together with the big playback speakers. We had about six cabinets and three heads. I wanted them to film me playing guitar, standing on top the amps. We set it up so one stack had two heads on it, the other had one. I got up there, and the crew and Stiv stood behind the amps to keep them from shaking. They grabbed my ankles to keep me steady. I had no fear. It fell over once while I was trying to get up on those amps, but there was no big crash. I didn't get hurt. Stiv caught me, and saved the amps by letting them fall on him.

Tony wanted to do a long shot where he started in with a zoom and panned back so you could see the Eastern Columbia Building. I changed to the pink jacket, and went up a higher section of the roof. We got those shots, and I sang another couple of passes in the corner wearing the pink jacket. I didn't know what to do for the last verse. Tony suggested that I sing in front of the amps. I thought maybe we could have some of the extras sit on the speakers. Tony set two girls on one side and two guys on the other. I wasn't really paying attention, and Stiv said, "No man, don't have dudes on your amps, get the chicks." Stiv really saved the video by telling me that.

For the rest of the shoot I just plugged in and played in front of the crew and extras while they danced. We didn't really have an ending for the video. My suggestion was to walk out with the four blonde girls in my street clothes, look over at Annie, dump the blonde girls, and walk off with her. It was getting late, and we rushed to do it while there was still enough light.

After the shoot was finished, I got the blonde in the red shirt's phone number, and thanked Annie for coming. Stiv and I drove back to Hollywood. I went across the street to Ray's and bought a gram of coke and did it all in one rip. I went back to my apartment alone, thinking that the cameras were still following me. I got paranoid and hid in the closet. After a while, I blacked out. I had no idea what I was going to do next on my mission to make it in music.

It was going to take some time to develop the film and edit the video. Tony Schiff decided he didn't have enough close-ups and asked me to come back and shoot the following week. It was just me singing in front of one Marshall cabinet. It took an hour.

I went out with the blonde girl from the video, and I got together with Annie and did her too. Sleeping with my music video starlets became a habit I'd carry on for years to come. I spent another month in Hollywood going out on the strip. Black 'N Blue had just got a record deal with Geffen Records - a boutique record company that had offices across the street from Gazzarri's on Doheny and Sunset.

Geffen didn't have many rock bands at the time, but they were on a signing spree. They only had one rock act, Sammy Hagar, until they started signing Hollywood hair bands in 1984. They were mainly a pop label with acts like Berlin, Don Henley, Asia, and Peter Gabriel. John Kalodner was the A&R guy who signed Black 'N Blue. Tommy and I thought that Black 'N Blue would be big like Quiet Riot or Def Leppard. Both bands had number one albums in *Billboard*. 80s metal was starting to take over the world. It just felt like our time to do it was now.

Tommy and I went out to see this band called Steeler and their guitarist Yngwie Malmsteen. We knew the bass player, Rik Fox. He looked like Punky Meadows from Angel, with straight black hair down to his ass. Yngwie was hyped around as the fastest guitarist in the world. Steeler was signed to Mike Varney and Shrapnel Records. Yngwie got everyone talking in Hollywood. He shredded on a vintage Fender Stratocaster with scalloped frets, and he used his guitar cable as a whip while he played.

Black 'N Blue opened for Quiet Riot at The Roxy on March 18, 1983. It was the emergence of the Hollywood Heavy Metal Explosion and Quiet Riot was the first of the new Hollywood rock bands to break big in the music industry. 36 weeks from that show, Hollywood metal had its first number one record with *Metal Health*. Quiet Riot kicked open the door for Motley, Ratt, and every LA band that followed. We saw Motley Crue and KISS at the Universal Amphitheater on March 27. Ratt had put out an EP, and did two shows at The Beverly Theatre on the Sunset Strip in July, and got signed to Atlantic. Another band called Rough Cutt was managed by Ronnie James Dio's wife, Wendy, and they got signed to Warner

Bros. Heavy metal ruled the industry. Record companies were signing rock bands.

I went to Day on the Green in San Francisco to see Journey with Dan Levitan. We'd just seen Randy Hansen, the amazing Jimi Hendrix impersonator from Seattle, at the Old Waldorf. Randy came out in blackface. He played behind his back and with his teeth. He played on the tables, and took a big hit off somebody's joint. He tore the house down. At the start of the Day on the Green festival, Bill Graham came out and said, "Please rise for our national anthem," and Randy Hansen came out and played *The Star-Spangled Banner*. San Francisco was a good alternative to Hollywood, but the new scene that attracted all the beautiful girls was in Los Angeles.

There were a lot of thrash bands playing at the Troubadour, like Armored Saint, Malice, and Lizzy Borden. A label called Metal Blade, run by Brian Slagel, was putting out compilations like Mike Varney and Shrapnel. Black 'N Blue had a song on Slagel's *Metal Massacre* release that also had a song from Steeler, Ratt, and the San Francisco band, Metallica. Mike Varney and Brian Slagel knew who I was. I spoke with both of them a few times, and *Metal Forces IV* was just about to be released. Bands didn't make money from these records. Back then, if you wanted to matter, you had to be on a major label.

Pete Holmes, Woop, Jaime St James, Gene Simmons, Patrick Young, Tommy Thayer

Tommy Thayer was meeting with different producers. He met with Danny Kortchmar, who produced Don Henley, and he met Gene Simmons of KISS who had a label called Simmons Records. Tommy said that he and Gene really hit it off. He didn't think Gene was the right producer for Black 'N Blue, but they were going to write songs together. Tommy and the band made the decision to record their debut album with Dieter Dierks in Germany, the producer of the Scorpions.

When Black 'N Blue left, I started going out a lot with Bruce Johannesson. Bruce introduced me to Ric Browde, a short older guy in his 30s that went to the Rainbow in assless chaps while parading young girls on a leash. He was with Herman Rarebell, the drummer for Scorpions, who was at the Rainbow with Ronnie James Dio. Ric was a producer, and he was interested in my solo tape. Ric asked Bruce to have me give Herman a tape for him. Herman asked me to drop it off at his hotel the following day. He was sitting at a table with this gorgeous brunette with huge hair and legs to the sky. She was stunning. Her name was Tammi Ventrella. Bruce said, "I grew up with Tammi. She's my best friend."

As Bruce and I left the Rainbow, Tommy Lee was trying to break up a fight between two smoking hot strippers who were going at it in the Rainbow parking lot. One of them was Tommy's new wife, Candice. She was dressed to the nines, and these Rainbow girls looked so amazing. They looked nothing like the high school girls I was used to. These girls looked like the chicks I saw in magazines and movies. Tommy Lee just gave up and watched them rip each other's hair out. I loved Hollywood. I wanted to be a rock star as soon as possible.

Bruce and I went back to my apartment. We did some coke and played guitar until the sun came up. We made a bet: "Whoever makes it big first has to give the other $100." We shook on it. He thought it was a bad wager. We were both pretty sure that I was gonna win that bet and have to pay him a C-note.

The next day, I went to the Sunset Marquis to drop off the tape. Herman was out, but his girlfriend Tammi was in. She invited me in, and we spoke for a little while. There were some empty wine bottles on the table, and the room looked so posh. As I was talking to her, I thought, "This is what it must be like to be a rock star." She gave me a kiss on the cheek as I left, and it depressed the fuck out of me. I thought I could never get a girl like that, or have a life like a famous rock star. I went back and wrote a song called *You'll Never Know.*

I was counting on something to happen once I got my video, but it was taking ages. It had been over three months since I heard anything from Tony Schiff. Out of the blue, Brad Sinsel got back in touch with me. He was reforming TKO in San Francisco with Dan Levitan and Mike Alexich, and he wanted me back on guitar. Brad was being managed and living with Toni Isabella, the girl who worked for Bill Graham Productions. It was a big connection, so I went up there to play with them and check out the music scene.

End of the Line

San Francisco was booming with heavy metal bands at the start of 1984. It was the adolescence of thrash and speed metal. I went with Sinsel to see the bands Exciter, Exodus, and Slayer at the Keystone. I didn't like these groups. They didn't make playing music seem glamorous at all. All of the songs were about death. It was just fast noise with bad guitar solos. I could see that this scene was drawing huge audiences, but you had 2% chance of getting laid at a thrash show. The only girls at these sausage festivals were overweight, zit-faced tomboys.

Brad was staying at his new manager Toni Isabella's house. Toni booked the bands at the Old Waldorf, which closed and reopened in a new location with a new name, Wolfgang's, after Bill Graham's son. I stayed with them when I first got there. I played Brad my tape that I made with Keefer. Brad said he thought I did a good job, but he didn't encourage me to sing. I wasn't blessed with a natural, gifted voice like him, but I was really proud of that tape. It was a touchy subject, so I didn't bring it up with him after that.

Wolfgang's was the place to be, and we could eat and drink for free. I went home with Toni's best friend, Rachel Matthews, who was a product buyer for Tower Records. I stayed with her for the rest of my time in San Francisco. We never really said we were a couple, but I started living at her place. I really liked her. It just kind of happened. She was the first girl I ever lived with. She had a cute little tiny house decorated with candles and Christmas lights. She burned incense, and we had fun together. Her place was on a hill in Oakland, a mile from Fremont.

I forgot to put on my parking brake, and my Alfa Romeo Spider rolled down the hill and wedged underneath a car. Rachel woke me up and said, "Adam, you better come outside." It was miraculously undamaged. She loved Rod Stewart, and she had tons of promotional items that Warner Bros. sent to her job. She worked during the day, and I worked on music with Brad and Dan Levitan. She taught me that Billy Idol's *Rebel Yell* is by far the best album ever to fuck to.

Finally, I got a copy of the video in the mail. It was February 2, 1984. I had to go to a store that sold televisions and ask them to play it for it me just so I could see it. I thought it looked a little too much like a commercial advertisement for Tony Schiff's video company, but I looked good in it. I got Toni Isabella to play it on the giant screen at Wolfgang's before the concert that was going on that night. It just worked out that one of my guitar heroes was playing, former UFO guitarist Michael Schenker.

The video wasn't announced or anything, but the whole club stopped what they were doing and just watched. I was with Rachel Matthews and Dan Levitan, and I was in seventh heaven. After the video played, I felt like the whole club was staring at me. I'd never seen Michael Schenker play in a small club; I was keyed up to see him. While I watched his show, a lot of people came up to me and told me that they loved my video.

During the concert, I saw Bill Graham talking to some guy that looked like Alan Alda from the TV show *MASH*. He was holding a metal briefcase, and he just looked important. After the show was over and the crowd had left, I saw Bill Graham still talking to the same guy, so I asked Toni, "Who's that guy? Over there, the one with the metal briefcase talking to Bill Graham?" She said, "That's David Krebs, he's Michael Schenker's manager."

Right away, I recognized his name from the back of Aerosmith and Ted Nugent albums, and the *CaliFFornia World Music Festival* concert program. That was my moment. I only had one copy of the video, and I had just got it that day, but I scrambled to get it back so I could give it to David Krebs.

I went into the video booth and got it, but when I looked for David Krebs, he was gone. I was crushed. I walked towards the dressing room, and right then, David Krebs opened the door. I went up to him and said, "Excuse me Mr. Krebs. My name is Adam Bomb. I just made this video and I'd like to give it to you." He put down his briefcase and took the video from my hand. He read the cover and said, "I hope it's as good as the title." He gave me his business card, and told me to call him the following week. I felt like that was my big break. I wanted him to be my manager. He was my fairy godmother. He was the one who could make my dreams come true.

Mike Alexich flew down. We rehearsed, and TKO played a show at Wolfgang's. Toni booked us a gig at The Troubadour in Hollywood for the following day. Yngwie Malsteem and Rik Fox had just quit Steeler, and they had a gig booked at the Troubadour the day after TKO's show. Mike Varney called Dan, and asked if we could fill in for Yngwie and Rik. In my heart, I knew it was TKO's last stand, so playing a one-night-stand with Steeler was a good distraction. Dan and I had only a few days to learn their set.

That was the only time TKO played in Hollywood. It was the best show that Brad Sinsel and I ever played together. I did a stage move where I walked like a drunk, and it got quite a reaction. We played every song that we recorded in Hawaii. It was a milestone for me, and a swan song for TKO. I spoke to a few old friends in the crowd. I saw Jeff Isbell, who changed his name to Izzy Stradlin, and his friend Bill Bailey, who changed his name to Axl Rose. We talked for a minute after the show. Izzy and Axl wanted to ask me if I would play in their new band, but they were too afraid I would've told them no. I wasn't living in Hollywood anymore, and Izzy knew I didn't think he could play. As a lead guitar player, I was on fire, and I really wanted to play with accomplished musicians. I was a one-guitar guy.

My anticipation of playing with Steeler overshadowed the TKO gig. We rehearsed at sound check with Ron Keel and drummer Mark Edwards. They had a big song called *Cold Day in Hell*. Other cool rockers on the album included *Backseat Driver* and *Hot on Your Heels*. I didn't have a problem doing the solos. They were just rock songs, and I shredded like me. Yngwie's lead playing on Steeler's record was untouchable. Ron Keel could never resurrect Steeler from the shadow of Yngwie Malmsteen. It was a three-day whirlwind, and a lot of fun. I finally played the Troubadour, not once, but twice.

We went back to San Francisco to write some new songs and I showed Brad some of my ideas. I had some AC/DC-type chords and he wrote a chorus, *She Talks Just Like a Devil*. For the riff Dan Levitan liked, Brad wrote something called *Sticky Situation*. Brad was fucking Toni Isabella, but he'd just gotten married to Susie Wimberly. Susie was pregnant, and moving to San Francisco soon. The new TKO just didn't gel, and as Brad put it in a December '84 interview, "The rats had left the sinking ship." Brad did his best to write me out of history but my guitar playing was bigger than his ego. I spent two months in San Francisco, and played there twice. Brad's personal life directly affected the band - it was just too much for me to take. It was the end of the line for TKO.

Tony Schiff had sent Rick and Donna Keefer the video, and they really loved it. Rick wanted me to cut enough songs for a full album. They were going to pay for the plane ticket to Hawaii, rent me a house to stay in, and get me a car to drive when I was there. They wanted to sign me to a production and publishing deal, like I had done for the TKO album. I had about a month before I was booked in at Sea-West. Rick was recording Cliff Williams of AC/DC and Laurie Wisefield from Wishbone Ash, so I asked Rick if he could get Cliff to play bass on a song with me. He encouraged me to go home to Seattle for a few weeks to write songs, and we'd put it all together in the studio.

I went home and back to work at the bakery so I'd have some money for my month in Hawaii. I was doing the night shift, running the oven. I brought my V to work, and sat on the flour sacks on the back and started writing. I put the bagels in the oven, set the timer, and went in the back to work on my song ideas. I started working on the song idea of the AC/DC chords I had in San Francisco when Brad had sung *She Walks Like a Devil*. I wanted to make a song about a kid going to an AC/DC concert and getting backstage. MTV had a campaign across the country, with Cyndi Lauper, David Bowie, and Billy Idol saying, "Call your cable subscriber and say I Want My MTV." So, I figured if the Rolling Stones could rip off Winston cigarettes, then I could plagiarize MTV. I wrote down in my notebook, *'I Want My Heavy Metal.'*

The words poured out of me; I was just writing about myself. The oven bell had been ringing for quite a while, but I was in another world. When I realized I was supposed to pull the bagels out of the oven, they were burnt. My Uncle Itsey had a shitfit and told my dad, "Ugh Joe, the little bastard burnt the bagels." My dad told him, "Leave him alone Itz, he's just a kid." Itsey started screaming at me, "Aw shit. God dammit you spoiled little son of bitch, you think you can get away with anything. You ruined a whole god damn rack. I'd kick the living shit out of you if you were my son." He took a black bagel off the pan and threw it at me. I screamed in his face at the top of my lungs in front of every employee, "Hey Uncle Itsey, Go fuck

216

yourself. Fuck off and die you cantankerous old bastard. Everybody hates you. Do you hear me Uncle Shithead? FUCK YOU!" After I said it, his face got so red, I thought that he was going to have a heart attack. He went home, and that was the only time Itsey Brenner had left work early in over 50 years. All of the bakers, drivers, and bread slicers were proud of me. From that outburst, I got more congrats and compliments than I did at gigs.

Weeks had passed since I came home from California. Whenever I called David Krebs' office, the receptionist always answered the phone by saying, "CCC" or "8900," then she'd say, "No, David's not available. He'll have to call you back." She'd hang up before I could ask a question. I left messages every day, calling at 7:30 AM Seattle time from the bakery phone after working the nightshift. After calling there 15 times in two weeks, I gave up hope. David Krebs wouldn't take my call, and the receptionist was a bitch.

I went back to Hollywood for a week to get some song ideas, but I just ended up partying with my friends at the Rainbow. I dreamed up a song about getting picked up by a starlet, in a limousine, but it was a fantasy. I called it *"Take Me In."* I parked my car at The Martel House, and Stiv took me to the airport with my amps and guitars. As I was checking in, Stiv talked to some hot girl. He told me, "I used to date that chick. Be cool Okay? Don't do anything." She was traveling on the same flight. It was an empty flight, and we sat next to each other in the back of the plane. I joined the mile-high club on that flight.

I got to Hawaii, and they got me a beautiful one-bedroom vacation home. Donna Keefer rented a car for me. They had a few more song titles for me look at. One was *Fatal Attraction,* taken from the title of an article in *Cosmopolitan.* I used it for the riff Brad wanted to call *Sticky Situation.*

We started out with a production meeting. I had some musical ideas for this title, *Fatal Attraction. I Want My Heavy Metal* was totally completed. *Take Me In* had a drop D tuning, and a cool guitar riff. I had another song I was working on called *All's Fair in Rock & Roll.* Rick thought *You'll Never Know* sounded like *Bette Davis Eyes.* I had a power ballad idea called *Edge of a Dream.* Rick thought I should do a cover song, and I thought about the song I saw Nick Panicci play at the apartment with Izzy - *All the Young Dudes.* I also had a Rolling Stones-influenced riff in an open G tuning. I wanted to write a song about paranoia. I called it *It's a Bust.*

This time, I wanted to use real drums. Rick said, "We can record basics on the computer and overdub live drums later. But for some of them, you might prefer the sounds I can get with Gary in a Box."

For the song *Fatal Attraction,* I wrote a chorus that fit the syllables of the title. Keefer brought in a live drummer to record the basic track to a click. I created the arrangement as we recorded it. The kid playing drums had never played rock before. He could barely keep up with me. At the end of the song, he fell off of his drum stool. He knocked over a tom-tom as his cymbal stand crashed on the floor. We kept it in, and that basic track was done.

Rick had the new LinnDrum, but I liked the MXR drum computer better. We used it for the rest of the basic tracks. Rick brought in Abbey Brazely, a local Honolulu singer he was recording, to help me with my vocals. Abbey was a big guy with short hair, and he was half black. He could sing really high, and Rick brought him in to do vocal harmonies.

Abbey had a voice like Smokey Robinson. He also knew girls and where to get drugs in Honolulu. He came in, and introduced himself - "I got a song for ya." He snapped his fingers and sang in falsetto: "I met a girl street rollin' - 90 miles an hour I'm arrested. You look so nice in my mean machine, high heels and wine, sweet sixteen. Get on in, take a ride with me - Drivin' on down the road in my SST." I immediately played the three chords of the intro, and sang *SST.* I quickly worked out a blues-type progression for the verse, and I wrote a bridge riff, added a little B section, and used the bridge riff for the solo and the outro. I finished the lyrics. Keefer loved it. He wanted to do a backwards echo effect in the middle part. We programmed the MXR, and recorded the basic track. We also recorded a the Aerosmith song *Kings and Queens.* Now we had more than enough songs for a full album.

Abbey took me to Honolulu, and introduced me to a photographer. Her name was Mary Ann Changg. She had a photo studio, and lived in a downtown Waikiki high rise. She painted me with weird makeup, and teased my hair like a new wave fashion model. We did a photo session, got really high on coke, and I fucked her on the moonlit beach at midnight. We should've brought a towel. Sand is a bitch. Donna Keefer used one of Mary Ann Changg's crazy hair photos for a promo shot. They picked it. I hated it.

ADAM BOMB

During a break in recording I got a phone call. It was Dennis Marcotte from David Krebs' office. They finally returned my call. I told him I was in Hawaii recording. Dennis said, "I saw the video. You kind of remind me of Steven Tyler. You need to come to New York. Here, David Krebs wants to speak to you." Then he put me on hold for three minutes. I was just about to hang up, and... "Hi Adam, this is David Krebs. I really liked your video. I like the name Adam Bomb too. It sounds very political. *Shape of the World* is a great title. Call me next month when I'm in LA and you can play me the songs you're recording in Hawaii. The Scorpions are doing two nights at the Forum. We can talk there."

David promised he would take my phone call. I hung up the phone, and I knew David Krebs was going to be my manager.

Keefer checked out Leber-Krebs. He said they were big, but I needed to be careful. Cliff Williams used to be managed by Leber-Krebs. A guy named Peter Mensch handled AC/DC and Def Leppard for them. He was the tour accountant for the Aerosmith Express Tour in 1978. AC/DC was one of the support acts, and Mensch developed a personal relationship with them. David Krebs thought Bon Scott was a huge star, and wanted to sign them. AC/DC agreed to sign with

Leber-Krebs if they set up an office in London to be run by Peter Mensch. Cliff Bernstein, who worked directly for David Krebs, had been an A&R executive at Mercury Records. Shortly after Bon Scott's death, Bernstein and Mensch started their own company, and took Def Leppard with them. AC/DC, Scorpions, and Michael Schenker stayed with Leber-Krebs. Their top acts were Aerosmith and Ted Nugent. They were the biggest rock and roll management company in the world.

Keefer said he would ask Cliff Williams about David Krebs. Cliff was doing a new project with Laurie Wisefield. They used to play together in the 70s British band Home. Cliff paid for his studio time, so I was recording on the days in between.

When I wrote *I Want My Heavy Metal*, I included a bass solo like the middle break in the AC/DC song *Sin City*. It was either a tribute or a complete AC/DC ripoff – even the backing chords of the guitar solo were A, C, D, and C.

Recording on *I Want My Heavy Metal* started with us listening to Mutt Lange's production of *Highway to Hell*. We tried to get the same snare drum sound using the MXR computer. Cliff was using the same machine for his recording. They were trying to mimic the same snare sound from his band's album too. I did the rhythm guitars on the V, and the solo on the Zebra. It was really high to sing, so Rick slowed the tape down just a fraction of a beat using vari-speed. I was able to hit the high notes. It hurt like hell, but I nailed it. Rick thought it was pretty believable. I sounded like a kid.

We originally started the song with a phone call I recorded with Jeff L'Heureux, having a conversation about getting backstage passes to an AC/DC show. I played a scratch bass track, and Cliff came in the next day to do a session. At the end of his session, Rick gave him a line, played *I Want My Heavy Metal*, and asked him if he wanted to play a bass track on it. I was waiting in the office for them and I asked Rick, "So what did Cliff say?" Rick shook his head with disappointment. I got scared, and then he said, "He thought the song was great! He loves it and he wants to play on it."

I went into the control room, and Rick introduced me to Cliff. He was tan, wore an aloha shirt, and he looked like a rock star. I wasn't allowed in the control room when Cliff recorded bass, but after 30 minutes they called me in to listen. It was perfect. It sounded just like AC/DC. He changed the part I wrote for the middle bass solo into something apocalyptic. We did a line of cocaine and I asked Cliff if he would sing the background vocals with me. We went out and sang the chorus. He sang really loud. I loved standing next to him, listening with one ear off the

headphones so I could hear him scream. We listened to the playback. When I first heard Cliff Williams shout *I Want My Heavy Metal*, I said to him, "This is going to be my anthem."

Cliff Williams thought it was a good idea for me to sign a management deal with David Krebs. I spent another three weeks in Hawaii. Rick brought in a drummer, Chuck Ruff, who was the drummer of Montrose, to play on *Shape of the World* and *Russian Roulette*. He also brought in Jerry Martini, a saxophone player, to play on *It's a Bust*. We cut everything else pretty fast. He rented me a Roland Guitar synthesizer for the song *Fatal Attraction*. On *Take Me In*, Rick did a backwards echo effect on the MXR drum track that sounded really cool. He also did some huge effect he called *London Drums,* on *I Want My Heavy Metal*. Some of these songs just sounded right with a drum computer, but I missed playing with Gary.

We recorded *SST* and *All the Young Dudes* at the same time. They were the last songs we recorded and my voice had really developed, but I was far from being a good lead singer. It still hurt to sing in the studio, but I was getting far better at it. Abbey and I sang backgrounds and I started figuring out how to harmonize to my vocal tracks. I did a three-part harmony in *SST*.

After we mixed and compiled the 14 songs, I signed a contract with Sea-West Productions, and Rick gave me a few tapes to give out in Hollywood to get a buzz going.

I had successfully bypassed having to rely on a band, or more importantly – a lead singer. Playing live was going to be a challenge, but I could make videos. I was buzzing about meeting David Krebs. It didn't seem so out of reach for me that I might have actually been able to take this rock and roll thing all the way. I could make a life out of it. For that there was no backup plan. The biggest hurdle would be finding myself along the way. I kept my promise to Eddie Van Halen - I never copied him. I wasn't like anybody else. I was me. It was a big step becoming a singer/songwriter but I still had a long way to go. I wasn't just a guitar player anymore. I started to feel like I had my foot in the door. I just needed to kick it open. This was my time.

SEA-WEST STUDIOS / HAWAII

An Invitation to Record in Paradise . . .

The City That Never Sleeps

I flew back to Hollywood to get my car, which was parked in Black 'N Blue's driveway, and I got a $35 room at the Tropicana Motel. There was another band staying there called Heavy Pettin'. We met by the pool in the afternoon. They were from Scotland, and were signed to Polygram Records. It was April 24, 1984.

David Krebs took my phone call. His secretary conferenced me to his room at the Beverly Hills Hotel, and I went there to meet him. We rode to the show in a black limousine, with his German partner who co-managed Scorpions, Olaf Schröter. We listened to my tape in the limo on the ride down to the Forum. After he heard *I Want My Heavy Metal*, David Krebs said, "I want to sign you."

The Scorpions were on Polygram Records, as was their opening act, Bon Jovi. I saw Ric Browde backstage, inside Scorpions' dressing room, and David Krebs introduced me to the band. Herman Rarebell was with Tammi Ventrella, and Matthias Jabs remembered me from Seattle. For the first time in my life, backstage at a concert, I felt like I wasn't just a fan, like I had business being there. I told Tammi about *You'll Never Know*, the song I wrote about her, and I gave her a tape. She was flattered. Her best friend, Bruce Johannesson, was backstage sitting next to her.

There was a party backstage after the concert. I met Bon Jovi. The buzz was that their singer, Jon Bon Jovi, was going to be a huge star. They had a video on MTV called *Runaway*, and I thought they were AOR like Foreigner. Scorpions had a few big songs on MTV, and their latest hit song was *Rock You Like a Hurricane*. Both bands really took a shine to me. I was shooting the shit with Gordy Bonnar and Punky Mendoza from Heavy Pettin' and Bruce Johannesson. Tico Torres, the drummer from Bon Jovi, came up to me and said, "I heard that David Krebs wants to sign you. Congratulations." He gave me a great big hug. The whole room was buzzing about me. The manager of Bon Jovi came up to me, and said, "I'm Doc McGhee. I heard your tape yesterday while we were out on a yacht in Marina Del Ray. It sounded really good. You're great. You should call me."

I had so much fun on the Scorpions/Bon Jovi tour, that I went to the second LA Forum show, and I drove up to San Francisco to see two more shows. I thought my hustling days were finally behind me, and I had a laminate all-access backstage pass.

Scorpions and Bon Jovi played at the Cow Palace. I stayed with Rachel Matthews, and took her to the show. We were standing right behind the stage, and Rudolf Schenker looked right at me just as the house lights went dark and the crowd roared. We saw Scorpions the next evening. I stayed with Rachel a few more days, and then headed back to Seattle. I wanted my family back home to know how well I was doing.

I showed my dad and Joanie the video I had made. They were having a party with every relative and hanger-on in the family. They all watched the video. They thought I was insane. Later that night, Joanie thought I was on drugs. She searched my suitcase, and started to ransack my room. Under my bed, they found an old brown sunglasses case with a burnt spoon, a razor blade, and a syringe. I never saw it before, but my dad thought it was mine. I had never even seen heroin before. Lisa told Joanie that it belonged to her, and she went to rehab. They assumed because she was on dope that I was too. I had to get out of Seattle.

I called Dennis Marcotte, and told him I was coming to New York. I flew to JFK with, a suitcase, my Flying V, and $200 in my pocket. Dennis picked me up in a blue Mercedes that belonged to David Krebs. Ric Browde came along to get me and I sat in the backseat. Dennis gave me a small bag of cocaine, and took me on my very first drive through New York City.

It looked just like it did in the movies. The big yellow Checker cabs, and steam coming up through the manhole covers on the street. I asked about police and Dennis said, "They never stop you in New York City." A minute later, we got pulled over, and Dennis got a ticket for an illegal turn. "That was a fluke," he said. "That never happens. Welcome to New York, Mr. Bomb."

Dennis Marcotte was from Detroit. He'd been working for Krebs for over a year. He had stories about Steven Tyler. "Steven's really fucked up on heroin. Rumor has it, he sent his girlfriend, Teresa, out on the street to prostitute herself, so he could buy dope when David stopped giving him money. He's living at the Gorham Hotel, a block down from the office. Leber-Krebs just dropped Steven last week.

Krebs was thinking about getting you to play guitar in Aerosmith but he just can't deal with Tyler's problems. Steven's a nightmare, but he's such a fucking good singer. He helped me a make a demo tape I made. He's got a set of lungs on him, boy. He can hold a note for days without taking a breath." He went on, "Aerosmith is finished. You should get Jimmy Crespo to play in your band. You don't do heroin do ya? If you do, don't tell David, and if he offers you coke don't do it. Well do it if he offers it, but he won't." I told Dennis not to worry; I had never tried heroin. I had no intention of ever doing it. It reminded me of my stepsister.

We dropped off Ric Browde on Riverside Drive, and went to the apartment where I was staying at 399 East 72nd Street. Dennis lived there with Debby Prisco, a pretty Italian girl with black hair, and a Boston accent. Debby was Leber-Krebs' in-house accountant. David Krebs didn't know that Dennis and Debby were a couple, and it was still David's apartment, but he lived in a penthouse he bought on 2 East End Avenue. Debby said, "If David found out Dennis was living with me, he'd throw us both out. You too - so keep your mouth shut."

399 was a two-bedroom with a sunken living room floor. It was plush. They had a spare bedroom, and I slept on a convertible pullout bed. In the morning, Dennis took me to the Leber-Krebs' office at 65 West 55th Street. I took my Gibson Flying V with me. It looked like a doorman apartment building where ordinary rich people lived. We went up to the 2nd floor. The sign on the door read: Contemporary Communications Corporation. We walked in, and the fat receptionist said to me, "So you're the guy that left all of those messages."

Dennis showed me around. David Krebs had an office in the corner. Next to it was Steve Leber's office. Steve was David's partner, and did more Broadway-type stuff than rock bands. He produced *Beatlemania* at the Winter Garden Theater, and hooked Aerosmith up with Robert Stigwood and the Bee Gees to do the movie *Sgt. Pepper's Lonely Hearts Club Band*. Leber was as bald as a cue ball, and was not a rock and roll guy at all. He was all business.

Next to Leber's office was Louis Levin, who handled Michael Bolton. There was another guy named Paul O'Neill, who was on the phone in a mailroom with a long desk. David had a secretary, Patti O'Toole, who was drunk. She put her arms around me and said,

225

"Who's this?" She was not pretty. Another person working there was Laura Kaufman, an overweight middle-aged lady who breathed heavy, and spoke with a bit of a lisp.

It was a normal looking office, except there were gold and platinum records all over the walls from Aerosmith, Ted Nugent, AC/DC, and Scorpions. There were photo books with hundreds of personal pictures of Aerosmith. Everybody ordered coffee from the deli downstairs, even though there was a coffee machine in the mailroom. We went upstairs where Debby Prisco worked. As well, it was the office for Blackheart Records and Kenny Laguna, who managed Joan Jett. She had just had a number one single with *I Love Rock and Roll*. Debby was nice, but everybody else in the office seemed to have that, 'Who the fuck are you, and what are you doing here?' attitude. We went back down, and went in David's office. He told his secretary to hold his calls, and David said to Dennis, "Leave us."

David looked at me, and pointed to the 10 platinum records on the wall, behind his desk. He said "Do you want to get one of these?" I smiled and said, "I'd prefer one of my own." He said "Cute. Do you want to smoke a joint?" His desk was covered with folders and papers. Little metal toy soldiers and little trinkets were scattered all over the office. There was a framed picture of Napoleon on the wall, and cassette tapes, albums, a stereo, and a television with two VCRs were on a shelf. There was a small mirror coffee table in the shape of a piano, a black leather couch, and a matching chair, which he sat upon.

He lit the joint with a match, sucked in a big hit, and passed it to me. There was a framed poster on the floor, of the CaliFFornia World Music Festival. I pointed to it, and said, "I went to that concert." Krebs wanted to know, "What do you think of Aerosmith?" I told him, "I grew up on them, Ted Nugent, Scorpions, Def Leppard, AC/DC and Michael Schenker." He laughed and said, "Those were all my acts." I told him about Hawaii, Rick Keefer, and the deal I made with Tony Schiff. I spoke about the bakery, and my family. David Krebs was Jewish, and he grew up in Brooklyn.

David Krebs graduated from Columbia University with a law degree and an MBA. He went to work at the mailroom at the William

Morris Agency with David Geffen, who became his best friend. A young Steve Leber was brought in as head of the music department at WMA. Eventually, they all moved up the ladder. David Krebs liked the Greenwich Village folk scene with Richie Havens, Judy Collins and Bob Dylan. Krebs was there in 1961 when Dylan forged his reputation as The New Poet of the Beat Generation. David felt a connection to the music. The audience was intelligent, and the lyrics mattered.

Dylan was a huge draw in the nightclubs, and Krebs got intrigued to find new artists for WMA. The WMA bookers discovered Simon & Garfunkel at a club called Gerde's Folk City on West 4th, and an unknown black comic, Bill Cosby, at the Gaslight Café on MacDougal Street. Krebs was the agent for Don McLean, and his

song *American Pie,* became a number one single. David Geffen wanted to start a new company with David Krebs in California - they were best friends, both of them Brooklyn boys, and Krebs had charisma. But David liked the gritty New York folk scene, and chose to stay behind. He started a  management company in New York City with Steve Leber, and they called it Leber-Krebs.

In 1972, Marty Thau quit his job as the head of A&R for Paramount Records to manage the darlings of the emerging New York City punk scene - the New York Dolls. He brought the two ex-William Morris bookers on as partners. They secured a deal with Mercury Records for the New York Dolls. David talked about the Dolls: "They could be the best band in the world one night and the worst the next. We booked them for the Mercer Arts Center, and they were fabulous. But, at another show, the guitarist, Johnny Thunders, came up to me before he went on, and said: Gimme a hundred bucks or I won't play. They self-destructed from heroin. Don't ever take it.

I've seen it ruin too many lives." The Dolls imploded, but Leber-Krebs started taking on other acts.

In 1972, Frank Connelly - the number one promoter in Boston, brought Aerosmith's demo to Steve Leber. They did a showcase at Max's Kansas City, and Ahmet Ertegun from Atlantic Records passed because they looked too much like the Rolling Stones. But they got them a deal with Clive Davis at Columbia. Aerosmith were about to lose their contract when David Krebs gave Columbia a free six-month extension, and the rest is history. Aerosmith happened, and outsold the Rolling Stones four-to-one. David signed Ted Nugent in 1975 and guided him to three multi-platinum albums and three gold records until they parted ways in 1982. Aerosmith and Ted Nugent were the two biggest selling American rock acts in the late seventies.

David liked Steve Marriott from Humble Pie. He signed him to a management deal on a napkin. He managed Bon Scott, and was devastated by Bon's untimely death. He had a birthday Western Union telegram from Steven Tyler on his wall that said, 'There once was a scholary Kreb who knew how to pick the celeb, so he signed up A. Smith and made them all rich, now he takes all his phone calls in bed. Happy Birthday, Love Steven.' I thought David Krebs was the coolest rock manager in the world.

I took out my guitar and played him *You'll Never Know,* and sang it right there in the office. No one had ever auditioned for him like that before. He called Dennis back in, and asked him to put on my video. Then he asked me, "So what do you want to do?" I told him, "I want to put together a band to back me up, play big concerts, and get a record deal." Dennis mentioned Jimmy Crespo. David wasn't sure about that idea, but I thought if I was going to be the lead singer, I could use a second guitar. The idea of playing with Jimmy Crespo from Aerosmith sounded good to me. David told his secretary, "Get me Jimmy Crespo." Dennis set up a meeting between Jimmy and me.

Dennis took me to a club in a big ballroom on East 11th Street called The Ritz, to see a band called TNT. There were only about 80 people there, but the place could probably hold 1,000. I was wearing my Zebra coat, looking like a rock star, and I met this motor-mouth in a green army jumpsuit who was completely insane. His name was Gregg Gerson, and he was the drummer for Billy Idol, who I saw play in Seattle. He was looking for a new band to play in. He had beady eyes, and was with some older guy named Arturo. They handed me a folded-up dollar bill with some coke in it. I loved New York. I told Dennis, "I want to play The Ritz on my 21st birthday."

Gregg said, "Phil Feit, the bass player that was in Billy Idol is looking for a band. I'll give him your number." Dennis wasn't so sure about Gregg. There was something fishy about the guy, but I liked him. He played with Billy Idol. I saw him play, and I knew he was good.

Phil Feit called me up the next day, and came over to 399 to meet me. I answered the door, and l saw this Jewish guy in his late 20s with a cool haircut who looked like a New York City new romantic. I told him I was a fan of the Billy Idol record, and guitarist Steve Stevens was one of my heroes. Phil had played the bass on *White Wedding* and the rest of Billy Idol's first album. He said, "I'm still good friends with Steve. I've known him for years, ever since he played at Great Gildersleeves with the Fine Malibus." Phil didn't elaborate on why he left Billy Idol. He just said, "There was a lot of bullshit and I just had enough, so I quit." I tried to pry further, but he wouldn't talk about it. We listened to the tape, and he was into giving it a shot. Dennis mentioned Jimmy Crespo, and Phil thought that was a great idea. The next step was for me to meet Jimmy.

When I met Jimmy Crespo, he was living in Harlem. He got a ride over to meet me with a heavy-set Dominican guy named Justin, who was driving a beat-up Cadillac. Jimmy wore scarves and leather. He had really nice eyes, and I liked him from the moment I saw him. He wasn't so sure that he wanted to work with David Krebs again, but he was interested in checking it out. Dennis said he'd get Krebs to pay for the rehearsal time, so we set it up.

Dennis put in a check request to David Krebs for $120. David signed it. Dennis went up to Debby's office, and she wrote out a check. He took it back to David, and he signed it. We went to SIR and met up with Gregg, Phil, and Jimmy. We took a room with amps and a PA for three hours. The Billy Squier band was rehearsing in the room next door, and I couldn't wait to plug in and play.

Phil had a red Fender Jazzmaster bass. Jimmy had a 1959 cherry sunburst Les Paul. Gregg just brought a stickbag. They had learned four songs from the tape; *Shape of the World, Russian Roulette, SST, and I Want My Heavy Metal.*

I started off *SST,* and Jimmy came in right after me. It worked. When it came time to sing, I just grabbed the mic with one hand, and slid my guitar behind my back and belted it out. We felt a little magic there. They knew the songs good enough to get through it. Everybody felt good about it, and I thought we looked great together. These were name musicians who had gone on tours and made records. I was in New York City just a couple of days, and I already had my band together.

After that first rehearsal, I met all of the guys in the Billy Squier Band except Billy. I was excited to meet drummer Bobby Chouinard. He was a big drum hero in Seattle. All of the guys were really cool. The bass player was Doug Lubahn, the guitarist Jeff Golub, and the keyboardist Alan St. Jon. I went with my guys across the street on 54th to the Ye Old Triple Inn to get a burger. Gregg stayed behind to talk with Bobby Chouinard about something. He met us at the bar about 10 minutes later.

I asked Jimmy Crespo. "So whadda ya think?" He responded. "I think it's cool, real cool." I asked Phil, "You into it?" and he said "Yep." Gregg was kind of restless, he didn't eat but he kept going on about how fantastic and perfect this was. Phil had a Cuervo and orange, Jimmy had a glass of wine, Gregg had a beer, and I had a Coca Cola. We raised our glasses and made a toast to our new group - "To the Adam Bomb Band."

Everything seemed like it was meant to be. There was just one problem - Dennis didn't want me to sign a contract with David Krebs. He was telling me that I should sign with Steve Leber so Dennis could handle things, like Kenny Laguna did with Joan Jett. I really liked David. I wasn't sure how to handle that situation.

The following day, I went to the office, and spent the day. Ric Browde was there, and he invited me to dinner at his apartment. I met Ric's wife Holly, and their guest, Cheryl Rixon, who was voted *Penthouse* Pet of the Year in 1979. Ric was producing a record for a band called Victory, who were based out of Hannover, Germany -

where the Scorpions were from. The guitarist, John Lockton, was staying at Ric's. Victory were managed by Leber-Krebs and Olaf Schröter. The singer was Charlie Huhn, an American who sang with Ted Nugent, and three other guys who were from Hannover who were friends of Rudolf Schenker. Ric had a huge apartment; it was three times the size of 399. It had a black-and-white checkerboard tile floor, four bedrooms, and a big dining room with a long table.

Holly Browde was a music-law attorney who worked for Polygram Records. The Browdes had some bizarre open relationship. Ric was very open about being into bondage and S&M. He said, "I don't drink or do drugs so I need to do something to make up for it."

It was a fun dinner party. Ric was telling me all kinds of things about the music business and Krebs. He wasn't a technical producer like Rick Keefer who could run machines. He could only give advice about the sick side of rock, and write really dirty lyrics. I liked Ric Browde. I trusted him.

By coincidence, Holly Browde had been going out with Gregg Gerson, and fucking him. It was a small world. Cheryl Rixon had a crush on me. Cheryl was in a movie called *Used Cars,* and she did a photo shoot with Judas Priest I had seen in a rock magazine back when I lived at home in Seattle. She was 11 years older than me. I gave her my number, and she came over to 399 the next day and fucked me. She came over a few times during those two weeks I was staying at 399. I loved her Australian accent and she was a *Penthouse* Pet. She was a living centerfold and every rock kid's wet dream. I thought she was one of the most beautiful girls in the world. I loved New York. It was amazing.

Dennis took me to a club called Danceteria on 21st Street. There were all of these different rooms on several floors. There were all kinds of people there. From rockers to punks, older guys in three-piece suits, drag queens, and all sorts of human trash. It was summer, and they had opened the roof and called it Wuthering Heights. They barbecued burgers up there, and you could look out over the city. Gregg Gerson showed up with his friend Arturo. He handed me a corner of a plastic bag that was full of cocaine. Gregg seemed to have it all the time. Gregg had another bag that had 10 little envelopes in it. That's how I found out that Gregg was a coke dealer. Dennis thought it might be a problem, but I didn't think it was a big deal. I thought it was a bonus. I met Billy Idol's keyboard player there, Judy Dozier, and I went home with her and fucked her. She wasn't the new wave sex goddess I imagined, but just a normal New York City chick, who lived alone with her cat. I felt like I was moving up a level.

Dennis did not want me to sign with David Krebs, he pleaded with me. I hadn't talked to David yet about signing any papers, so I told Dennis I wouldn't sign anything just yet. My trip to New York was ending, and I had to go back to Seattle. I was going to get all of my amps and guitars and move there for good in a couple of weeks. I left my V at 399, and Dennis put me in a taxi back to JFK.

I didn't stay home long. I got rid of my car, and packed up my music gear and everything I owned that could fit in two suitcases, and moved to New York City. I spoke to Dennis on the phone before I left. He was having problems at Leber-Krebs, Dennis said something to David about him wanting me to sign with Steve Leber, and David got pissed off and fired him. Dennis said, "You can't stay at 399, I quit CCC, and do not call David Krebs under any circumstances. Just stay with Gregg and don't sign anything, You hear me? Don't sign anything!"

Dennis sent Gregg Gerson to pick me up at JFK. Gregg got me at baggage claim. Billy Squier was collecting his bags at the same time from a different flight. I tried to talk to him, but he was very arrogant. He just smirked at me, and looked the other way. He said hello to Gregg, but not to me.

Gregg came to get me in his friend Arturo's car, a beat-up brown Chevy Impala. I sat in the back, and they passed me a bag with two grams of coke in it and a straw. By the time we got to Gregg's place at 110 McDougal Street, I was too high to speak. Next to his flat was a tiny clothing store that sold rock and roll gear called CC Star. I went inside for a minute, and looked around. They had a black leather jacket with a red snakeskin lapel. I bought it, but I was too high to deal with anybody. We took all my stuff up three flights of stairs to Gregg's place.

Gregg Gerson called himself The Gersonic Flow. He had these two chicks staying at his tiny studio apartment. He sectioned off a loft bed with a little desk underneath where he listened to cassette tapes and did cocaine. The room didn't have an air conditioner, and it was really hot and muggy. The place was a rathole. Gregg had two cats, Mr. & Mrs. Doobie, and I was allergic to both of them. Both girls that were staying there were butt ugly. It got dark and I calmed down a bit, got a falafel, and Gregg played me cassettes of Steve Stevens' rough song ideas that he was working on with Billy Idol. By 5:00 in the morning I was able to sleep. I got up at 10:00 AM, Gregg hadn't slept, and I felt like shit. I called David Krebs from a pay phone, and he told me to meet him at the Parker Meridian Hotel for lunch.

When I got there, David was already seated. He ordered a lobster salad, and I ordered a steak. He pulled out a contract and wanted me to sign it. I looked at it and said, "I need a place to stay and I don't have any money." He said, "I'll put you in the Gramercy Hotel, and give you a salary of $200 a week." I signed the contract, and we ate lunch. David Krebs was now my manager. If I wasn't under the weather from my drugged-out ride from the airport, I might have screamed.

David took me back to the office, and had Debby bring me a check for $200. She took me down to the bank on 55th and 6th and told me who to speak with to cash checks so I could do it on my own. David had his secretary Patti O'Toole book me a room at the Gramercy Park Hotel, and once I got there, I felt like I could breathe again.

When I went to 399 to get my guitar, Dennis was furious. He spoke in a very mean tone "Don't talk to me or I'll beat the shit out of you. I swear, I'll fucking kill you. Don't say a word." He handed me my guitar, and I backed out quick. I tried to explain, but he felt betrayed. I just couldn't survive another day in Gregg Gerson's apartment. I grabbed a taxi to the Gramercy Park Hotel, a place I would call home for the next month.

The following day, I took a taxi to the office and there was a copy of the *New York Post* in the backseat. I looked through it, and started reading *Page Six*. I read a few items, and then I put it down. When I got to the office, Patti O'Toole smiled like I had done something wrong. She grabbed me, showed me the *Post*, and said, "Did you see this?" Right below the last item I read, before I put the paper down in the taxi, I saw "Record companies are fighting to sign the latest heavy metal rocker, Adam Bomb, A competitor for Adam Ant?" All of New York City reads *Page Six*. I was starting to feel like a 'somebody,' like I really mattered.

There were lots of bands playing all around New York in 1984. The Ritz always had shows, and The Cat Club had rock bands on Wednesday nights. A big venue for rock and metal was L'Amour, which had clubs in Queens and Brooklyn. I got Gregg's friend Arturo to take me out there. Arturo owned a limousine, and had a business card. He called his company Kadillac Car Service. He also sold blow. He drove me out to L'Amours in the limo, and he'd always give me free coke. Life was pretty good. I had no trouble getting female attention in New York City.

There was a club called Nirvana on 42nd Street at 1 Times Square on the top floor where they drop the ball on New Year's Eve. It was an Indian restaurant the rest of the time, but on Sunday nights there was a big music party where people could get up and play. It was usually blues jams with sax players and three singers, but sometimes cool people would get up and play. I met the Raspberries singer, Eric Carmen, and Joe Lynn Turner from Rainbow. He looked like he wore a wig. After my band with Phil, Jimmy, and Gregg rehearsed a few more times at SIR, we did a jump-up at Nirvana. We tore the house down.

I met a good-looking singer named Ray Gillen at Nirvana. He looked just like Ian Gillan from Deep Purple. He had a pretty girlfriend with blonde curly hair named Daisy Cohen. I was buzzing around, and he kept stopping me and wanted me to sit down and talk to him, so I did. We became friends, and I brought him into Krebs' office, and he became friendly with Paul O'Neill. They talked about putting a band around Ray with Bobby Rondinelli on drums. Krebs thought Ray Gillen was a star. He definitely had that look. Out of nowhere, Ray got offered the job to be the lead singer in Black Sabbath after Glenn Hughes dropped out mid-tour. Just two days from getting the call, Ray Gillen was singing *War Pigs* at Meadowlands with Tony Iommi, Geezer Butler, and Eric Singer on drums, touring the arenas of America.

Arturo took me to The Ritz, and we floated around the VIP room and just hung out, no matter who was playing. He knew the club manager, Michael Scopino. We'd always go down in the office and do coke. Arturo was popular. He got excited over musicians like Joey Ramone, who was always hanging out at The Ritz. Arturo was friendly with a black security guard who wore a bullet-proof vest, Jerry Adams. We had free rein at The Ritz, and all of the crew there loved to party. I was friendly with the soundman, Charlie Martin, and the video controller, Richard Zimm. The Ritz had an amazing sound system and a $100,000 video setup that was just like a TV studio. I asked Scopino if my band could play there, and I got my first gig at the Ritz booked for August 14, 1984. My 21st birthday.

I went out to some after-hours clubs called Save the Robots and AM/PM, and they were just drug dens. I just went by myself and observed. There were a lot of bridge and tunnel mobsters. I didn't mix in; I just looked at girls and stood around like a wallflower. I went to a club called The Limelight where I spoke the doorman who was an aspiring television actor for about 20 minutes; his name was Bruce Thomas. I wasn't really dressed up, but he let me in for free to go see the inside. It was in a church, and it was all painted up decadent with dark lighting. It had a main disco room with a huge stage six feet off the ground and three levels of balconies and stairways. It was big enough to get lost in. I wanted to play there. I didn't know who to ask, but I was going to find out.

My band rehearsed for a month at SIR. Victory and Billy Squier were also rehearsing there. I was playing Jimmy Crespo's 1959 Les Paul, and the strap fell off. The guitar hit the ground and the neck broke. I freaked out. I thought that was the end of my band. Jimmy wasn't mad. He was always really mellow. He told me, "I thought I was going to have to sell it but I guess I can't now. I was really looking for a way to keep that guitar, so thanks." I gave him the money to fix it, but I always felt really bad about breaking Jimmy Crespo's guitar neck.

Rick Keefer got a deal for my album in Japan with JVC Records. We called it *Fatal Attraction*. Even though the band didn't play on it, we shot a cover with photographer Geoffrey Thomas. He also shot the album cover for Victory, which was a photo of a girl wearing fishnet stockings, panties and bra, lying on her back, with her legs spread in the air to make a V.

I let Phil Feit wear the red vest I had worn in the *Shape of the World* video. Crespo wore a leather jacket and his hat. I wore jeans and a white top that had Japanese letters on it. Gregg showed up late wearing the same green army jumpsuit he always wore. He looked like he had cut his hair himself with a bowl on his head. He wore an army surplus utility belt that had a concealed knife for a buckle, a beeper, some pouches where he kept his blow, and his nunchucks which he'd pull out and demonstrate like he was Bruce Lee. Phil was kind of pissed that Gregg was up all night. While we were getting made up, Gregg fell asleep on a table, flat on his back. It took us about 15 minutes to wake him up from his three-day coke binge before we could start the shoot.

Geoffrey Thomas also shot a girl's body wearing see-through lace to be the background of the album cover. In a few days, he sent the contact sheets to Krebs' office. On the band shot we picked, I thought I looked like a 15-year-old girl. Krebs thought it was an image he could sell around the world. He had Geoffrey Thomas take out the band and use that photo for the album cover, and the whole band photo for the back.

The layout was done by Spencer Drate. I was searching for a band logo. He had ten drawn up, but I didn't like any of them. We had a deadline for the Japanese release, so I closed my eyes and picked one.

Krebs had showcased the band to Derek Shulman of Polygram. Derek used to play bass in Gentle Giant, who opened for Yes at the very first concert I saw. He thought *Russian Roulette* was a hit. He wanted to sign the band. Derek took me to see Rush at Madison Square Garden, and he introduced me to Alex Lifeson, who was also on the label. Polygram wanted an act to follow Bon Jovi. I wanted to take Derek's offer, but he was only offering $80,000, so David kept bringing more A&R people down to SIR to see us.

I saw Derek again at a dinner party at Ric Browde's apartment. I felt bad that David didn't take his offer. I could've forced him to sign with Derek, but I took Krebs' advice. He was sure he could get more money. In hindsight, that might have been the biggest mistake I ever made in my life.

Nearly every label came down to SIR to see us. MCA, Chrysalis, Warner Bros., Epic, Columbia, A&M, and Elektra Records were all interested in signing Adam Bomb. It was like auditioning for Wall Street cokeheads in cheap suits. One lady in her 40s came in that was kind of bubbly. Her name was Carole Childs. She watched us, and she really liked it. She gave me a big hug before she left. She was from Geffen Records.

Debby Prisco had broken up with Dennis, and she moved out of 399 East 72nd and got a place on Second Avenue. David had me moved into his place at 2 East End for a few weeks, and when 399 opened up, David put me in there. I went out and had a late night. I was awakened with a phone call. It was David. He said, "Geffen Records offered us a six-album deal with a $125,000 advance." I wondered, 'Am I dreaming?'

Super Rock '84

The contract for Geffen Records was as thick as a phone book. I couldn't understand any of it. I just trusted David Krebs. The contract was handled by Rick Keefer's lawyer, Bernie Fishbach. All that I really understood was we had two guaranteed releases at $125,000 for the first record and $150,000 for the second. There was a variable allowance for tour support, $10,000 for music gear, and two videos per record with a budget of $40,000 per clip. Then they had two options to extend the deal. I signed the back page and wrote, 'Thanks for being there David' right under my signature. To celebrate, he took me out to dinner. "Where would you like to go?" Krebs asked. My answer was, "McDonald's."

Leber-Krebs and Sea-West Productions were partners on my first album. Keefer got around $60,000. Geffen paid off Tony Schiff for the *Shape of the World* video. David made a $50,000 publishing deal with Warner/Chappell, and Keefer got half of that as well. David also got a $10,000 advance from a merchandise company called Brokum.

David signed me with CAA, a company who handled movie actors, as he thought Geffen would try and break me into movies. CAA's strengths were definitely not rock tours, and they put a kid who was just starting out in charge of booking us in clubs.

I didn't get any big check. I never asked for one. I didn't even have a bank account. I just wanted David Krebs to take care of me and get me on giant festival stage like CaliFFornia Jam, or a big gig at Seattle Center Coliseum.

I went home to visit my dad and the dog. I showed my dad the contract. He didn't know what to make of it; I already signed it anyway. All of my friends were completely blown away that I got a deal on Geffen Records. It was huge news all over town. I had pulled off quite the coup.

Brad Sinsel formed a new version of TKO using Scott Earl, and the guitarist from Culprit, Kjartan Kristoffersen, and to complete his lineup, he used the drummer from the band Ridge, who beat Tyrant at the Battle of the Bands, Ken Mary. Keefer made a deal with Combat Records for a $5,000 advance for the TKO *In Your Face* album. Brad took a photo with him standing in the air raising his fist while Susie Wimberly, Brad's wife, was on her back, knocked out, wearing boxing gloves. On the back was a band photo. Nowhere on the album credits did it say that I played all of the guitars on that record; Kjartan was taking credit for my guitar playing. It was misleading, but everyone around town knew I did that record. I had my deal with Geffen, so I didn't think too much about TKO. I was moving on, but that record was my baby too. I wanted the world to know it, and I think Brad wanted to take that away from me.

I went to visit Chris DeGarmo while I was home. I went to their rehearsal room where they practiced with headphones, in drummer Scott Rockenfield's parents' basement. He was packing his suitcase to go on tour. They had tour jackets with European flags on them. Chris was really doing well. EMI was really behind them. Rail had just won the MTV Basement Tapes competition. The prize was a record deal with EMI. I saw Rick Knotts, and he said, "It's so cool; I can't believe it. All of my students are getting record deals."

I overheard Terry Young complaining that EMI was not giving Rail enough support, like they did for Queensryche, but I thought we all were pretty lucky to have record deals.

In August of 1984, David Krebs flew me to Tokyo to do press at Super Rock '84, a show headlined by the Michael Schenker Group, Whitesnake, Scorpions, Bon Jovi, and Anvil. The first version of *Fatal Attraction* was being released in Japan in September, and the record company had organized for me to be included in the press interviews at the festival.

Every band and the staff from Leber-Krebs stayed in the Tokyo Prince Hotel. I met with a guy named Aki Morishita from my label JVC Victor, and I did an interview for *Burrn!* Magazine. We sat at table while he smoked Mild Seven cigarettes and ordered $20 cups of coffee. The hotel was bustling with business men. It looked like the expensive hotels in Honolulu, but the rooms were like broom closets.

Backstage at Super Rock, I watched one of Krebs assistants, Paul O'Neill, run around and do errands for Krebs and the other bands. He acted important at Super Rock, but I never understood what his job was. Paul played guitar in a band called Slowburn. He failed to get a record deal, and went to work for David Krebs as an all-purpose flunkie. Paul O'Neill was the first name in the special thanks on the

Japanese release of *Fatal Attraction,* even though he had nothing to do with the album. David Krebs had high hopes for him.

In New York, Paul handled Victory and another band called Cathedral, with guitarists Mark Cunningham and John Corabi. He was also putting together a band he was selling called Heaven, with an Australian singer who was the lead vocalist for AC/DC for a day, until they shattered his dreams and hired Brian Johnson.

Paul said, "I like the Tammi song," but I could tell that Paul O'Neill didn't take me seriously. I was in the way of his agenda with David, who he always called Boss. Ever since Dennis quit working for David and started working for Steve Leber, the staff's attitude towards me changed. There were a lot of inter-office politics going on, and a ton of gossip. I no longer had anyone on my side who was working for David. Krebs did warn me, "Familiarity breeds contempt." It certainly didn't take long. Eventually Dennis warmed up to me and we became friends again, but the damage was done. As far as I was concerned, I did what I wanted to do, and signed a contract in blood with David Krebs

Tammi Ventrella was at Super Rock. I talked to her while David met with Olaf Schröter and Herman Rarebell. The backstage was crowded, and Doc McGhee congratulated me on signing with David Krebs. He said, "David Krebs is the best manager in the business. You'll do really well with him. Everything I know, I learned from him." I walked over into a corner and talked with Jon Bon Jovi. He was writing lyrics in a notebook for his second album. He was a really nice guy, but like most of the other rock stars, he wondered what the fuck I was doing there. I wasn't playing. I liked watching the groups on the video feed, but I hated being there and not playing. I had no idea what it took to play gigs like that. That was a manager's job.

There were no drugs in Japan. The only people who had a joint were the guys in Anvil. Paul O'Neill introduced me to the singer, Lips. He was smoking a little roach and he passed it to me, but it was finished.

After Michael Schenker played, we all went back to the hotel in buses. It was only midnight. Herman Rarebell and Matthias Jabs took me to Roppongi with a preppy guy named Rob Steinberg, who did press for Scorpions. He carried a list of phrases you could say in Japanese to get by. Outside of the rock shows, people spoke no English in Japan.

We took a cab, and got out and walked for a few blocks, I was a million miles from Seattle. There were street vendors selling mystery kebabs, and the streets were packed. Everywhere was lit up like Times Square. We went to a bar called Lexington Queen. Matthias was complaining that Ratt had made it to number six on the *Billboard* album charts. Nobody in metal liked to see other bands do good. It was all a big competition.

We sat down next to some attractive American models who might have been hookers. My song *You'll Never Know* was getting a lot of attention, so I explained it to Herman. "It's not really about her. It's about wanting what you've achieved. It's my dream to go out and play big shows, and have a life like you live. When I went to bring over my tape, seeing her in that hotel room was like looking at a trophy of a man who had it all." Herman hugged me. Then he looked at me with a cold face and said. "Did you fuck her?" I said, "No." Then he said, "Do you wanna fuck her?" He had a bit of a jealous streak. I said, "Who wouldn't? But I didn't write the song with that intention. It's just a song; don't worry. You're one of the biggest rock stars on the planet. I grew up on Scorpions, I played the songs you wrote in my first band. C'mon Herman, give me a break. I'm just a fan." Then he started to chat up the three American models who were sitting at the table.

I rode back from Roppongi in a cab with Rob. He picked up a girl he'd been talking to at the bar while I was being lectured by Matthias and Herman. Rob took her back to the hotel. She was the Hollywood movie actress, Diane Lane. She acted like a real bitch when I saw them the next morning at the hotel breakfast.

I didn't have anything to do on the day off. I got bored, so I let a groupie come up to my room. All of these girls would just wait in the lobby for some rock star or roadie to take them up to their room, so I picked one and invited her up. Once we were alone, it was too strange for me. I didn't feel like Van Halen. It was no fun to go to Japan and not play a show. She couldn't speak English, and the room was so tiny. I couldn't understand her, and I told her, "I don't want to do fuck with you, just leave." I wandered around close to the hotel and tried to shop but found nothing, went to McDonald's, and spent whatever yen I had that Krebs have given me. It cost around $30. I wasn't really McLovin' Japan. Those three days were longest time I had gone without smoking pot since I was 15. I felt like shit.

That evening, the Scorpions had a dinner party in a fancy Japanese restaurant. I sat silent the whole dinner. Everyone was talking in German. Herman was telling his bandmates that I wrote a song about Tammi, and then he started talking in German. The girl next to me asked me if I'd ever been to Germany. I said, "No. They'd probably put me in a camp." Nobody heard me but David, and he said to me, "Not smart." I wanted to play Japan, not tag along, and I thought the whole trip was stupid. It was a long way to go to do just one interview. Watching the other bands have all the fun was a waste of my time. I didn't want to be a fan anymore. I wanted to be taken seriously.

When we got back to New York, my band played a show at The Ritz on my 21st birthday. David hired a road manager named Bob Kelleher, who worked for Aerosmith before they split, to handle the day-to-day issues with Adam Bomb. They called him Kelly. David told me, "Kelly had a very bad cocaine problem. The aftermath of Aerosmith had too many casualties, and I want to give Kelly a break. He's a nice guy. I always liked Kelly." He came in and met me. He was a stalky guy with short hair, an alligator shirt, and a metal briefcase. If he worked for Aerosmith, those were good enough credentials for me. He got the job, and David paid him $500 a week.

Rick Keefer came to New York to finalize some deals. We went to see a new movie called *This is Spinal Tap* that was playing at the Gramercy Theatre. We thought it was hilarious. David Krebs and Scorpions saw it and they didn't think it was funny at all. They thought *Spinal Tap* was a parody about them. So did Aerosmith. That movie was my rock and roll bible. But they only scratched the surface of the humorous problems a rock band could face, and I was about to learn them all first hand for the next 35 years.

Ric Browde invited me over to his apartment for lunch. When I got there, I was really surprised to see Tammi Ventralla. She had just cut her hair a bit shorter. It was a hot, muggy summer, and she looked great. Ric left to go to a meeting, and I was alone with Tammi in the laundry room. She was just wearing a skimpy little top and shorts. By the way she looked at me, I knew I was in trouble.

Tammi kissed me. I knew it was a bad idea, but she looked so good, and she smelled great. She had teased eyebrows, just a little bit of makeup, and her lips were perfect. I asked her, "Are you sure we should do this? I could get in real big trouble if anyone found out and Herman would kill me." She said, "He'll never know. He'd kill me

too." I thought about it for a split second, Was I willing to chance screwing up everything to fuck this girl? One look at her eyes was all it took to answer that question, I dove in head first. We fucked for hours. I left before Ric got back. I was infatuated with Tammi. I didn't have the power to say no.

I saw her again the very next day. I came over to Ric's. She was alone, and we had sex. She wanted me to come with her in

a taxi to the airport. I loved her smell. I felt safe in that taxi with her. We made out the whole way. She flew home to LA, and told me to call her when I came to Hollywood. The next time I saw Ric Browde I could tell he knew. He set it up, I never said anything about it. He was at Krebs' office, and he smirked, and said, "So how's Tammi?" I said, "Umm, I think she's fine. I don't know, I left a few minutes after you did." He said, "Don't worry; I won't tell Herman."

When the band wasn't rehearsing, I went to the office and helped David. He'd give me money do go do errands for him, like go buy weed. We smoked pot everyday together. Olaf Schröter got pissed off at me because David was always calling me in to interrupt their meetings. He'd say, "Adam, roll me one." David wanted Olaf to be his co-manager on my career, but Olaf just thought I was a crazy kid.

I loved hanging out at the office. It was like hanging out at a friend's house after school. We listened to music, talked about bands, and smoked pot. Musicians would come by and hang out all the time. I was David Krebs' pet project. I had free rein at CCC.

David Krebs signed my band members to a management contract, and put them on a salary of $100 a week. We played shows in New York at Danceteria, a small club called Trax, and another show at The Ritz. This time, Steven Tyler was in the audience. He was hanging by the soundboard, and by the urging of Nitebob, the former soundman, for Aerosmith, he went up close. I freaked when I saw Steven Tyler in the front row of my show. I went right up to him. I think it made Jimmy feel a little strange.

We played shows at L'Amour in Brooklyn and The Cat Club in Manhattan. These club gigs were always packed. When we weren't playing, I'd go around town in Arturo's limo, picking up rock sluts at clubs, while Arturo made his rounds. I was doing a lot of cocaine, and we got into every club for free. We were VIP everywhere we went. It was easy as pie to get chicks in the back of a limo.

New York was full of nightlife. We spent many nights at the China Club next to the Beacon Theatre. I wasn't allowed to bring girls back to 399, but I did occasionally. I took home a hot blonde waitress from the China Club, and somehow, Krebs found out and yelled at me. 399 was just a temporary place for me to stay until David Krebs came up with a better solution.

After 15 years of success, David Krebs and Steve Leber were slowly dissolving their partnership. They still got credited as co-managers on their baby band records, but David wanted to move to California, and run his business from the West Coast. He rented a house on Broad Beach in Malibu. His next-door neighbor was Goldie Hawn. After he got set up, Laura Kaufman moved out to California as his assistant, and he worked out of an office he set up at his beach house. It made sense for me, since Geffen Records was based there. Kelly arranged for the band to go to Hollywood.

Kelly and I went to LA first, and we went shopping. I bought music gear with the $10,000 budget allocated by Geffen Records. I bought four Marshall cabinets, ordered two Energy Group bass cabinets from Charlie Kester in Seattle, Anvil road cases for everything, and a big case to hold six guitars. I bought a Gibson Hummingbird acoustic and a 1958 TV Model Les Paul Special from Norman's Rare Guitars in Reseda. It was called TV Model because of the yellow paint job. Back in the 50s if you wore a white guitar, it wouldn't show up on a TV screen. I sent it to Mike Lull, and he installed two vintage PAF pickups in it. I used my two 50-watt Marshall heads; you could never improve upon those. I also got some money for clothes.

I saw Tammi when I was in Hollywood, and went over to her place to spend the night. The phone rang, but she didn't answer. Whoever was calling kept ringing back. She finally picked up the phone, and it was Herman. She insisted she was alone, but he was having jealous fits. He knew something was up. Of course, Ric Browde had told him. Herman was his best friend.

I told Tammi, "We gotta cool it before I get in deep shit. Just deny it." She responded, "It's no big deal. I'm breaking up with him. He's fucking every groupie in America. I won't let anyone hurt you. I promise." I knew it was going to come back to haunt me. Once it became office gossip, I was doomed. Ric Browde had played me like a cheap guitar. I didn't think he was out to get me. But many people in New York are supportive until you get some sort of success, and then they take joy in trying to shoot you down. I gave them some pretty heavy ammunition.

Tammi was a goddess. I thought she was the most beautiful woman in the world. If I was going to get winged for falling in love, then that would be my fate. I knew I couldn't keep her. I didn't want to. I had a whole world waiting for me to discover. It was just like the song depicted. We had a love affair, drifted apart, and Tammi will forever own a small space in my heart. Before I left she told me, "That's my song and no matter what anyone does, they can never take that away from me and I love you for that."

Herman and Tammi did break up. She was going out all the time with my friend Bruce Johannesson, but they were just friends. She used the stripper name Fasha, and was *Penthouse* Pet of the Month of April '85. She got wasted a lot, but she was always beautiful. The next time I saw Herman was at the Rainbow, he threw a drink in my face and said, "You fucked my wife." At least he didn't kill me. A few months later, they got back together, and he married her. They got divorced a year later.

It only took a little while before it got around, and I got lectured. Krebs was pissed. He said that I blew my chance to be the support act on the next Scorpions tour, but it had already been given to the band Victory. Out of all the mistakes I made, Tammi was my favorite.

David Krebs signed Victory to a management contract solely on Rudolf Schenker's personal recommendation. They also had the same agent, Nick Caris. The members of Victory were from Germany and only came to New York to go on tour with Scorpions. It was the plan way before I ever came into the picture. I had no chance of supporting a Scorpions tour. I could tell that when I was in Japan. It was always meant for Victory. Scorpions were also meeting secretly with Doc McGhee behind David Krebs' back. But I surely did not help David Krebs' relationship with Olaf and the guys in Scorpions.

David Krebs did not encourage wild behavior. He already partied his legend. He'd seen that movie before, and witnessed the casualties. It was very confusing from everything I had ever read, learned, or knew about rock bands. Some managers encouraged artists to go off the deep end, but not David Krebs. He became like more of a father figure than a manager. I was afraid that if he saw me on drugs or doing bad stuff, he'd drop me, and I had nowhere to fall to. So I just went wild out of Krebs' eye like everyone else did.

The Beverly Sunset

For the first week in LA, I had been staying alone at a notorious dwelling for rock musicians - the Oakwood Apartments. The room was left behind by Dennis Feldman of the Michael Schenker Group. There was a skanky groupie packing up as I arrived. Kelly had made a deal with the Beverly Sunset Hotel, a two-story motel with a pool, next to Tower Records on Sunset Blvd. He got three rooms at a monthly rate. I wanted to get a house like Black 'N Blue, but Kelly thought it was more practical to stay at Beverly Sunset. It had a diner, and was walking distance to Geffen Records and the Rainbow. We had a rented van, and Kelly hired a guy named Terry to be our roadie. The band members were now getting $300 a week.

Jimmy Crespo, Phil Feit, and Gregg Gerson all flew out on the same plane to Hollywood. Gregg was his usual nightmare-self. He said he only brought along a small bag of blow and the guys said Gregg drove everyone crazy on the plane. Gregg told me that he finished it by the time the flight arrived and he was going to dry out in Hollywood. I didn't want him to fuck things up for the band just because of his cocaine addiction.

Jimmy and I shared a room on the second floor. Phil and Gregg took a connecting room, and Kelly had his own room on the first floor. In the morning we ate in the hotel coffee shop downstairs. Gregg ordered breakfast, ate it, then he immediately ordered lunch. He lied, and had brought an ounce of coke, not just an eight ball, so he was going to eat two meals and go on a coke binge. The waitress brought Gregg a salad, and he recognized some guy who wandered in the diner. Gregg said, "Hey my brother. Do that voodoo that you do so well. What ya doing here? You wanna taste?" The guy responded, "Taste of what, your salad?" Gregg said, "No, a taste. You know, a bump," and Gregg started sniffing. The guy laughed, and shook his head no.

Tommy Thayer and the rest of Black 'N Blue were all impressed that I got a deal with Geffen. Their manager Garo was taken aback by it. Tommy said, "Bro, you got a deal on Geffen. That's huge. It really shook Garo up." He regretted not trying to sign me. Garo cornered me at the Roxy, and said "Listen Son. You're making a big mistake. You should be playing with my son Peter."

Aerosmith had a new manager, Tim Collins, who was very anti-drug. He met with David a lot, and always got down on him for smoking pot. He was trying to settle with Krebs, who still had Aerosmith under contract. Tim Collins wanted David to give up all of his rights for nothing. Aerosmith planned a tour without a new record or a label. I met Joe Perry at the Sunset Marquis swimming pool. He was raving about Bedrock Amps, but I preferred my Marshalls. I felt a little weird talking to him, since I played with Jimmy Crespo, and I was Krebs' new boy. At this point, I idolized Steven Tyler. I had no choice anymore but to be a lead singer, and Tyler was the coolest that ever was. But Joe Perry did say something more prolific than anything anyone's ever said, *'Let the Music Do the Talking.'*

I got a telephone call at the pool at the Beverly Sunset. Joey Kramer, the drummer of Aerosmith, wanted to talk to me. He sounded really high, and he talked my ear off for 45 minutes about Krebs, Kelly, and Jimmy Crespo. Rock stars were calling me out of the blue.

The Beverly Sunset was a real shithole, and hookers were always throwing furniture into the pool. I saw the guitarist of Metallica, James Hetfield, checking into a room at the motel. He just nodded at me like a redneck trucker. Gregg Gerson tore off the door between our connecting rooms because I took one of his sodas. There was a Mexican caretaker that fixed the problems caused by our destruction. The owner was an old Iranian dude named Mr. Savis. He would always talk over the public address system and say, "Danny to the desk, Danny to the desk," and this guy that looked like Cheech Marin would come to repair the daily damage or fish the furniture out of the pool.

A cop car stopped to let me cross at a crosswalk, then they gave me a ticket for jaywalking. That same night, I was walking back from the Rainbow at three in the morning, and I got mugged. A car with five black dudes pulled over in the middle of Sunset Blvd. Two guys beat the shit out of me, and the other two tried to steal the girl's purse. There were no cops around. I had over $300 in my zipper pocket, but they didn't get it. I picked myself up off the street, and I knocked on Kelly's door. I was a bloody mess. I told him I wanted to move, but we never left the Sunset Strip. That shithole cost over $3,000 a month for three rooms. We wound up staying there for almost a year.

Our first gig in Hollywood was at the Pomona Valley Auditorium. The support act was a group called Poison. The blond singer, Bret Michaels, was really cute. He was about my age, and he was an Aerosmith fan. He was really excited to meet Jimmy Crespo. He wore a button with a picture of Steven Tyler on it. I thought the drummer Rikki Rockett had a really cool name. The bassist Bobby Dall, and the guitarist Matt Smith, were not very good. They had an original called *Rock Like a Rocker,* and they played a lot of covers. They were just kids, but they looked cool.

The guys in my band were pissed at me that I took my own dressing room. Carole Childs, from the label, was there with David Krebs and Laura Kaufman. The band did really good, and it was a packed crowd. People went to see metal no matter who was playing, and my band had a big buzz on the Sunset Strip.

I told Carole that I was bored during the daytime in Hollywood, so she invited me over to the office, and she introduced me to the Geffen staff. We went to lunch at Palm Restaurant. I kind of felt like her toy boy. She didn't know much about rock or metal. She just liked *SST* and AC/DC type rock. She signed me as her rock act and she was in direct competition with the other two A&R guys at Geffen - Tom Zutant and John Kalodner, who signed Sammy Hagar, Whitesnake, and Black 'N Blue.

Carole Childs hooked up with Bob Dylan at his son Jakob's bar mitzvah. She was his secret wife for three years, and he'd go to parties with her as her date, and leave with other women. They broke it off around the time Carole signed me. When I asked her why they split, she said, "The answer is blowing in the wind."

Carole Childs signed Terri Nunn and Berlin, the band Quarterflash, and Maria McKee - a singer she had been nurturing for three years for a band called Lone Justice who opened for U2. David Geffen himself had made the deals with John Lennon, Peter Gabriel, and Don Henley. The company president was a big guy named Ed Rosenblatt. I thought since David Krebs was close friends with David Geffen, we had a direct line to the top, and we did. The A&R guys knew this too.

John Kalodner didn't like David Krebs or my record. He also didn't like Carole Childs, who was David Geffen's friend. I always liked David Geffen. He was a nice guy who was always full of encouragement. I saw him at the movie theater when Phil and I went to see *Desperately Seeking Susan*, Madonna's first film. Geffen offered me to sit next to him, but there was only one seat, so Phil and I sat together somewhere else.

David Geffen   *industry giant*

Jimmy Crespo had a lot of girls coming around to the hotel. One of them was a former Aerosmith groupie, a cute chunky blonde with huge tits, but her eyes were really pinned from smoking heroin. I hated that shit, and I didn't want anybody doing smack around the band. I thought if David found out, he would dump us, so I had to get rid of these girls. I just didn't want anything to do with heroin. We had enough problems with drugs.

I was going to the Rainbow every night, and there was a lot of coke. If I got too high, I would try to hide my face when I got home by tilting my head so my hair would hide my face. Kelly and the band would say I was tilting, and take the piss out me. But I wasn't always wasted. For my 21st birthday, David Krebs took me out to the Rainbow. I showed my ID to the doorman, Steady. He looked at it, and said, "So you're finally legal."

I wanted to put the band on the record, but I didn't want to recut the songs. I wasn't sure that the live band would sound good enough to record as a group. I created my songs differently than most bands. I made these songs by creating them in the studio with Rick Keefer. I wasn't sure if I could even sing in another studio. Rick Keefer brought the tapes to LA, and we overdubbed tracks at Cherokee Studios on Fairfax.

Jimmy Crespo now had a Charvel guitar with a Floyd Rose, which had been updated with fine tuners. Mine was still the one made in

Floyd's basement that took ages to tune. Jimmy played a lead on *SST*, and lead and acoustic on *All the Young Dudes*. Phil Feit played on *SST, Dudes,* and *Fatal Attraction.* Gregg Gerson played drums on *SST, Dudes,* and *Fatal* as well. Gregg was high during the sessions. He was always high. His fills sounded like someone throwing a drum set down a flight of stairs, but it worked. Gregg was a pro, and did good takes on *Fatal* and *Dudes.* Now that the band had their touch on the album, Keefer flew back to Hawaii and mixed.

There was an issue with certain people at the label about Keefer's mixes. Carole Childs wanted us to remix *SST* and *I Want My Heavy Metal* with David Thoener, a remix artist who worked on Aerosmith's *Toys In The Attic* and David Bowie's *Young Americans*. The thing was, Rick Keefer had printed all the effects to tape so there was not much Thoener could do to change the sound. He put my voice through a tape echo, and that was about it. Geffen paid him $5,000. I hardly noticed a difference. Neither did Rick Keefer, who mastered the finished album in Hollywood with Bernie Grundman. There were a lot of changes from the Japanese version. I loved it. When I watched the test pressing spin in Carole Childs' office, I started to cry. I couldn't believe how far I'd come.

We had a big gig at The Troubadour. My father came with Joanie and Lisa Silverman. Lisa made me some white silk lab coat, with ripped lace on it. It looked like a bad wedding gown. Everyone from Geffen Records had come to the show. The front bar was full of scene makers, and Gregg was talking to some girl. He tried to escort the girl into the venue, but the security guard would not let her in with a drink. Gregg started arguing with the guy, pulled out his nunchucks, and started his Bruce Lee routine. The huge black security guard threw him out on his ass. They didn't want to let Gregg back in to play the show. Gregg wasn't the only rocker to get 86'd from the Troubadour. John Lennon got ejected in 1974 for heckling The Smothers Brothers. Kelly had to pay the security guy $50 to let Gregg back inside. We did the show. The band was tight and aggressive. The label people loved it, but I could tell we were skating on thin ice.

At another gig at The Hollywood Palace, we couldn't find Gregg for hours. We were all frantic looking for him. About five minutes before the show was supposed to start, we found him. Terry took me outside, and he slid open the loading door of the equipment truck. Gregg was in there, holding a glass pipe and a torch, freebasing coke with Ray, the hellion who lived on Martel Street across from the Black 'N Blue house. Gregg looked up and said, "Where were you guys? I've been looking all over for you." His eyes were big black circles. Things were getting out of hand.

Black 'N Blue were playing in Fort Lauderdale, Florida, opening for Aerosmith on December 18, 1984. David Krebs was putting together a live album from old Aerosmith tapes for Columbia Records called *Classics Live.* David wanted me to go see Aerosmith to see how they were holding up. He flew me to Florida. I got backstage with Black 'N Blue, and I saw Steven Tyler. He was hiding in his dressing room with a guy named Richie Supa, and I heard he was still doing heroin. Steven Tyler was amazing onstage. When he saw me, he gave me a big hug. They hadn't put a record out in over two years but they were selling out big venues, all across the country. John Kalodner signed Aerosmith to Geffen Records, and they were about to record an album called *Done with Mirrors.* They didn't need David Krebs, but I thought maybe, David Krebs needed them.

I went back to LA, and saw Krebs. There was nothing going on until the New Year. It was getting near the holidays, so Gregg went back to New York for Christmas. While he was away, Jimmy, Kelly, and I had a discussion, and decided Gregg's coke problem was affecting the group in a bad way. We all did a ton of coke too, but Gregg was just way too out of control. We had to get rid of him. I was the one who had to tell Gregg he was fired.

I was really upset about it. We had just added him to the album. But Gregg was causing too much shit in front of the Geffen people. On New Year's Eve, I called him up. He was screaming and crying on the phone, telling me his cat, Mr. Doobie, had just died. He was holding his dead cat in his arms. I told him, "Gregg, I have to fire you." He dropped the cat, took me off speaker, and changed his tone.

He couldn't believe what I just told him. He started screaming and begging, and I said, "You need to go to rehab." It was not a great moment. "I'm sorry my brother, but I have to let you go, We're going to get another drummer for now, and if you get your shit together, maybe you can get back in the band, but you need to fix yourself first or you're gonna die." He checked into a hospital, and they said he had a swollen heart. Firing him saved his life.

Jimmy and I went out later that night for New Year's Eve. We picked up two girls, and brought them back to the Beverly Sunset. The resident hotel hookers had done a 21-drawer salute at midnight. The swimming pool was full of furniture. Jimmy asked me, "Which one you want?" I didn't really care. I pointed to the one named Patti. Jimmy took the girl named Cynthia. Patti liked to do dirty things – she literally ate my insides for breakfast. When she came up for air from giving me a mouth enema, we could hear bones cracking from under the covers on Jimmy's bed. We were laughing 'til the sun came up. Jimmy Crespo and Cynthia wound up getting married, and they've been together ever since.

Gregg Gerson, Adam Bomb, Phil Feit, and Bob 'Kelly' Kelleher

1985

With the drummer spot open, I called Gary Thompson, and asked him if he wanted to try out for my band in Hollywood. He was still playing with Q5, but they weren't doing much. I could have forced it for him to be the new drummer, but I wanted Jimmy and Phil to be happy so I told Gary he had to audition for the guys. Gary flew down and played with us at SIR. I think he played so loud that he scared Jimmy. It didn't really feel right. Now that I was also a singer, everything we played had to be worked around my vocals. I didn't really realize that I had changed direction in music since we last played together. I was trying to become something that I wasn't already; a rock front man and a lead singer. It broke my heart to tell Gary he had to go home. Phil and Jimmy wanted to keep looking.

Phil was keen on Sandy Slavin, a drummer he used to play with in a group called Riot. Phil rang up Sandy, who was living at his grandmother's house in New Jersey. He was between bands, and looking for a gig. I saw him play with Riot, opening for Black Sabbath with Ronnie James Dio in Seattle, so I knew he was good. We flew him to Hollywood to audition for the band.

When I first met Sandy Slavin, I thought he had a nice smile. and looked very New York. He didn't drink or do drugs, and he was just into playing. Sandy moved into Phil's room, and we started a month of rehearsals at SIR, where I had auditioned for KISS.

We did a low-profile gig at Madame Wong's. There were only about 10 people there. I had my Seattle friends, David Morris and Paul Passerelli, come to Hollywood to be our roadies. During the previous year, David Morris got a job as a guitar tech for Queensryche. They went on tour with Dio and he went to England with them when they recorded their first full-length album, *The Warning*. Forcing David Morris to learn how to tune a guitar really paid off. Paul Passerelli had formed a band called Lipstick with his friend Brett Miller. They wrote a cool song called *Daily Grind,* and broke up. I liked having my Seattle friends around. I hoped it would keep me grounded, especially since I didn't hire Gary Thompson.

Sandy was a much stronger drummer than Gregg. He liked harder super-cranky music like Motorhead. He decorated his hotel room with food delivery menus, centerfolds, rock posters, and band ads from magazines. When he had covered the whole room, he dubbed it The Party Suite. We had a good rapport, and we were always bantering stupid jokes back and forth. The only time I ever saw him freak out is when somebody brought some balloons and put them in his room. Sandy Slavin had a fear of balloons and clowns. He didn't like to go out. He spent most nights with his practice pad watching Letterman.

Left to right: Phil Feit, Adam Bomb, Jimmy Crespo, Sandy Slavin

We played gigs at the Country Club, the Troubadour, and Gazzarri's. Before the Gazzarri's show, Carole Childs and Laura Kaufman took me out to dinner at Sushi on Sunset. They ordered over $200 of sushi. I got so drunk on sake, I missed the soundcheck. I didn't even have time to change for the show. The roadies had put my guitar volume on so quiet that it sounded like shit. I couldn't get a proper sound during my solo. My two Seattle friends came on stage during *All the Young Dudes* and started singing. It was a disaster. Laura said, "Carole thinks you're gonna be a really big star." I thought we sucked.

Signing the record contract:
Sandy Slavin, Jimmy Crespo, Phil Feit, Adam Bomb, Carole Childs, Rick Keefer

Carole Childs wanted us to try some other songs. One was called *Cherry Baby*. It had a really high vocal with lots of harmonies. I didn't want to do it. David Krebs insisted that I go into a studio and try to record it, or they won't release the album. I thought it was a boy band song. No one ever said it was Starz, and I could never sing like that anyway. I couldn't make a proper record in one day, not without a producer that could do what Rick Keefer did. We went into Cherokee Studios and did a really quick cover version of *Cherry Baby*, *Time Is on My Side* - a song we used to play live where I just sang without a guitar while Jimmy played guitar on encores, and three originals that I wrote with Jimmy.

Two of the new songs were joke songs. One, called *Black Girl*, was about a white hooker who married black. The other was a homage to David Krebs and Rick Keefer's lawyer, Bernie Fishbach. The song had no title; it was just Jimmy playing ragtime guitar with me singing, "Never happened but it could have been, look it baby, look at the state I'm in, never happened but it shoulda happened could have been, You took my money, you said I'd be a star, the only stars I see are up there in the galaxy. Never happened but it could have been, never happened but it couldn't be. Call the Fishbach before he swims home free. "

We recorded a song called *Feel It Rock* that was heavy, but it didn't have the magic of the songs from *Fatal Attraction*. As much as I wanted to have a real band who wrote music together with Jimmy, I couldn't force it. We had nothing in common, and he was really only in it for a paycheck. It took years to become a perfect two-guitar team like Joe Perry and Brad Whitford from Aerosmith. Playing with a second guitarist was holding me back, but I loved him because he was my guitarist. It didn't hurt that he used to be in Aerosmith. Jimmy told me, "Steven would always crank up the Sex Pistols in the limo on the way to shows. Once Steven gave me a line of white heroin and told me it was cocaine. Steven thought it was really funny but I could barely play the show. I was sick for weeks. Steven Tyler was a fucking skooch."

Jimmy showed me how to play Aerosmith songs. He loved to play *Cry Me a River* and he knew all of the strange tunings of *Toys in the Attic*. He told me, "When Steven was cool, he was one of the nicest, sweetest guys in the whole world, but when he was fucked up he was a total nightmare. "

Kelly told lots of stories about Steven, too. "When Steven Tyler stayed up for longer than three days, he had to cover one eye with his hand to stop him from seeing double. We called him Mondo. When they played the last song of the night, Toys in the Attic, the crew would all cover one eye and give the Mondo Salute." Kelly said he used to check his metal briefcase at airports, collect it at the baggage claim, and rip off the tag. He'd declare it as missing, and collect baggage insurance from the airline and credit card companies. He called it, "The Ol' Haliburton Briefcase Trick." Kelly would initiate pranks - like put Vaseline on the hotel doorknobs, Saran Wrap the toilets, or put razor shavings in room service pepper shakers. If you had a bindle of coke, Kelly would ask for a hit and do the whole thing in one sniff. Then he would hand you back an empty paper. Kelly was definitely an old pro.

Geffen Records paid for me to take vocal lessons from Seth Riggs, a flamboyant Hollywood character who had a picture of Johnny Carson on his piano. He told me, "You have to quit smoking marijuana for your instrument." I quit voice lessons instead. Geffen also sent me to a Beverly Hills health spa.

I went out to a bar called Coronet, just to go somewhere other than the Rainbow. I was talking to a guy for about 15 minutes. I thought he looked familiar. It was Sean Penn from the movie *Fast Times at Ridgemont High*. I spent the whole time talking to him. These two girls were all over me, so I went home with them. One of the girls spoke a little French; her name was Jessie. We started making out, but I was sort of attracted to her blonde friend who wore a short fur coat with no shirt. She had enormous tits. She took her clothes off, and got in her bed which was in the living room. Jessie went to the bathroom. I sat on the bed next to her friend. I played with her chest, and she started to rub my crotch. She pulled it out, and put her mouth on me. When we heard Jessie open the door, we quickly stopped, but it was too late - I started to buckle, and came all over myself. Jessie didn't know her roommate had just given me a blowjob, and asked if I was alright. I just picked myself up off the floor, and told her I was drunk. I gave a wink to her friend, and took Jessie back to the Beverly Sunset. I saw Sean Penn a few weeks later at Sushi on Sunset. He introduced me to his date. She stuck her hand out for me to kiss it like she was royalty, and Sean said, "This is Madonna."

I saw Bruce Johannesson play at the Troubadour with his band Sarge, and a few days later I saw the singer of Poison, Bret Michaels, at the same bar. He told me his guitarist, Matt Smith, quit Poison and went home to Pennsylvania, and he asked me if I knew any guitar players. I recommended Bruce from Sarge. He got the gig with Poison, and he changed his name to CC Deville.

I was getting VIP treatment at the Rainbow. The owner Mario took Phil Feit and myself up to On the Rox, and gave us a private tour. The tables were all full at the Rainbow, so Mario snapped his fingers, and they set up a table in the kitchen for us and covered it with a red and white checkered tablecloth. It was like a scene out of *Goodfellas*. While we were eating we saw a coked-up David Lee Roth coming out of the back toilet. He stumbled, and fell flat on his ass in the kitchen. He picked himself up laughing, and said, "Bottoms up!".

A few days later Phil and I were at the Geffen office, and we saw David Lee Roth and Pete Angelus sitting in the waiting room.

They were meeting with someone to try and pitch a movie. Carole Childs approached them to direct a video for *SST*, but they weren't interested in making clips for bands. I asked Pete Angelus if he remembered me. He said he did, but I don't think he had a clue that I was that little kid who followed them around the West Coast.

I went to a party for Kramer Guitars, and Eddie Van Halen was there. I started talking to him. He had a drink in his hand. He still was my all-time hero. After about 10 minutes, I asked if he remembered me. Finally he goes, "Oh you're that kid." He sort of remembered. I told him that I got a record deal on Geffen. He said to me, "Whatever you do, don't end up like these guys," and he pointed to Robbin Crosby and Stephen Pearcy. Robbin was trying to get Ed's attention, but Eddie ignored him. The guys in Ratt looked wasted. Their record was huge - *Round and Round* was a huge MTV hit, and Ratt's album went platinum. They made it part of their act. Girls in bikinis came onstage every night to give them their RIAA awards in whatever town they happened to be playing.

I met Dennis Berardi, the president of Kramer Guitars, at that party and he told me, "I got a feeling about you. I want you to play a party at my house. I think it would be really good for you. Eddie Van Halen will be there. What do you say?" I told him, "If Eddie's gonna be there, I'm in."

Kelly took me to see Queensryche, who were playing at Long Beach Arena. He pointed out a British photographer and said, "That's Ross Halfin, Go over to him and say: I thought you were dead." I went over and spoke to the guy for a minute. He shot pictures for *Kerrang!* - an important rock magazine out of the UK. I pointed to the guitarist, Michael Wilton, and told Ross, "I gave that kid a guitar lesson for $12." He wasn't impressed. Queensryche were doing some double guitar solo, and it reminded me a lot of Rail & Company. Ross Halfin set up a photo session with me for the following day. He had me come to the Sunset Marquis, and he shot me in the room with backlighting using a fisheye lens, so it looked like you were looking at me through a peephole. I thought he was going to cover me in blood or do something outrageous. Ross had a reputation for getting metal bands to do weird shit in photos. I brought my Zebra guitar, but he didn't want me to hold it. The photo shoot was boring, so I thought the photos would be too.

The whole band did an interview with *Kerrang!*. I just told the story of the band getting together. I was told to not talk about drugs or anything bad that had been going on in Hollywood. I was strictly coached by Laura Kaufman to say nothing offensive. She wanted a puff piece. We did the interview in a booth at the Rainbow with Sylvie Simmons, an older female journalist who couldn't have cared less about my band. Paul Passerelli told me to say, "I'm drunk, I'm tired, and I'm done hunting," just to see if I could get it in print. When the article came out, it wasn't flattering, but it wasn't damaging. It was just bland. Laura Kaufman successfully got me to keep my monster hidden, but the interview was lame, and I thought the photo sucked. Paul's quote made it in print. It was the last thing I said in the interview.

I had agreed to play the party for Kramer Guitars. We set up by the pool. No sound system or lights, no stage. Just a few monitors by the diving board. There was an open bar. I felt really strange because there were all of these metal guitar players there, and nobody got wasted. It wasn't a fun party. The guest list included Floyd Rose, Madonna guitarist Paul Pesco, Eddie Ojeda from Twisted Sister, Mike Wilton, Chris DeGarmo, and Eddie Jackson from Queensryche, Jeff Golub from Billy Squier, and bunch of other guitar players from bands who had record deals. There were no girls there; just 30 guitar players hanging out in the daylight, one-by-one trying to out-ego the guy next to him.

We played a short set, and nobody watched or paid attention. I used the Zebra guitar that Floyd built the tremolo bar for in his basement. Floyd Rose didn't even acknowledge me at this party.

There was this strange air about him ever since he joined Q5. When he made his deal with Kramer and became an instant multi-millionaire, he became unreachable. Floyd never even thanked me for helping get his invention off the ground and in the hands of some major rock stars. It went on to become a billion-dollar product. All the guitarists at the party took a group photo with Floyd that became an advertisement for Kramer Guitars in *Hit Parader* and *Circus* magazine. After the photo was taken, Eddie Van Halen showed up at the party, for 10 minutes. I briefly said hello to him. That was the last time I ever saw Edward Van Halen.

The recording of *Cherry Baby* was really bad. It sounded like a joke compared to my recordings with Keefer. All of the other kid metal singers in Hollywood worked with great producers and studio magic. I kept Carole Childs from hearing it as long as I could, stalling for weeks. I think after she heard it she lost faith in me. I stopped hanging around her office after that. Carole Childs' advice to me was, "The best thing for you to do, is to just keep writing songs." David Krebs thought she wanted to fuck me; I only thought of her as my rock and roll mom.

I'd spoken on the phone to a Geffen stylist earlier in the week, and I got her to order me a $600 white leather coat I could wear on the album cover. Geffen had sent the band to the Warner Bros. office in Burbank to shoot it. Kelly dropped us off, and we waited around for an hour. I had to go up three times and ask the receptionist what the holdup was. Finally, a little college girl with glasses came out and got us. We went into a room that had two racks of clothing; everything on it was ridiculous. It was like they went into the fancy dress section of a department store and picked out some tacky striped jackets and really baggy pants. They also had a makeup artist who wanted to overdose us with rouge and colored eyeliner.

I let Sandy wear my leather with the red snake lapel, and we all used whatever we were wearing. The only thing they got right was the $600 white jacket. I used a few of the scarves they had bought but these girls had no sense of style when it came to rock clothing and a cool band image. Sandy wasn't comfortable at all getting made up, but I was used to it. I wanted clothes like Aerosmith, who had a personal tailor named Francine, not some prep school graduate, who wanted to dress us up like shopping mall drag queens.

When I returned to the Geffen office after the shoot, I got yelled at by Ed Rosenblatt because I asked the receptionist three times to get the stylist. When David Geffen saw the photos, he said, "That's the wrong image. It's too glamorous. You need to be more street." They spent $5,000 on that photo shoot and Geffen Records didn't even use one of the photos.

I found a photographer from a large painted photo of Billy Idol thqt was up in a hair salon window on Sunset Blvd. It had silver stars painted on it and it looked really glam. His name was Eddie Wolfl, and we did a photo shoot, on Hollywood Blvd. in front of Frederick's of Hollywood. New Edition were taking photos nearby at the same time. They scowled at me like the kids at Graham Hill looked at me on the first day of school. I wore a borrowed leather jacket from Juliana Roberts; she stopped working for Roger Fisher and moved to Hollywood to work for a film company. David Krebs picked a photo that he thought looked fabulous. Eddie Wolfl gave it to the guy who painted the Billy Idol photo. Instead of painting stars and stardust, he decided to paint my hair bigger and make some violet texture that I thought looked like the inside of a purple sewer.

For the back cover, the band just took a photo outside a Hollywood 7-Eleven against a brick wall. I wanted the layout to look like a movie poster. Geffen had just made a movie called *Risky Business*, I asked for layout and typeface just like that poster. For the band logo, I gave them a button that someone had given me in Japan that had 'Adam Bomb' in shattered block lettering. They duplicated the logo from my tiny button. I thought *Fatal Attraction* was a good album title. It became the title of a major motion picture three years later.

I went over to Malibu to see the proofs at Krebs, and he seemed pleased. He handed them to me and said, "Here's your first album cover." When I saw it for the first time, it was a horrifying disappointment. I complained to him, "The colors are awful. You can't read the title, and what the fuck did they do to my hair?" David said, "Well, you better like it. Anyway, it's too late, I already signed off on it."

It looked nothing like the movie poster typeface I requested that was used on the layout of the Japanese version of *Fatal Attraction*. I had to trust the professionals at Warner Bros. were going to at least make the cassette look right. I was so wrong. For the cassette cover, they split the logo in half, making the shattered block letters off-center. It was even worse than the LP cover. I had no choice but to live with it.

Billy Idol was in Hollywood and staying at the Le Mondrian hotel with his manager Bill Aucoin, who used to manage KISS. Phil Feit had gone over to a party there, and he said they wanted to meet me. Phil warned me, "Bill Aucoin is really gay and they can get kind of freaky so watch out. Just stay close to me."

We went in the five-star hotel, and up to the penthouse. Bill Aucoin answered the door. He had a huge suite with four connecting rooms that took up half the floor. He greeted Phil and I at the foyer, and shook my hand. I gave Bill an advance copy of my album, *Fatal Attraction*. He looked at it and said, "Great cover." He asked Phil to come with him while he put the record away, and told me to go sit in the main room and say hello to Billy. I went into a large adjacent room with a grand piano, and there was Billy Idol, sitting on a couch alone. He was butt naked except for a pair of cowboy boots, looking at his dick, and twirling it in a circle. I knew one thing for sure; he wasn't Jewish.

Billy looked dazed. He said, "Eh mate, right, yeah, how's it going?" like he was dressed and greeting somebody on an ordinary day for tea. I felt a bit uncomfortable. I didn't say much. He sat there for about 30 seconds, got up and left the room.

After five minutes sitting in there alone, I went down the hallway towards the other rooms. As I walked by the first door, I caught a glimpse of three or four guys sucking each other off on a bed while Bill Aucoin was filming them. I said, "Whoa," and did an about face. I went to a different room and Billy Idol was sitting on a bed wearing a white hotel robe. There was a bottle of amyl nitrate and a huge pile of coke next to the phone. He said, "Help yourself mate," so I did a big hit of blow. Billy had a boom box. He played a dub remix of *Flesh for Fantasy* from *Rebel Yell,* which was a multi-platinum album. Billy was just on the cover of *Rolling Stone* wearing nothing but jewelry and black leather underwear. Phil Feit came back in, and Billy played another remix. They both raved about working with producer Keith Forsey. They were chit-chatting like old bandmates. All of the state-of-the-art studio effects sounded really futuristic. It was incredible. I wanted to make music like that.

We went back to the main room, and Phil disappeared again. Steve Stevens entered wearing a white hotel robe. He briefly said hello, and went back into the hallway to his room. Then Phil reappeared. He grabbed me, and pulled me into a bathroom, and said, "We got to put on these," and he handed me a pair of black leather underwear like Billy wore on the cover of *Rolling Stone*. "What the fuck, Phil?" I said. "Are you kidding me?" He made some joke about Wild Bill and said, "Just do it, Bill doesn't want us to make everyone else uncomfortable. You don't have to do anything with anybody. Just put them on." I was high so I said okay. After all, it was just like wearing a bathing suit.

We went back out into the party, and there was about seven guys jumping around in their underwear. We talked with Bill Aucoin. He was about pushing boundaries, and he bragged about how he created KISS and got Billy Idol to wear the same black leather underwear I was wearing on the cover of *Rolling Stone*. I did not want to ask him, "What's it gonna take for my band to open for Billy Idol?" That was a manager's game, and I wasn't so desperate to sleep my way to the bottom in Hollywood. Bill Aucoin was a freebase addict and a chicken hawk. He liked to prey upon young boys, and got off on challenging straight guys.

Bill Aucoin walked over to me holding my record. The front cover had a noticeable wet stain on it over my face. He said, "I checked out your record. It's really good. Actually, I just defiled it in the bathroom." It was a little hard to believe that this was the guy who turned KISS into superstars. "So you think it's a hit, do ya?" was all I could really say. I walked off to talk with Phil.

Aucoin had a silver briefcase full of

nitrous oxide cartridges. He filled up balloons, and gave them to the party boys. They were most likely picked up on Santa Monica Blvd. They were passing around a plate with cocaine. I took a line, and then I saw Bill Aucoin in the reflection of a mirror, holding a large video camera. He was filming me and Phil snorting coke. I asked him to stop, and he said, "Okay, I'll put it away, but you look real good." He went in the other room, and put the camera away. He came back, and started talking to me while freebasing with a torch and blowing the smoke out his mouth into a balloon. He offered the balloon to me, I politely declined, and he handed it to one of his rent boys. I didn't do freebase or poppers; I only snorted coke. Then Bill told me, "You need to have sex with somebody if you want to stick around," and I said, "I'm not gay." Bill was trying to pressure me into it, to broaden my horizons. He wanted me to pick somebody, so I said, "Okay, go get Billy." Aucoin got excited, and said, "What makes you think Billy would want you?" I told him, "I'm not gay; I only like girls." Aucoin laughed and said, "We'll see about that," and dashed off to get Billy Idol.

I put my clothes back on over the leather underwear, and told Phil, "Grab your clothes, I got to get the fuck out of here," and I headed for the door. I liked Billy's albums, but I was not about to let him fuck me in the ass. On the way out, I quickly waved goodbye to Billy Idol. He laughed, and said, "Don't listen to Aucoin mate. He's off his fuckin' head." Phil got dressed in the hallway. As we rode the elevator back to the safety of Sunset Blvd., Phil said, "Now you know why I had to quit Billy Idol."

We were booked to play at the Hollywood Palladium on Sunday, March 10, 1985 as the third act opening for Armored Saint and Metallica. The Palladium was huge. Carole Childs took me to see Dokken play there the night before our show. I thought Dokken were boring. The crowd was full of rockers and music industry people in the balcony VIP section. The floor was packed, but the audience was sedate.

I was looking forward to playing our gig, but Sandy was really apprehensive about it. He said to me, "I don't know about this show man. These bands are real hardcore. This crowd is gonna hate us." I'd seen the headliners Armored Saint at the Troubadour. In small places like that the crowds were never that rowdy, but this was a big place. I didn't know what to expect.

We had a dressing room, and when people started coming in, you could feel an energy, but it was dark. Thrash metal was exploding, and the Palladium was sold out. Metallica was in the next dressing room. They had amp stacks in there, and bassist Cliff Burton was warming up. The lead bass coming out the room next door was so loud, we could barely hear ourselves talk. Metallica looked like greaseball hippie serial killers. The crowd was nothing but an angry mob of denim and leather. My band hid in our dressing room, and we talked about what we were going to do. Sandy took a peek at the front row. He said, "If you ask me, I say we should run." We decided to play the fastest, heaviest stuff for our 20 minutes. Our set was *Fatal Attraction, Russian Roulette, I Want My Heavy Metal,* and *SST.* Kelly came to get us to play, and as we walked to the stage, Sandy said, "I still think we should run."

When the house lights went down, there was a roar like death from above. When the crowd saw me with a zebra guitar and ripped T-shirt - they went ballistic. They wanted blood. We blasted through the set to 1,000 middle fingers. So much spit and shit was thrown at the stage that it took 30 minutes to clean it up. I went out there like it was war. I was drenched in spit, but I wasn't afraid. I gave them a face full of guitar, and dared them by saying, "Come and get me." I nearly incited a riot. The crowd would have literally torn me apart if I jumped in that audience. They loved to hate me.

The Geffen people and David Krebs were stunned and confused. No one really knew what to make of it. It was a huge error in billing, and Krebs knew it. They put me headfirst in the lion's mouth, and I went for it with all I had, but it was far from a win. The show was reviewed in the LA Times by Duncan Strauss: On a different night - or a different bill - perhaps Adam Bomb's opening set of hard rock would have carried some distinction. But Sunday the local band was simply outclassed by Armored Saint, and outcrassed by Metallica.

It seemed like Krebs and Geffen were making a lot of bad moves. They were trying an old-school 1960s, grassroots, word-of-mouth approach, without pulling any strings. I was getting my throat cut at every corner. I had no clue but I had faith. I was starting to have doubts about Geffen Records making Adam Bomb happen but wherever David Krebs wanted to take me, I'd be riding shotgun.

ADAM BOMB

Geffen promo shot outside Frederick's of Hollywood – 1985

Just Check Out These Names

David Krebs and Marco Babineau from the Geffen marketing department came up with idea to do a giveaway of 40,000 singles of *I Want My Heavy Metal* and *SST*. They designed an ad that was the tackiest thing I'd ever seen. They used really gaudy colors and the full-page ad read: When was the last time you heard a new group that you were dying to tell your friends about? Make it now with your free record from Adam Bomb! Just check out these names: Jimmy Crespo formerly of Aerosmith! Phil Feit formerly of Billy Idol, Sandy Slavin formerly of Riot, and 21-year-old singer/guitarist Adam Bomb!.

When I saw the proof of the ad, I was mortified. Geffen bought full-page ads to run in *Hit Parader* and *Circus*.

I went home to Seattle for a visit. I went to a 7-Eleven and looked at *Circus*. When I saw the ad, I threw up in my mouth. It was not something I would've invested a stamp on, but it did get a good response. They mailed out 40,000 records, and Geffen collected the data. My hometown friends were impressed, but I'm pretty sure the talk behind my back was negative.

Geffen printed up 12-inch radio promos. They couldn't figure out what song to make as a single, so they made two different ones –The first was a *Limited Edition Metal Explosion* with *I Want My Heavy Metal* and *Fatal Attraction*. The promo record had a grey spinning background and the logo. The other radio single was *All the Young Dudes* with *SST* on the B-side, which had some lame Art Deco design on it.

I met Peter Napoliello in the radio promo department at Geffen. He was excited about a single he was working on - a promo on a new format called Compact Disc or CD. When I asked Krebs if we could get my record on CD, he said, "It's an experimental format; it will never take off. Waste of time. Next." I wanted to make a video but there was still was no talk of it. I met with a few directors; one was Mark Resnik, who worked with Juliana Roberts. Mark drew up and pitched a treatment with the look of the movie *Rumble Fish,* a black-and-white film that only used colors on the fish. Krebs rejected it. He wanted me to make a video with his friend Hart Perry. So I met with Hart, and he wanted to shoot the band using a wind-up film camera called a Bolex.

We decided to make a clip to *You'll Never Know.* I went to Geffen Records and asked Carole Childs' secretary Beverly Lund if I could get a reel-to-reel to copy of the song. I got in trouble for coming over unannounced, and she told me, "This is not a bank. You can't just come over here and request anything you want. This isn't an authorized video shoot so I can't order you a tape. " When she told me that, I started to think my days at Geffen Records were numbered. They called Krebs and he told me not to go over there anymore, so we had to shoot the video without a playback.

I needed to hire an actress, so I got to look through head shots and pick one. I found a girl I liked named Teresa Crespo (no relation to Jimmy), who was in the Michael Jackson video, *The Way You Make Me Feel.* We didn't have a script so we shot a bit by the Hollywood Sign, and at Juliana Roberts' apartment. Hart was not really an artistic director, and it just looked like bad acting. We shot the band walking down the Sunset Strip at night by the Roxy. I saw Izzy and his singer Axl as we were shooting it. Izzy said something to me while we were shooting, and we just kept walking. I heard him say, "What a dick," as we passed him by. When we finished the scene, I turned to look, but he was gone. After the walking scene, we shot a clip of the band sitting at a table in the Rainbow. I spent most of that day hitting on my co-star.

The video ended up being useless. It was completely out of sync, and we shelved it. The only good thing that came out of that was I eventually got to fuck Teresa Crespo, but it took some doing because she was a lesbian. That plus I got to shoot a video at the Rainbow.

I got picked up at the Rainbow by Tommy Lee's ex-wife Candice. They had split up, and Candice had her sights on me. She was screwed up on heroin but I didn't care; she was hot as fuck. A few days later, I got a call in my room at the Beverly Sunset. It was Tommy Lee.

"Hey is this Adam Bomb?" I said, "Yeah." Then he went, "This is Tommy Lee. So dude, I heard you fucked my wife Candice." I was terrified, and I said, "Yeah, but she said you split up." Then he said, "I'm gonna kick your ass." I was silent and I got a chill of fear. Then he changed his tone and started laughing, "Nah, I'm just fucking with ya dude. I could care less, but hey I taught her well, didn't I? Go ahead and fuck her. You have my blessing. Aren't I the coolest motherfucker in the world?" I said, "Yes you are Tommy." We spoke for about 20 minutes. Chicks were trouble, and every rock star in Hollywood was a target, even if you weren't quite a rock star just yet.

Vince Neil had just gotten out of jail for a car crash where Hanoi Rocks drummer, Razzle, was killed. I was asked to host a local access video program in Hollywood where I introduced videos, so for a Motley clip I said, "This next video is by vrmmm vrmmm pow, Motley Crue." A few days later, we were rehearsing at SIR, and so was Motley. Vince came up to me and said, "Are you Adam Bomb? I don't like your sense of humor. I should punch you in the face." I looked down and said, "I'm sorry man, I didn't mean anything by it. I just kinda said it without thinking. Sorry." I was too small of a guy for him to want to hit me, so he walked away pissed off. He came back to me later and said, "It's cool dude, We did stupid things when we were first starting out too. You're alright. Tommy says you're cool. Just watch your mouth." That was a close call.

I did a ton of press and interviews. We did a photo session with Mark Weiss, a famous rock photographer. Geffen printed up promo shots, and we were slowly being promoted by the Warner Bros. distribution network.

When the record came out in May 1985, there was no big fanfare, no release party, no arena tour supporting one of my heroes, and no big tour bus to go across the country on. I heard the intro to *Fatal Attraction* on KLOS. I got excited, but after five seconds, there was a voiceover, and I realized that it was the background for a car lot commercial.

I figured I'd get a song on the radio once we had a video on MTV like every other band that had a record deal. I was supposed to be a video artist; The *Shape of the World* video was how I got signed in the first place. When I asked Peter Napoliello about getting a record on the radio, he told me, "Adam, I don't know what's going on but I'm not allowed to work your record, and I could get it played in a heartbeat. I'm tight with practically every program director in the country, but boss's orders."

Tommy Thayer wanted me to play some guitar solos on Black 'N Blue's next record. They were recording in Vancouver, British Columbia, with producer Bruce Fairbairn and a studio engineer named Bob Rock. They flew me up from LA, and Fairbairn really liked me. He wanted me to just go as wild on the guitar as I possibly could, make the craziest sounds I could come up with, for a solo on a song called *Bombastic Plastic*. I just went apeshit on the Zebra guitar. Fairbairn and Bob Rock were really excited that this loud, fun, rock and roll kid, came into their studio and brought the energy back up. This was supposed to be Black 'N Blue's breakout album.

Fairbairn pulled me aside and told me, "You've been produced all wrong. I listened to your Geffen album. I don't think the sound is the problem as much as the direction of the music you're playing. You're Adam Bomb. You should be doing the most out-of-this-world, explosive, wild guitar music, not these mid-tempo songs and ballads. Geffen should have spent more time on you. I'd do it but I just don't have the time right now, but you need to make the most of your guitar playing."

Bruce Fairbairn could tell I was just starting out and he probably had a good sense of what I would become, but I was also stuck in a world where I had to please David Krebs, and he wanted me to be as big as Aerosmith. Fairbairn said he'd love to work with me again someday. Jon Bon Jovi loved the sound of that album so much he hired Fairbairn and Rock to record his breakout success - *Slippery When Wet.* That record launched the career of Bob Rock, who went on to produce Metallica's self-titled *Black Album*.

David Krebs wanted to put us on a headline club tour of the Southwest. He had the kid at CAA book about two weeks of shows. It started with a date at The Roxy on June 10. Geffen paid for a half-page black-and-white ad in *BAM* to promote the show and advertise the album. For the tour, Kelly rented an 11-seat passenger van and a U-Haul truck for Terry to drive with the gear. We had dates booked in San Diego, Phoenix, Tempe, Albuquerque, San Antonio, Houston, Dallas, and San Francisco.

The show at the Roxy sold out. There was no support act. Everyone from Geffen came, as well as the guys from Black 'N Blue, and Keel featuring Steeler vocalist, Ron Keel. I did the best show I ever played in Hollywood. It was my debutant ball. For the opening night of my first tour, it felt like it was a big success.

Moments after the show, I was alone in the dressing room, and Ed Rosenblatt, the president of Geffen Records, was the first to come up. He said, "You did great. I'm really proud of you." Then he kissed me on my forehead, touched my face, and left. For some reason, I thought about the movie *The Godfather,* where if the boss kissed you like that, you were going to be the next guy to get whacked.

I changed, and went downstairs. There was a photographer who had interviewed me, Jodie Summers Dorland. She wanted a photo of me with the guys from Black 'N Blue and Keel. My interview with Jodie was done weeks before. She was a famous name journalist, and I hit on her like everybody else did that she interviewed. She wondered why every rocker wanted to fuck her, and that's what we talked about during my interview. We became friends but we never dated. She rounded up the guys, and when she was about to snap, all of the guys grabbed me, held me up in the air, and tried to rip my legs apart. It was a stupid photo, and she published it in *Hit Parader.*

Marc Ferrari, Tommy Thayer, Ron Keel, Adam Bomb, Jaime St. James

273

The next day, we checked out of Beverly Sunset for the very last time, and drove to the gig in San Diego. There were only about 50 people at the show. Three kids were waiting for us to arrive with albums for us to sign. I thought that was a good omen, but I never saw those kids at the show. The next date in Phoenix, I did a radio interview before the gig. The heat was unbearable, and I got them to play *SST* for me so I could hear in the van. There were only 20 people at the show, and it was in a big bar. Rob Halford from Judas Priest was there. He lived in Phoenix. He went home halfway through the gig.

We went to New Mexico, and did an empty club there. This club tour was pointless; nobody had heard of us. There was very little or no promotion in most of these places. Geffen Records did nothing but sit back and watch it not happen.

Texas was a little better. We did an outdoor gig that was put on by a radio station. The last gig of the two-week tour was in San Francisco at Wolfgang's. The band was just starting to get really good. The show was packed. My Uncle Sam came down to see me, and so did Rachel Matthews. She was very excited, and I  went back home with her after the show. There was no end-of-tour party. There was no immediate plan except to go back to Hollywood and make a video with Marty Callner, who did videos for David Krebs with Scorpions. That was the hope to jumpstart the album. I was supposed to be a video artist. Krebs told me that was why Geffen signed me in the first place - from the *Shape of the World* video. MTV was the only way to break national.

When we got to Rachel's place, she looked at me and asked me what was wrong because I looked like I was going to cry. I said, "It's over." She told me, "No it's not. You're being silly. It's just beginning. I just ordered 100 copies of your album for Tower Records." She tried to reassure me that it was fine, but I was haunted by this gloomy premonition. I told her, "Listen, something is really wrong; I can feel it. I can't explain it but I just know it. Something's up. It's over." I couldn't shake the sadness. The feeling of depression was so strong it frightened me. I was warned about the end-of-tour-blues, but this was worse than I imagined. I had it so bad, I wanted to curl up and die. Rachel wanted to have sex, and I told her, "I can't; I just really need a friend right now." She held me until I fell asleep.

The next morning, I was awakened by a phone call. "Adam, are you awake? Wake up. It's David Krebs. Kelly gave me the number. Are you listening? Geffen just told me in a meeting that they weren't going to give us the fifty grand for the video that was in the contract. They said radio is no longer playing any metal, and 20 other groups released this month didn't get played either. He thinks we should just take the $150,000 for the guaranteed next record in the contract. They actually said to me, 'If you want the video money then you'll have to sue us.' Fuck Geffen. I want to take this record to another label. I going to tell them I want out of our contract."

My intuition was dead-on. I said, "Are you sure you know what you're doing? $150,000 is a lot of money." David said, "Don't worry about that; I'll back you myself if I have to. Go home and see your family, and we'll talk in a couple of days."

What David Krebs didn't tell me was he had been in meetings that had not gone well with Aerosmith's manager Tim Collins, David Geffen, John Kalodner, and Ed Rosenblatt. He said it was just a normal record company meeting like he'd done since 1974. David Krebs said he was negotiating a settlement for Aerosmith who he still had under contract to Columbia. Krebs threatened to sue Collins, Aerosmith, and Geffen Records as a negotiation tactic. When I found that out, he told me that was unrelated to my deal at Geffen. That might have been a factor in Geffen's actions towards me, but David Krebs always denied that.

Before the deal was signed with Geffen, Krebs had a meeting with David Geffen and their top A&R man, John Kalodner – the guy who signed Black 'N Blue and Aerosmith. Geffen asked Kalodner to go down and listen to the *Fatal Attraction* album and tell him what he thought. Kalodner's answer was: "I didn't hear any good songs." Krebs thought that was odd, because if anything *SST, Shape of the World,* and *I Want My Heavy Metal* were great songs. Geffen sent out his other A&R person, Carole Childs, to watch the band showcase at SIR in New York. They offered us a huge deal, but Krebs should've been wary of John Kalodner's power at Geffen. We had an enemy at the label before we were ever offered a recording contract.

David Krebs ultimately blamed me, the artist, for what happened at Geffen, saying I turned them off by going to Carole's office unannounced, getting wasted, or fucking Tammi. We never discussed the tacky ads, lack of tour promotion, or things they did that I had no control over. According to them, radio stopped playing new metal the week my album dropped. Krebs wrote if off as an unfortunate succession of uncanny bad luck. He insisted, "You could've toured with Scorpions. But you couldn't keep it in your pants, could you? So it went to Victory." Tammi or no Tammi, whatever the reason was, it didn't matter. As far as I was concerned, Geffen Records was just another hot chick in my life who got into bed with me and conveniently lost my number. Krebs was confident he could get a deal with one of the six other labels that gave him offers, but I was still crushed. I was going to have to learn the hard way that real rock and roll didn't have anything to do with record companies or record deals.

David Krebs took Geffen's money for the second record, and we had to give them first right of refusal. Basically, they paid for a record they were going to pass on before they even heard it. When it came down to it, Geffen Records lost over $400,000 on our deal. I heard reports that the album sold 25,000 copies. I also heard numbers of 50,000 and 80,000, but I never saw statements. I didn't care. I didn't need a college degree to know they killed it, but I sure was getting a hard education in record company bullshit.

That money was nothing to them compared to the millions they were tossing around with Black 'N Blue and Aerosmith. I felt like a pawn in a chess game. I wasn't the first reckless rocker in Hollywood to have problems with a record company. Sadly, it happened just as fast as it started. When a big label like that gives up on you and shatters your dreams, it can be a tough pill to swallow.

Carole Childs got pushed out of Geffen Records by Kalodner and the other A&R guy, Tom Zutant. I wasn't surprised. She had the best office, with a window right on Sunset Blvd. When we went out on the club tour, somebody embellished my album cover, which was hanging above Beverly Lund's desk, to say Adam Bomb'd. Even though they would've put out my second record if we just stayed at the label and they honored the contract. For me, this Hollywood dream company turned into a nightmare factory. David Krebs got us out of our deal, and got the rights back to *Fatal Attraction*. They gave us $150,000 to make the next record in the settlement. And just like that, my time on the Sunset Strip had come to an end.

Sandy Slavin, Adam Bomb, Phil Feit, Jimmy Crespo – San Francisco 6/24/1985

High or Low

After our last stand in San Francisco, Jimmy Crespo, Sandy Slavin, and Kelly went back to Hollywood. Jimmy's girlfriend worked for Singapore Airlines, so she could get him free flights back to New York City so he could still work with us. Sandy Slavin met a girl in Hollywood named Mimi, who was Gregg Gerson's friend. She tried to help us with Gregg until we fired him, then she set her sights on Sandy. He married her. Gregg went to rehab and was now completely sober, but just as much of a freak as he always was.

Phil went back to his wife in NYC, and I went home to Seattle. My dad had moved into a new house in Kirkland. John Bogohosian got addicted to heroin, lost his job at A&M, and was back in Seattle staying at my parents'. He borrowed my dad's car, and backed over the neighbor's dog and killed it. My dad and Joanie were always generous to my friends. They threw a big pool party with all of my friends and every relative from the bakery. I didn't really mention what was going on with my career. As far as they knew, I was a big success. I just had a major label record released with my picture on the cover that was in all the stores. My dad bought a box of 50 cassettes from a record distributor. After a few weeks at home, I was anxious to get back in the game for round two of my mission to rock the world.

Krebs sent me to Hawaii to work on new songs with Keefer and Abbey Brazely. We did a demo of a song called *Fallen Angel,* which I wrote about my Uncle David who died in the war, and *Lost in Time,* a song with a very haunting clean guitar sound. I wrote the words about getting lost in the spiral and the pain of coming down. 'Every night's a nightmare. I felt the darkness closing in on me, my only light was lightning. Lost in time, going out of my mind, lost in time.' I was unconsciously becoming a real artist, writing songs about drugs and anxiety. I had more in common with Steven Tyler than I realized. I finally could chase my feelings and have something to write about.

Rick asked me if I wanted to play a guitar solo on TKO's new album with Scott Earl, called *Below the Belt.* Brad had a song called *Sticks 'n Stones,* a title he was playing around with since 1978. He sang, "You led me down like a lamb to the slaughter." Brad always did have a way with words. "Sticks and stones may break your bones tonight, I don't give in without no fight." I played an emotional double lead, reminiscent of what I played on *Without You* on *In Your Face*. It was my parting gift to Brad Sinsel.

That was the very last session at Sea-West Studios in Oahu. Rick and Donna Keefer made enough money from my deal with Geffen to relocate the studio from Oahu to the Big Island of Hawaii. They bought a bigger house, and constructed a room next to it where they built a new studio. The Big Island of Hawaii was a much nicer place with a volcano, black-sand beaches, and fewer tourists.

After Hawaii, I went to New York, and David let me stay at his penthouse apartment at 2 East End; one of the richest neighborhoods in Manhattan. One of Cheryl Krebs' friends, Debby Barish, was living at the penthouse, and watching it while they were in Los Angeles. She became the house mom, and made sure I didn't bring any girls up to the penthouse.

I started to work on more song ideas to make my next record. I met with Phil Feit in Washington Square Park, and he told me that he had a title for the new record, "What do you think of this? *Dangerous When Lit.*" We went into a store on 8th Street called It's Only Rock and Roll. They sold everything rock related, and the guy that worked there, Peter Ascher, took us in the back and smoked pot with us. There were little pot parties all over Greenwich Village. We ended up at some flat that looked like The Freak Brothers' apartment, with 10 people passing around bongs. A shop next door to It's Only Rock and Roll was called Psychedelic Solution, they sold vintage rock posters. It was run by Jacaeber Kastor. He had pot parties in the back of the store, had a connection to *High Times*, and had the best grass in the city. Sex, drugs, and rock and roll were everywhere in the summer of '85 in NYC.

I was going out most every night, usually with Arturo in his limousine. Since there was a house mom at 2 East End, I usually did chicks in the toilets of these nightclubs. It was easy to party in New York City. I was meeting all kinds of people at the China Club, Nirvana, The Cat Club, The Ritz, The Mudd Club, L'Amour, and after-hours bars. We started hanging out at a small bar called the Pit Stop. Then, a bar opened right below Gregg Gerson's apartment called The Scrap Bar. I was with a different girl every night, and doing a lot of coke. NYC was a non-stop party. They weren't kidding when they called New York, The City That Never Sleeps.

Without the band's involvement, Krebs was creating an Aerosmith live album called *Classics Live.* They were still under contract with Columbia for compilations, and Geffen was about to release a new studio album, *Done With Mirrors.* He had Paul O'Neill take the tapes to the Record Plant to mix them. It was a Joe Perry recording, but Paul O'Neill had Jimmy Crespo fly in to fix some of Joe Perry's guitar parts. I went to the studio to see Jimmy. Everybody kind of thought it was strange that Paul O'Neill was producing an Aerosmith live album, and I saw Paul doubling the rhythm track himself on *Train Kept a Rollin'.* It was rumored that I played on it. Paul O'Neill probably tried to deflect the backlash he was getting by blaming it on me; I was an easy target for trouble. I don't think Krebs was aware of what Paul was really doing in that studio. I thought it was sacrilegious, and I didn't want anything to do with it.

Paul took me to Playland and Tad's Steaks. When I was alone with Paul, he was very sweet guy. He would always give a homeless guy $20 on our way out to eat, but he never took any interest in my music. If Krebs tried to pair us together, we both did it out of obligation. Paul was starting to be taken seriously with A&R at record companies and his passion for progressive metal was something I couldn't pretend to believe in. The only common ground we found was steak and pinball.

The Adam Bomb band went into the Record Plant with Paul O'Neill and his recording engineer to cut one song called, *What's Your Secret.* We rushed through takes as Paul O'Neill offered me $5 for every time I recorded something in one take. I did every overdub in one take. The song sucked.

I saw Ray Gillen around the office. His version of Black Sabbath imploded after recording the album *The Eternal Idol.*

Drummer Eric Singer left the band with Ray, and they formed Badlands with Jake E. Lee. Paul O'Neill got them a deal with Atlantic, and produced their debut record. They played The Cat Club, had a video on MTV, and got a lot of press. When that record failed, arguing with management led to Jake self-producing the next album, *Voodoo Highway* with Paul's long-time studio engineer, Jim Ball. When that album didn't sell, Paul gave up on Ray and he struggled in New York for the next two years. Ray died of complications due to AIDS. I never knew him to be a drug user. It was rumored that he got it from gay sex, but I never knew him to be gay or even promiscuous. Only his girlfriend Daisy knows for sure, and they were close until the day he died.

Motely Crue played in New York City on my 22nd birthday. It was their *Theatre of Pain Tour,* and Nikki Sixx wore a jester outfit like Steven Tyler. Tommy Lee made his dream come true, and played his drums upside down at Madison Square Garden. Motley had really improved since their first album. They spent millions making their record, and it really paid off.

Motley threw an afterparty in a seedy loft on West 41st Street. Phil Feit and I were in the freight elevator with Tommy and Nikki. They were snorting coke out of a vial on the way up. I said, "Hey Tommy, remember me - Adam Bomb? It's my birthday dude. Gimme a bump." He looked at Nikki, and they broke out in laughter. Tommy said, "Aww dude, the krell is gone man, I just finished it. Happy birthday!" The lift was a really slow old loft elevator, and Tommy told me a joke: "Why do Indian girls have a red dot on their forehead? So you can go..." and he pushed his index finger into my forehead and said, "Get the fuck outta here." They slid open the large door, and got out of the elevator laughing.

The party was really dark, and everybody just watched Motley as they showed off their platinum records while being snapped up by paparazzi. I met some fat guy who worked for Megaforce Records, and he took my photo. His name was Bill Ketch, and we became friends. I told him I'd get him a job working for Leber-Krebs.

Motley's manager, Doc McGhee, always said hello to me. He knew what had happened with Geffen. News traveled fast among managers. He encouraged me to stick at it, and he raved about David Krebs. He was a little coked up so he didn't sound very sincere, but I still appreciated that he took the time to talk to me. I thought Doc McGhee was amazing. He took Motley from a Troubadour band with a record deal to becoming the biggest act in rock in 1985. He saved Vince Neil from prison. He knew how to hustle for the world's biggest game.

I had a friendly meeting at Doc's office on Central Park South. His operation looked exactly the same as Leber-Krebs' office. He was working hard on breaking Bon Jovi because the second record didn't do well. David was like family to me, and Doc could see that. He took me seriously, and that was enough. He had his own problems. Rumor had it that Doc McGhee was involved in a huge drug smuggling operation that eventually got busted bringing 40,000 pounds of marijuana into the USA from South America. That was supposedly how he bought his way into the rock management business. I was sure he'd buy his way out of that one too. It only took a good lawyer and one concert a few years later in Russia, under the guise of the biggest drug-addled bands on the planet promoting a worldwide anti-drug message, to pull it off. It was produced as a charity gig, but it more than likely cost more to put on than they took in. He arranged a multi-million dollar party in Russia for his bands, and they fired him. Doc McGhee is the epitome of the American dream. He's *Scarface* with a happy ending.

David Krebs never really respected Doc because of the drug money rumors, but I always thought that Doc was a great rock manager. Regardless of what he had to do to get the money to bankroll his major management firm, and pay off his prosecutors, Doc always appeared as squeaky clean as his next superstar, Jon Bon Jovi. He currently manages KISS, the most successful and biggest anti-drug band on Earth.

While Jimmy Crespo was in New York, we did another gig at the Ritz. I loved Jimmy, but I wanted go back to being just a one-guitar band. I had enough experience doing gigs as a front man. I could now handle singing and playing without a second guitarist. With Jimmy living in Los  Angeles, we were already heading in that direction naturally.

I was working on a song called *High or Low*. I tried to sum up my experiences of the past year, and make a subtle cry for help. It had a cool intro like *Shape of the World* and it was a happy-sounding song. Krebs liked the lyric line: I still dream for free. He was more interested in the lyrics that I was writing, than the music I was creating. He'd always say, "I love the guitar," but he was a word-man. His roots were in Bob Dylan.

I went to Hollywood to see Krebs and write a song with Jimmy. I went to Crespo's house. We stayed up all night with a huge bag of coke, and talked about our adventures, and wrote a song called *Know Your Rights*. Back in New York, Louis Levin at Krebs' office introduced me to Bob Kulick. Bob used to be in the Leber-Krebs act Balance. Bob was a guitarist who did a lot of outside writing for KISS, Michael Bolton, Alice Cooper, and Motorhead. His brother, Bruce Kulick, was the lead guitarist for KISS at the time. I went to his place, and I told him Phil's title, *Dangerous When Lit*. I came up with a chord riff based on the syllables of the title and a verse. Bruce came up with a three-chord bridge but nothing lyrically. It was fairly simple, and we demoed it. It was easy to collaborate with other name songwriters if you just let them add a chord or two to a song idea.

Krebs was always pitching rock operas. He wanted records that could be turned into Broadway shows like *Beatlemania*. He introduced me to a keyboard player, Chris Meredith, who lived on 57th street. Chris was writing a rock opera called *Tale of Two Cities*. He was trying to make a modern musical twist to the Dickens novel. Steven Tyler sang on a song called *Think Fast*. Chris wanted me to sing a song on it called *Treason*. After I did it, we started writing. Chris played a piano melody, and we built a song around it called *You Take Me Away*.

Phil and I started rehearsing with Gregg Gerson. I didn't know it yet, but this revolving door of drummers was something that would plague me for life. Gregg was 100% clean but he took to Narcotics Anonymous as much as he took to cocaine, so it was kind of annoying. He had a new girlfriend named Melissa that he met in rehab. She was gorgeous. She was also a troublemaker.

On December 10, 1985, Black 'N Blue opened for KISS at Madison Square Garden. I went to see them and catch up. After the show, I went backstage to see Tommy Thayer. We talked for an hour, and he showed me his tour bus. Geffen Records was spending a boatload of cash trying to break Tommy's band. They had already played every giant arena in America. I was a little disappointed to tell him about my current situation with Geffen. He told me "Don't worry, Bro. You got a long way to go. I got a feeling we'll be rockin' out for a lot of years to come. We'll be talking about these days when we're old. Look at me; I just played Madison Square Garden opening for KISS. We're having the time of our lives. Just keep on rocking. You'll get there. I'm sure Krebs will look after you and make the right moves. Just have faith and it'll happen. I believe in you."

I gave him a big hug and told him, "I don't know if I ever said it but thanks for naming me Adam Bomb." I left their tour bus and I could hear the echoes of KISS playing *Rock and Roll All Nite* from the stage as I walked alone up the limousine entrance of Madison Square Garden and into the streets of New York City. It was all lit up for Christmas, and I flagged a taxi back to 2 East End.

As I walked past the doorman and took the elevator up to Penthouse E, I felt like I'd been through so much for a kid from Seattle with big dreams. Things didn't happen the way I imagined they would, but the stars had a different path for me to follow. I was still dying to learn as much as I could about rock and roll, and get my music outta my head and into the world. I wasn't sure if I'd ever get a tour bus, or play that coliseum stage, but I knew one thing for sure - I was gonna live a rock and roll life.

Jimmy Crespo flew in and we played L'Amour East in Queens on New Year's Eve. It was a sold-out show and the last gig that Jimmy Crespo played as the guitarist of Adam Bomb. We killed that audience. I had total control. When I screamed, they roared. I was the front man. I had my debut album out on Geffen Records. I was 22, and I had all I needed to kick New York City's ass. We had an afterparty next door at the Pan  American Hotel until noon. We trashed the hotel so badly that they stopped letting other bands stay there who were playing L'Amour. It was going to be a very big year for me, and I had no idea what fate had in store. I called David Krebs in LA from the party and said, "Happy New Year David. You know I love you."

He laughed and told me, "Happy New Year Adam, I love you too. You're gonna be a huge star!"

END OF PART I

Adam Bomb, Johnny Thunders (New York Dolls), Steve Jones (Sex Pistols)

Acknowledgements

Cover and back cover photo: Mick Rock
Additional photos: Adam Brenner, Yetta Brenner, Miss Chickie,
Mark Weiss, Ross Halfin, Eddie Wolfl, Bill Hale, Mary Ann Changg,
Jodie Summers Dorland, Claire O'Connor

Special Thanks: Harry Papazian, Teddie Dahlin, David Krebs,
Blaise Brenner – you are my rock and roll legacy, I love you
eternally. Anne-fleur Oltmans and Doggyvel – for all the love and
support you gave to me for the eight months we lived in Haarlem,
Netherlands, where I wrote this book. Douglas Smith, Dennis
Marcotte, Debby Diamond, James Tolin, Scott Earl, John Paul Jones
and Mo Baldwin, Darian Brenner, and all of the rock bands and their
guitarists who made the music.

911 is Disconnected – Part 1

To each and every girl I shared a moment with - *Même si vous n'êtes pas dans ce livre, je vous aimerai pour toujours*

Research and listen to the songs listed in this book

See you in Part II - Druggy Stardust and the Empress of Clubland with love, AB

Discography

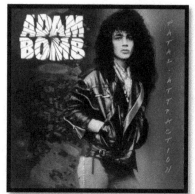

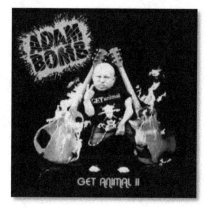

(from previous page)   www.adambomb.com
Fatal Attraction   *Pure S.E.X*
Grave New World   *New York Times*
Get Animal 1   *Get Animal 2*
(pictured above)
Third World Roar   *Rock Like Fuck*
Crazy Motherfucker, Rock On, Rock Hard, Rock Animal
TKO: *In Your Face* - John Paul Jones: *The Thunderthief* - Michael Monroe: *Whatcha Want*